What People Are Saying About
Living the Law of Attraction

"Nothing inspires a person who is learning about the Law of Attraction more than hearing about how others have found outrageous success using these principles. Sometimes the simple reminder that all of this really does work is all a person needs to keep going when things don't seem to be going as planned. This book will uplift, educate, and inspire you to live the dream that you so richly deserve."

—**Bob Doyle**
Teacher featured in *The Secret*
Author of *Wealth Beyond Reason*

"What a wonderful gift this book is! You can feel the love of the people who so generously shared their own personal experiences for the benefit of those who read it. Living the Law of Attraction brings people together in a way which will enhance the lives of all who are involved with it."

—**Marie Diamond**
Teacher featured in *The Secret*
Feng Shui Master and Transformational Speaker and Author

"This book provides the missing link for all those who have read about the Law of Attraction but don't have the results they want in their lives. Rich and Robin's book shows us how the Law of Attraction meets inspired action!"

—**Pat Finn**
CEO and Senior Course Leader
Rubicon Results Institute

"In addition to providing real life examples of people applying the Law of Attraction, in this book coauthor Rich German explains in practical terms, and in a very enjoyable fashion, how you can do the same in your life."

—**Steven S. Sadleir**
Director—Self Awareness Institute

"Living the Law of Attraction brings to light the success stories that we, as a collective consciousness, are experiencing due to the recent phenomenon that has brought it to the forefront of our attention. It provides us the moral support of 'If I can do it, you can too' that helps make active and participating believers of us all."

—**Morgan McKean**
Producer and Host of "Morgan—The Empowermentor"

"Living the Law of Attraction is a phenomenal book that shares inspirational success stories from those who constructively use the Universal Law of Attraction in everyday life. It also manages to provide a great deal of impactful and practical information that will literally change your thinking, hence change your outcomes permanently. After reading this work, I'm further convinced we are the true masters of our Universe and have the ability to attract anything we want into it. I have never felt so much gratitude, peace, and happiness as I do today after reading this amazing work!"

—**Matthew J. Loop, DC**
Author of *Cracking the Cancer Code*

"People have been living the Law of Attraction for a long time now yet never really knew that they were doing it. While The Secret brought the name to the public, this book brings the names … of real people with real stories. It demonstrates how miraculous this law really is. This book isn't just their stories; it's our stories as well. Here's to Living the Law of Attraction!"

—**Stu "GuruStu" Rosen**

"*The Law of Attraction is age-old wisdom, and yet we're always finding new ways to apply this wisdom to manifest all the good things that life has to offer us. Living the Law of Attraction offers beautiful stories of success, wonderful examples that inspire us to tap into and live up to our creative potential.*"

—**Lissa Coffey**
Author of *What's Your Dosha, Baby? Discover the Vedic Way for Compatibility in Life and Love*

"*I love it! Doubt is the number one reason why dreams are not realized. This book can help you eliminate your doubt so you can work with the Law of Attraction and create what you truly desire. If all these people can do it, you can do it!*"

—**Christy Whitman**
Author and Founder of *7essentiallaws.com*
Certified Law of Attraction Coach

"*To the people who tell their stories in this book, The Secret is no longer a secret. They have aligned their thoughts and feelings, paired with action consistently in harmony with the law that is universally active in our lives. Take a life-changing journey with this book of awe-inspiring tales and read about how you can start living the Law of Attraction today.*"

—**Lydia Proschinger**
Life Coach and Author

"*The Law of Attraction works absolutely, all the time. This book shares how real people are living with conscious and deliberate intentions and experiencing a better life. The book is plentiful with stories that are sure to reach most everyone with some inspirational thought, idea, or pathway another has already taken—and achieved success. Thank you for putting this book together."*

—**Erica M. Nelson**
Author of *Prospect When You Are Happy:
Move the Law of Attraction into Action*

"This book is a must-read for anyone who really desires to implement the principles of the Law of Attraction into their life. The stories are inspirational, powerful, and practical!"

—**Bill Loucks**
Author of *The Committee*

"Reading about the Law of Attraction or hearing someone inspiring speak about the Law of Attraction is a whole different experience than living it successfully ourselves. Often people stumble and fall into the gap between insight and application. This book can help by delivering clues, inspired actions, and support for our own personal journey in recognizing and perfecting our own manifesting skills. Pick up this book when you're feeling a bit frustrated or discouraged, and connect with ordinary people, just like you, who are finding their own inspired answers and 'next steps' and see if you don't find your own next, inspired actions in the direction of your desires."

—**Deborah Ivanoff**
Master Life Coach
Author of *How to Make More Good Stuff Happen*

"The Law of Attraction matters and the real life examples in this memorable book shine light on the possibilities for all. We love and appreciate its focus on contribution, connection, and conscious creation. These success stories from everyday life are inspiration to create your reality and experience self, with responsibility and action. This practical and powerful guide will grace

the shelves of The Cafe of Dreams, as a reminder to be truly living the Law of Attraction."

—Cris Van Cleemput and **Jane McCarthy**
Co-Creators, Cyres Cafe * The Cafe of Dreams

"This wonderful book, Living the Law of Attraction, reminds us that life is great, and we are blessed to be able to create, activate, cultivate, participate, and appreciate. The stories shared within it are inspirational and powerful."

—Robert H. Glover, D.C.

"This book is a must-read for all cynics and disbelievers of the Law of Attraction. These stories prove the power of combining the principles of attraction with taking action."

—Thach Nguyen
Entrepreneur and Philanthropist

"The Law of Attraction is working all the time for all of us. Realizing the truth of this and understanding it will free us from the restrictions imposed through our own negative application and expectation. All of us are capable of improving our lives by changing our beliefs, our thinking, our dreams. Living the Law of Attraction gives the readers insights and examples of how this wonderful law works to better all aspects of life."

—Paulette Bethel
Author of *The Power of Mentorship—The Law of Attraction*
and *The Power of Mentorship—For the Woman Entrepreneur*

"Living the Law of Attraction inspires the reader and reminds us of the important things in life—love, happiness, and gratitude."

—Shannon Duncan
Author of *Present Moment Awareness* and creator of Audio Serenity

"Skeptics of the Law of Attraction be forewarned. These stories prove that the law is real. Just like you cannot deny the existence of gravity, you cannot deny the power of attraction!"

—Joe DiRaffaele
Author of *The Gifts from W.T.*

"A powerful collection of stories … ordinary people achieving extraordinary things! The Law of Attraction in action!"

—Jody England and **Kim Yardlay**
Co-Founders—BuzZen

LIVING
THE LAW OF
ATTRACTION

LIVING THE LAW OF ATTRACTION

REAL STORIES OF PEOPLE MANIFESTING HEALTH, WEALTH, AND HAPPINESS

RICH GERMAN
AND ROBIN HOCH

FOREWORD BY BOB DOYLE,

FROM THE SECRET

iUniverse, Inc.
New York Bloomington Shanghai

LIVING THE LAW OF ATTRACTION
Real Stories of People Manifesting Health, Wealth, and Happiness

iUniverse books may be ordered through booksellers or by contacting:

iUniverse
1663 Liberty Drive
Bloomington, IN 47403
www.iuniverse.com
1-800-Authors (1-800-288-4677)

Because of the dynamic nature of the Internet, any Web addresses or links contained in this book may have changed since publication and may no longer be valid.

The views expressed in this work are solely those of the author and do not necessarily reflect the views of the publisher, and the publisher hereby disclaims any responsibility for them.

ISBN: 978-0-595-47411-0 (pbk)
ISBN: 978-0-595-49410-1 (cloth)
ISBN: 978-0-595-91689-4 (ebk)

Printed in the United States of America

CONTENTS

Health and Wellness

Business and Career

Happiness

Everyday Miracles

CONTRIBUTION

Because this book was originally born out of the desire to contribute something to the world, we will be donating a percentage of every book sold to the Boys & Girls Clubs of America. The Boys & Girls Clubs enable young people, especially those in need, to reach their full potential as productive, caring, and responsible citizens.

The Boys & Girls Clubs provide a safe place to learn and grow; ongoing relationships with caring, adult professionals; life-enhancing programs and character development experiences; and hope and opportunity for children. For more information, please visit their Web site at *www.bgca.org*.

It is our hope that everyone who reads this book will find at least one story that changes their life in a positive way. It is our intention that our readers will benefit and the world will benefit as well.

As I have spoken with others about the Law of Attraction, it is always the stories of success that most seem to motivate. Until a person really starts to live such magic they live it vicariously.

—Carole Baskin

FOREWORD

By Bob Doyle, from The Secret

The Law of Attraction is getting more attention than ever before. Thanks in no small part to the movie, *The Secret*, the message has moved from prominence in the New Age or metaphysical communities into the mainstream. This is a wonderful thing, and part of my personal mission has been to facilitate just that.

Several years before I was approached about being a featured teacher in *The Secret*, I first put together our online curriculum in the Law of Attraction with a focus on communicating these principles to those people who might not normally be open-minded to the concepts of "creating your reality" or "living your life by design." I was driven by the profound impact that finally having my own breakthrough in this area had in my life.

While I was aware of what many would call New Age principles, I was hardly a New Ager. My mother was a school teacher and extremely practical and logical in her approach to life and thinking. This is something I most definitely inherited, and although I was intrigued and excited about the concept that we could actually take conscious control over our destinies, I needed more than just concepts to be able to fully integrate and utilize these types of ideas in my life.

When I finally learned the science behind the Law of Attraction, I experienced profound shifts and one of the biggest "Ah ha!" moments of my entire life. These insights eventually led to the creation of our "Wealth Beyond Reason" program, because I was so inspired to share what I had learned with anyone who would listen. I've dedicated myself to providing what I call a practical education in the Law of Attraction, targeting the bulk of my teaching at people who would normally never give these ideas any serious thought.

While this scientific approach definitely does open the door for many otherwise skeptical and left-brain individuals, I've found that all the intellectual knowledge in the world is no replacement for concrete examples of these ideas at work in the lives of everyday people.

People want stories. As many as they can possibly get.

A very important piece of the whole Law of Attraction puzzle is what I refer to as resistance. Because the Law of Attraction is all about getting into "vibrational resonance" with what you want to attract, understanding the nature of resistance is key. Resistance is simply a vibration you're putting out that is *not* in vibrational resonance with what you're trying to attract. This resistance literally acts like an energetic force field keeping your desire at bay.

While there are many tools available to help a person interact directly with this energy that is out of whack, I've found that one of the most powerful tools in the elimination of resistance is very simply a true success story. Often, just knowing that others have successfully and powerfully implemented these ideas into their lives with tangible and undeniable results is all a person needs to lower their resistance to the oddities of these new and often challenging ideas.

This book is full of these stories, and as such, may very well prove not only to be an enjoyable source of inspiration (as good stories are), but more importantly one of the most powerful tools available for creating the breakthroughs you're seeking in your work with the Law of Attraction.

I applaud Robin and Rich for acting on their inspiration to create this and hopefully future collections of examples of just how amazing the Law of Attraction truly is.

Share these stories with your friends and family and watch miracles begin to unfold all around you!

WITH GRATITUDE

Our parents, **Bob and Fran German**, have been our biggest supporters since the day we decided to write this book. They raised us to believe we could do anything we set our minds to and always encouraged us to pursue our dreams. They have helped us tremendously with the proofreading, editing, and organizing of this book. But it is their love and support that has truly meant the most to us.

Bob Doyle has been extremely supportive throughout this project. He understands the importance of sharing these success stories and how much they help people realize that the Law of Attraction will work for them, too. It is a tremendous honor for us to have one of the teachers from *The Secret* endorse our book and write our foreword.

We would also like to acknowledge and thank the following people for helping make this book possible:

Lori Bowers is a top-producing real estate agent in La Quinta, California. She and her team of eight agents live their lives following the principles of the Law of Attraction. She can be contacted at *www.loribowers.com*.

Elizabeth Callaway and **Sally Schoeffel** are a top-producing mother-daughter Realtor team in San Diego, California. They are grateful for the opportunity to powerfully serve their clients as well as build their personal real estate portfolio. They can be contacted at *www.RBVrealestate.com*.

Greg Harrelson has been in real estate sales and development for over fifteen years. He has successfully helped thousands of clients make profitable investments and move into their dream homes. He can be contacted at *www.gregharrelson.com*.

Pete Hawk is a recording artist, producer, and a successful EFT practitioner in Las Vegas, Nevada. He can be contacted at *www.petehawk.com*.

Carol Hinson is a real estate coach and mentor specializing in making a difference in the lives of others.

Kathleen Kramer is a Realtor, investor, and certified mortgage planning specialist in Huntington Beach, California, who is dedicated to assisting her clients with wealth building and creating passive income streams for retirement. She can be contacted at *www.The-Kramer-Team.com*.

Jennifer Mannion is a young woman who has successfully used the Law of Attraction to triumph over the chronic pain of fibromyalgia and other illnesses and become healthy. She can be contacted at *www.thankfulformyhealing.com*.

Mike Morawski specializes in creating real estate syndications that provide passive income and long-term wealth. He can be contacted at *www.michaelfranksllc.com*.

We would also like to thank **Betty Bogart** and **Elizabeth A. Grant** for not only contributing their own success stories to our book, but for volunteering to edit and proofread the entire book as well.

And, of course, we are extremely grateful that so many people generously shared their personal Law of Attraction stories so that others could learn from their experiences. We received hundreds of stories from all over the world and want to thank everyone, whether we were able to use their story or not. Their generous contribution will help many people realize their own dreams.

Rich would like to thank all of the incredible friends and teachers he has had in his life. It is hard for him to express in words the impact they have made on his life. He is eternally grateful for them and the love that they share: **Joe DiRaffaele, Ty Leon-Guerrero, Mark McEachren, Joel Rico, Steven S. Sadleir, Tom Ferry, Carol Hinson, Morgan McKean, Lisa Leslie, Snow Nemeth, Christina Banaga, Barnet Meltzer, Mike Morawski, Jocelyn Singh, Hillary Caston, Linsey Planeta, Gantry Wilson,** and **Andy Wong**. He apologizes if he has left anyone off this list.

He would also like to thank his sister and coauthor, **Robin Hoch**. Not only was the idea for this book hers, but this project would never have been completed if not for her passion and tireless effort over the past year.

Robin would like to thank her husband, **Gary,** for his constant love and support. She also appreciates the support of her two amazing daughters, **Jordan** and **Taylor,** who even helped by providing quotes and other creative input to this book. She enjoys watching them grow into strong, independent young women and is very proud of them both.

Robin would also like to thank her brother and coauthor, **Rich German,** for introducing her to the Law of Attraction. It was his visionary thinking and strong desire to contribute to the world that led to the birth of this project.

And last but not least, we would both like to thank and dedicate this book to **Grandma Eve**, the happiest person we know. She has always been our best example that having a positive attitude is all it takes to live a happy and fulfilling life!

INTRODUCTION

By Rich German

Everyday Miracles

You hold in your hands a book that can change your life in absolutely monumental ways.

The teaching of the Law of Attraction has become mainstream. What was once only known to a few is now known and applied by the masses. This book is a compilation of real-life stories written by people who are truly *living* the Law of Attraction. You will notice that those who have applied this law into their everyday lives are experiencing what used to be considered miracles. What was once miraculous is now commonplace ... *everyday miracles.*

There are many excellent books written by powerful teachers discussing the Law of Attraction. This book, as the title implies, is about the *application* of the law. It will show you that anyone, in any situation, regardless of age, sex, economic background, or previous mindset can practice it and experience greater levels of happiness, love, and abundance. **We are all incredibly powerful manifesters ... we just need to apply the principles.**

The world is changing right before our eyes. The consciousness of the planet is growing. While the Law of Attraction is nothing new, a new understanding of it has created a shift in the overall awareness of human beings. People are more focused on contribution and improving the planet. We are quickly moving into an age in which love and truth will prevail. The more people live the Law of Attraction, the more they will experience prosperity, and the less suffering will exist.

If you can accept the fact that you have created everything in your reality that does *not* work, then you have the power to manifest a reality in which everything *does* work. This is called taking 100 percent responsibility for your life—this is called *freedom*. This power, as more people become aware of it, is literally changing the world in this moment. We have entered a new revolution of thought, understanding, and consciousness. This is a revolution in which individuals will experience more happiness as selflessness replaces selfishness. "How may I serve?"

will replace "What's in it for me?" as the social mantra. People will see that when they focus on others, their personal needs are always met. This service-based way of living is creating a higher collective consciousness. The entire world will experience more peace, love, harmony, and abundance.

As a business and life coach, I have been practicing and teaching the Law of Attraction for several years. I have personally seen the lives of thousands of people changed almost immediately after being exposed to the Law of Attraction.

Like the law of gravity, it applies to everyone whether they believe in it or not. As you begin to believe in and implement the principles, you can create the life of your dreams. **The life you want, wants you.**

My own life is one full of incredible amounts of gratitude, passion, love, joy, contribution, great relationships, health, happiness, and abundance. If you live by the simple principles, you too will enjoy exactly whatever it is you desire.

◆   ◆   ◆

Do not believe what you have heard.
Do not believe in tradition because it is handed down many generations.
Do not believe in anything that has been spoken of many times.
Do not believe because the written statements come from some old sage.
Do not believe in conjecture.
Do not believe in authority or teachers or elders.
But after careful observation and analysis, when it agrees with reason and it will
benefit one and all, then accept it and live by it.

—Buddha

As with any subject that captures the attention of so many people so quickly, the Law of Attraction has garnered its share of negative press. Since *The Secret* took off and Oprah hosted shows on the topic, some people have said it is not true and that it is misleading the public. That is the beauty of this book. Included within the following pages are real stories from real people who are experiencing the power of this law. Don't tell them it is not real. And whether you call these experiences miracles, magic, coincidence, or just luck is irrelevant. What is relevant are the results people are experiencing.

We hope you enjoy reading this book as much as we enjoyed creating it. We hope it inspires you to envision and attract the life you truly desire. We hope you experience a life full of abundant wealth, vibrant health, and incredible amounts of happiness. Millions of people around the world are now living the Law of Attraction. Enjoy the following stories of people who have put the Law of Attraction into action!

Keep spreading the word, and keep sharing your stories. Let's change the world. Let's create a world full of peace and prosperity for all.

◆   ◆   ◆

As previously mentioned, there are many great teachings available on the Law of Attraction. *The Secret* (both the movie and book) does a fantastic job of explaining both the power and simplicity of the law. Esther Hicks does a wonderful job of teaching the principles, and we recommend any and all of the teachings of Abraham (*www.abraham-hicks.com*). Lynn Grabhorn's *Excuse Me, Your Life is Waiting* is another superb book on the subject. Also, all of Wayne Dyer's more recent material is excellent in describing the power of the law.

Before getting to the stories, let's define what the Law of Attraction is and then walk through the process (the exact steps) required to manifest what you desire. Our intention is that you understand the following process, get inspired by the stories, and then go out and attract the life of your dreams.

The Law of Attraction is one of the most powerful laws in the Universe. Like gravity, it is absolute, constant, and unwavering. It works whether you know about it or not. So what is the Law of Attraction? Try on this definition:

You attract into your life anything you give your energy and attention to.

In other words, like attracts like. In even simpler terms, it is fair to say:

Think good thoughts, attract good things …
Think bad thoughts, attract bad things!

Let's expand the definition by stating that you draw toward you everything you focus on, *whether you want it or not*. Whatever you think about, talk about, and feel—either good or bad, positive or negative—will be pulled like a magnet into your experience. You truly are the creator of your own reality.

Now that you understand conceptually what the Law of Attraction is, the key is to be able to use its power to create a better life … a life full of health, wealth, happiness, and anything else you desire. The answers lie in the six simple steps to follow.

The Attraction Process
Six Steps to Manifestation

Step One: Feel Good!

We all live with the objective of being happy;
our lives are all different and yet the same.
—Anne Frank

All manifestation begins with feelings. If you are feeling good, you will attract what you want. If you are feeling bad, you will attract what you do *not* want … period. Your state of being attracts everything to you.

You cannot attract wealth if you are feeling poor.
You cannot attract health if you are feeling sick.
You cannot attract love if you are feeling unworthy of it.
You cannot be happy if you are feeling undeserving of happiness.

You must see yourself as you want to *be*. From that point of being, you will attract what you desire. So the key is to consciously *choose* to feel good and then just stay in the joy.

Unless you are one who just naturally feels good all the time (which makes you a very rare individual), there are some powerful tools you can use to cause you to consistently feel good. Let's discuss three proven tools for you to consider:

The Tool of Gratitude

There is always a time for gratitude and new beginnings.
—J. Robert Moskin

When you consciously choose to live in a state of gratitude, you will automatically begin to feel good. It is not possible to think about the amazing things in your life and not feel good! By focusing on what is good you will attract more good into your world. (Conversely, if you act like a victim and focus on what is bad, more bad will come flooding your way!) It sounds so simple … because it is!

Try this exercise for the next thirty days. Each morning, ideally as soon as you wake up, make a list of at least ten things that you are grateful for. You can write the list in your journal or on your computer, speak the list out loud, call a friend and share your list with him, or scream it out loud on your morning walk. There is no wrong way to do this. The key is to just begin each day focused on what is working in your life. Focus on what you are grateful for. It does not matter how messed up you think your life might be; you still have plenty to be grateful for. The fact that you had the means to buy this book and read it tells me you are doing okay. In fact, I'd bet there are millions of less fortunate people around the world who would change places with you in a second.

I have personally been doing this exercise every single day for over two years now. I type it up and e-mail it every day to my buddy Mike in Chicago, and he sends me his in return. Why do I do it? Because I know I have the option each morning to either be grateful for the new day, or to whine and complain. And you know what? Gratitude feels a whole lot better than whining and complaining! Plus, I understand the power of feeling good.

In fact, try it right now. List ten things you are grateful for. In case you need a little help to get started, consider things like: your body, your mind, your soul, your children, your spouse, your significant other, your lover, your friends, your home, your car, your pets, money in your bank account, your job, your business, your country, the weather, your mother-in-law, whatever....

Ten things I am grateful for:
1–
2–
3–
4–
5–
6–
7–
8–
9–
10–

Again, try it for thirty days, and just see what happens.

The Tool of Meditation

All men's miseries derive from not being able to sit in a quiet room alone.
—Blaise Pascal, French philosopher, scientist, and mathematician

I cannot stress enough the importance of meditation. Whether you meditate to simply calm your mind and feel a little more peace, or if you do it to make conscious contact with your Source and experience complete, utter bliss, meditation is an important tool when it comes to feeling good.

There are many forms of meditation to consider. I personally practice something called Shaktipat meditation. Shakti is the life force energy that beats your heart and sustains the Universe. In this technique, you connect with that energy and feel an amazing natural high. It is an effortless third-eye technique I learned from my teacher, Steven S. Sadleir, director of the Self Awareness Institute. (Steven is also a story contributor in this book.)

I personally sit for an hour or more each day, and quite honestly, it is hard to express in words how this has impacted my life. Meditation can lead to a greater sense of calm, peace, love, and joy in your life. It allows you to feel connected to the world and everyone and everything in it. This connection leads to a wonderful feeling of gratitude for simply being alive. Imagine being happy regardless of any external factors and conditions. Most importantly, in this conversation of attraction, meditation will make you feel good!

Even sitting in meditation for ten or twenty minutes a day is beneficial in your desire to feel good. Again, I recommend you practice some form of meditation on a daily basis.

(Note: I am a certified meditation teacher and lead meditations via teleconference call. For information on meditation and how you can join in on these live weekly calls, please send an e-mail to richgerman@cox.net and reference "meditation" in the subject line.)

The Tool of Exercise

> *Exercise is an expression of the soul; it is a philosophy*
> *and a discipline to a much higher order of life.*
> —Rich German

Beyond the obvious health benefits of a good exercise routine, let's be honest: exercising makes you feel good. Maybe not always while you are doing it, but when you are done, you always feel better!

So if you are committed to feeling good each day, commit to some form of exercise each morning. You can walk, run, lift weights, do yoga, make love (that got your attention) ... just do something each morning to get the blood pumping and create some energy. The more energy you have, the better you will feel. I recommend exercising outside if possible ... breathe in the air ... connect with nature ... connect with the Universe, God, or Source (whatever name you give to the power that created this magnificent playground we get to play in).

While there are obviously many other tools you can utilize in your quest to feel good each day, I strongly advise you to incorporate these three into your routine. In fact, the best guidance I can offer is to create a powerful morning ritual (routine) which includes gratitude, meditation, and exercise. Again, try it for yourself and see how good you feel.

My advice is to **make feeling good your highest goal**. Live in a state of gratitude and you will undoubtedly attract to yourself all you desire and experience a joyous life. When you feel good, everything just flows.

Step Two: Set Forth the Intention

The greater danger for most of us is not that our aim is too high and we miss it,
but that it is too low and we reach it.
—Michelangelo

Now that you are feeling good, it is time to decide what you want. We live in an existence where we truly can have anything we want. Your main "job" is to decide what you want and focus on it! As my good friend and mega-manifester, Thach Nguyen, states: *over 90 percent of manifestation occurs in the declaration*. So decide what you want and ask for it.

In the first step, we discussed creating a list of the ten things you are grateful for. In addition to that list, add the top ten intentions you have in your life. These intentions can include things like:

- The state of being you desire. (I intend to feel good, to live in a state of unconditional love, to be happy, to laugh and smile all day long, to be unattached, to have eternal patience, to have fun.)

- The health you desire. (I intend perfect health and my ideal body, to wake up with great energy, to lose ten pounds within thirty days.)

- The mindset you want. (I intend to think empowering thoughts all the time, to be in the moment, to be present.)

- The spiritual desires you have. (I intend to be completely connected to my creator or the Universe, to be conscious all day.)

xxxii LIVING THE LAW OF ATTRACTION

- The material things you desire. (I intend to attract $20,000 in the next thirty days, a black Mercedes convertible, my dream home with an ocean view in Southern California within twelve months, $100,000 cash in the bank by the end of this year.)

- The relationships you want. (I intend to find an amazing, passionate, intimate relationship, to create a close bond with my children, a strong connection with my parents.)

You can also set intentions you have for other people. For example, every single day I write down that: *"I intend great health and safety for all my loved ones today."*

Your intentions can be things you want to manifest today, this week, this month, this year, or within several years. There is no wrong way to create your intentions—just make them specific and clear.

Another piece of advice is when you ask for what you want ... **ask like you expect to get it!** Each morning I type up my lists of gratitude and intentions, and then I passionately read them out loud. I put energy and feeling into what I am grateful for and also what I want. It feels good to do this; plus, I know the Universe is made up of energy and will respond to the energy—the vibration—that I emanate.

Let me point out here that I know deciding what you want can be extremely hard for most people. Hopefully, you easily came up with ten things to be grateful for. However, you may find it a little tougher the first time you are asked to list ten things you want.

It is common for people to say they desire happiness, and that is a noble intention for all. But what do people really want when they say they want happiness? I believe the things they really want are: energy, experiences, and excitement.

Think about it ... when you are feeling energized, you are feeling good, and when you are feeling good, you are happy! When you are experiencing life, you are happy. To me, *a great life is a life of great experiences.* We also want excitement ... excitement increases our energy.

So if it is hard for you to answer the question, "What do I want?" then try these questions instead:

What experiences do I want?
What will excite and energize me and lead to happiness?
What will be good for me and for the greater good of others?

The last item to look at here is the subject of worthiness. It is critical you feel worthy of attracting that which you desire. **If you do not feel worthy of that which you desire, you will not attract it into your existence.** Your energy must be vibrating in line with what you want. This is why feeling good comes before setting the intention. You must intend a state of being in which you feel good. This will automatically raise your vibration (your energy). When you are energized, you will draw your goals and desires toward you like a magnet. When you are vibrating at a high level, you are connected to Source Energy/God/the Universe. And when you are connected, you become a channel to receive (to allow) your thoughts (intentions) to manifest! You and your intention become one in the same.

My favorite quote regarding worthiness is Marianne Williamson's wonderful words, "Our Deepest Fear" spoken by Nelson Mandela at his presidential inauguration. Anytime I feel any doubt, fear, or thoughts of unworthiness creep into my brain (which happens more than I'd like to admit), these magical lines quickly bring me back to a space of abundance and infinite possibilities:

Our Deepest Fear

Our deepest fear is not that we are inadequate. Our deepest fear is that we are powerful beyond measure. It is our light, not our darkness that most frightens us. We ask ourselves, Who am I to be brilliant, gorgeous, talented, fabulous? Actually, who are you not to be? You are a child of God. Your playing small does not serve the world. There is nothing enlightened about shrinking so that other people won't feel insecure around you. We are all meant to shine, as children do. We are born to make manifest the glory of God that is within us. It is not just in some of us; it is in everyone. And as we let our own light shine, we unconsciously give other people permission to do the same. As we are liberated from our own fear, our presence automatically liberates others.

Step Three: Take Inspired Action

If one advances confidently in the direction of his dreams, and endeavors to live the life which he has imagined, he will meet with a success unexpected in common hours.
—Henry David Thoreau

You cannot spell attr*action* without action!

Okay, so now you are feeling good and you have set some intentions. Congratulations. You have done much of what is needed to attract what you want. Now, the key is to take action! "But wait a minute," you say, "I thought all I needed to do was decide what I want and then kick back and wait for it to magically appear." Like you, I wish this were the case. "But that's what they said in *The Secret!*" you declare. Well let me let you in on another secret. You know all those fabulous people who were in the movie ... they all worked their butts off to get to where they are! Believe me, if I could just say, "Hey, Universe, plop down a couple of those Victoria's Secret models for me, and make sure they are carrying about a gazillion bucks in cash ... each," and then go sit on the beach gazing and smiling toward the heavens waiting for their angelic descent, I would do it! But it doesn't work that way. Trust me ... I tried.

But here's the good news ... if you properly do steps one and two, step three just happens. **If you are feeling good and know what you want, you will automatically get into inspired action. When you are taking inspired action, the line between work and play ceases to exist and life just becomes a series of pleasurable moments.** Read that sentence again. Is this not an ideal way to live your life?

Another thought to consider, is that to powerfully manifest what you want, you do not need to go out and quit your job (unless, of course, you want to). Just continue doing what you do, and do it with passion and joy. Staying in the joy and taking inspired action will help to quickly bring your intentions into your reality.

Additionally, make sure to tell everyone what your intentions are. Tell your friends, your spouse, and your family. Tell your neighbors, co-workers, and even the strangers next to you on the airplane. (Seriously, if you are on a plane right now, turn to the strangers next to you and tell them what you are up to. It is no accident they are next to you and they just might know someone or something that will create a great opportunity for you.)

Telling people is a great way of putting energy out into the Universe regarding your intentions. Plus, you will most likely need the support of other people to get what you want. As my good friend and coach, Tom Ferry, says, **"All opportunities lie in people!"** So tell everyone what you want, be open to their support, and connect with as many people as you can. You never know when you will meet someone who will lead you one step closer to manifesting what you desire.

Step Four: Release the "How"

Living is a form of not being sure, not knowing what next or how. The moment we know how, we begin to die a little. We never entirely know. We guess. We may be wrong, but we take leap after leap in the dark.
—Agnes de Mille

This is a critical step to manifesting, especially big stuff like launching new businesses or amassing large sums of money. Think of a time when you had a fabulous idea and quickly got completely inspired out of your mind. I am talking about a really amazing idea that was going to change your life forever and possibly make you the ruler of all time, space, and dimension, and of course, lead to world peace. You come up with this astounding idea and stay up all night because you are so absolutely thrilled you no longer feel the need for sleep. Eventually, just before dawn, you peel yourself off the ceiling and fall asleep. Then you wake up. You still like the idea but immediately ask the question: "*How* the hell am I going to do it?"

Asking "how" stops most people dead in their tracks. In fact, **getting stuck in the *how* will kill your intention**. If you need to know the exact process that must occur to reach your goal, you cannot become a super-manifester. Here's the good news: **It's not your job to figure out the "how" in detail**—it's the Universe's job. What you may not know is that you have a business/life concierge who works for you. This concierge works twenty-four hours a day, seven days a week. Your concierge never asks for vacations and happily works for free! Its job is to provide you with everything you ask for. Your job is to just allow ... to be open to receiving.

Yes, you can still brainstorm and plan; these things are important. Just don't underestimate the influence of your intention and the magnetic power of allowing things to come to you. In the midst of your planning and action, always be flexible and make sure to always go with the flow. Think about the time of your life when things were best. Were you paddling hard upstream or going with the flow? Were you banging your head against the wall or trusting your heart and intuition?

Also, **consider that if you know exactly how you're going to reach your goal, you're probably thinking too small!** Dream big, play big, act big, *be* big ... and be unattached to the results. It is normal as a human to have certain expectations, yet expectations quite often lead to disappointment. Instead, be flexible ... go with the flow ... and trust that the Universe will always deliver.

Step Five: Be a "Yes" to Life

Life needs to be lived in a constant state of discovery.
—Kobi Yamada

The next step is to be a *"yes"* to life. What this means is to get in the habit of saying *yes*. Once you have decided what you want, it will start coming your way. Sometimes, (okay most of the time!) we get in our own way. Opportunities show up that will lead us toward our desire and we reject them—we say *no*. Remember this: *No* **cuts off the flow!**

In the circles I run in, we play a game called "The Perfect Game." Here are the rules:

1. Whatever is offered to you, take it. (Your co-worker offers you tickets to the concert tonight; you smile and say *yes!*)

2. Whatever is suggested to you, do it. (Someone says, "Hey, you should read this new book." You say, "Okay, I will!")

3. No matter what happens, you declare everything to be perfect. (Get a flat tire— *"Perfect ...* I'll walk ... I could use the exercise." It rains on your day off— *"Perfect ...* I will stay home and read or meditate." Boyfriend dumps you— *"Perfect ...* I will use these principles and find a better one!")

Again, the idea is that once you set forth your intention, the wheels of the Universe start moving, and your desire starts coming to fruition. Your job now is to stay in resonance with the process (*stay in the flow*) by saying yes to whatever comes your way.

Now, for the few of you saying, "Well, what if someone suggests I should jump off a building; should I say *yes* to that?" To you, I say to use a modicum of common sense here. And honestly, has anyone ever suggested that you jump off a building?

Like everything else mentioned above, try The Perfect Game. You will notice that "bad" things will happen less frequently, and when they do, you will simply not be affected as much. I know many, many people who have taken on this technique as a way of life, and they all experience more ease and happiness as a result.

Step Six: The Intention Manifests

The final step is not so much a step as it is an act of receiving or allowing. A key to attraction is being in a receiving mode … again, being open and feeling worthy.

It is important to note here that **your manifestation may not look like you thought it would, but you'll always get the *essence* of it**. Webster's defines essence as "the most significant attribute, quality, property, or aspect of a thing."

So you may not get exactly what you want—the black car might by red … the blonde might be a brunette … the _____ might be _____—however, you will get the essence of it.

That's it. Don't believe it can be so simple? Try it for yourself. Start by intending to manifest something small. Intend to attract an unexpected $100 in the next three days … to set a date with someone new by the weekend (not recommended if you are married!) … to strengthen a relationship that needs strengthening … to receive a phone call from someone with whom you've lost touch … anything. Follow the steps and put them to the test.

The Missing Piece to the Puzzle
The Real Secret

There is one final piece to the equation you must understand in order to truly create and enjoy the life you desire. While the process outlined above, along with the techniques given, are very useful, the truth is there is really only one thing you must know. Here it is: ***The energy that created and sustains the Universe is the same energy that created and sustains you.*** Both scientists and spiritual masters agree on this point. So if this energy is everywhere, this means it is in you. There are many names given to this energy—Life Force Energy, Source Energy, Chi, Shakti, Essence, Spirit, Soul, God—and while the words are different, they all mean the same thing.

You are pure energy in a body. This energy is what runs you. It is the ghost in the machine. Just like your car won't run without gasoline, you won't run without this energy. You grew out of this Source Energy—you are it. And as it, you have the innate power to manifest and create anything.

You merely need to accept this (which is not easy for most people as the thought can be quite overwhelming), and then choose to create whatever you desire. We are powerful beyond measure but just don't know it. Or perhaps we cannot accept our true power, so we fear it and sabotage it.

The choice is up to you. Accept your power. Choose to feel worthy of it. Choose to feel really good. Choose to have an amazing experience of life.

◆   ◆   ◆

Now, let's get to the stories from our incredible contributors who are *living* the Law of Attraction.

On the following pages, you will find wonderful stories from people all around the world. The story contributors are all honored to share their personal stories and hope their stories touch, move, and inspire you to create a better life for yourself. Each story has a moral built into it. As a whole, the moral of this book can be summed up in one word … ***love***. These writers all express, in their own special way, a love for themselves … a love for life … a love for creating the life of their dreams. They also express a love to make a difference for others … that is the real reason each has decided to share their story in this book.

You attract what you put your attention on. Consider that **attention = love**. Ideally, you are putting your attention on that which you love. The more you put your attention on what you want, the more love you cultivate. The more love you bring into the world, the better the world becomes for everyone and everything. It has been said that love is the glue that keeps the world together. We all have different dreams, desires, and intentions. We all have different questions. Just remember, whatever the question is … *love is the answer.*

Here's to your *health, wealth, and happiness!*

With love,
Rich German

HEALTH AND WELLNESS

STORIES OF
HEALTH AND
HEALING

LEARNING TO DANCE IN THE RAIN

By Ross Craft

Life isn't about waiting for the storm to pass.
It's about learning to dance in the rain.
—Anonymous

This is a story that needs to be told. It is my intention that you will be filled with hope as you walk with me through moments of great despair and learn how I overcame blindness and two fatal diseases. I was told I had Wegener's granulomatosis vasculitis (WGV), severe cardiomyopathy, and at one point I was blind.

I was too old, too sick, and too weak to get on the list for a new heart, which seemed to be the only solution to the heart problem. I was also told the heart doesn't heal itself. I have to admit, it was always difficult for me to say, "I have" Wegener's granulomatosis vasculitis. I much preferred to say, "I have been diagnosed with it." It seemed that if I said it that way, I didn't own it or it didn't "have" me.

WGV is an autoimmune disease that is very often fatal. It is also difficult to diagnose. It can attack any organ. In a way, I guess I was lucky because when I got really sick and required emergency hospitalization, the disease was affecting everything. I had sore joints and little purple sores indicating a blood infection. I was coughing up blood, and my kidneys were also affected. While doctors say this disease can be controlled, I think when you read my story, you will realize one's life expectancy is short. You may not die from the disease immediately, but either it or the treatment will get you.

My ordeal took five years. In the course of the five years I became good friends with my lead doctor, Dr. Katz. He is one of the finest men and the best doctor I have ever met. One day, after the lab reports said I was in good health, he said, "Did you know how sick you were? If I were a betting man, I would have lost big money on you. When I met you, I didn't think you would be here now."

I once read a two-line quote from an anonymous author that described my journey. It went like this:

**Life isn't about waiting for the storm to pass.
It's about learning to dance in the rain.**

During the first four years, I experienced a series of life-threatening events. Each time, I would just get the best medical treatment I could find and sit back and wait for the storm to pass. The problem was, my health and my outlook for survival kept getting worse.

At the point of my greatest despair, I was blind, my heart had a 15% ejection fraction, and my immune system was really out of whack. I couldn't walk to the bathroom without getting chest pains. To relieve the inflammation in my eyes, I had to take very strong immune suppressant drugs usually used in cancer treatment. After taking one of the drugs for about three months, I was still blind, and my blood crashed. By crashed, I mean my white cell count went down to less than two, and my red cell count was also very low. In the process of suppressing my immune system, we had stopped my bone marrow from making new cells. In the middle of December, we had to stop everything and wait to see if my bone marrow would recover.

If my bone marrow did recover, the next drug of choice of a world-renowned eye specialist was a stronger immunosuppressive drug, Cytoxan. Our research showed this drug had damaged good hearts when used in cancer treatment. We didn't know what it might do to a bad heart. In addition, this drug causes bladder cancer if you don't drink at least four liters of water every day. With cardiomyopathy, I was on a restricted fluid diet.

Looking at what seemed like an impossible situation, I considered just getting up out of my chair and seeing how far I could run before my heart failed. Then, I just decided to get well. I immediately realized I didn't know how. For four years, I had been getting all the best medical advice and treatment and kept getting worse. I knew it would have to be something more. I decided on a shotgun approach.

I would continue getting medical treatment, continue with my program of nutrition, and start working on my mind. I had been a meditator, and I had some experience with the power of the subconscious mind. I don't know why I didn't use it sooner. I guess I was just waiting for the storm to pass with each health episode.

I started visualizing good health and started feeling better right away. I knew I had to get that feeling of "belief" in order to make it happen. I must say that when the men in white coats, armed with lab reports or x-ray film, tell you something, it is hard to "believe" what they say is not true.

I decided I needed some real work on my subconscious. I went on the Internet and bought several subliminal CD's on health and healing. I also bought one on guided visualization of health. When I got these CD's, I started listening to them all the time. When I went to bed, I listened to the sleep version. I thought if a little bit of this helps a little, a lot should help a lot. (Besides I didn't have anything else to do.)

My mind was being bombarded and saturated with phrases like, "You are healing, you are healed, you have perfect health, etc." I started feeling much better, and within a week, I had that feeling of "belief." Here is what I came to believe:

My body is repairing itself twenty-four hours a day, seven days a week. It has the blueprint to do it right. My body is now rebuilding itself perfectly. It is back on track.

I had learned to dance in the rain. Trips to the doctor's office, in my mind, were to verify what I already knew. I was getting well. I got the CD's around Christmas, and by the middle of January, my blood had recovered enough for me to take the more potent immune suppressant drug. By the first of February, my vision had started to return. I went to Boston to consult with a world-renowned eye specialist, and he confirmed the treatment I was getting was the best I could get for my eyes.

While I was taking this drug, I drank at least four liters of fluid every day to keep from getting bladder cancer. With cardiomyopathy, drinking large quantities of liquids is a big no-no. I did it anyway.

By the end of March, the inflammation in my eyes was gone, but I still had a big cataract from long-term, large doses of Prednisone. Near the end of April, Dr. Katz called and said, "Don't take any more of the cancer drug (Cytoxan). The lab tests show your blood has crashed. Your white cell count is 1.5 and your red cells are about as bad." (White cells are the backbone of your immune system. When the cell count is that low, your immune system will not function. A cold could turn into pneumonia and be fatal.) We discussed a transfusion but decided to wait the weekend to see if my blood would recover. (I just knew it would.) The tests on Monday confirmed that I didn't need a transfusion. Dr. Katz told me I should not take any more of the Cytoxan because there is no safe dose, and nothing says your blood has to recover. If it didn't recover, we would be looking at a bone marrow transplant to stay alive.

I had not had the eye inflammation for a month, and I didn't believe it would return. I just knew I wouldn't need any more of the Cytoxan. The eye inflammation was the last trace of WGV in my body.

The first week in May, I went to St. Luke's hospital to see if I could get into a national study for heart patients. In order to get into the study, I had to get a complete set of baseline tests of my heart. I completed the tests, and the doctor and a nurse said, "We're sorry but you can't get into the study. The reason you don't qualify is that your heart is normal. The normal ejection fraction is 50%–75% and yours is 50%."

Just think about that. After I started visualizing perfect health, the WGV went away. During the time I was taking potentially heart-damaging drugs and drinking large amounts of water, my heart healed itself. (When I first received the heart diagnosis, they told me the heart doesn't heal itself).

Now, a year and a half later, my corrected vision is 20/20 in both eyes, and all my lab tests look great. At the urging of my wife, I have written a book about my ordeal and the power of visualization and the Law of Attraction.

Message: No one can make you sick, and no one can make you well. You have to take control of your own life. If you want things to change, you have to get a mental picture of the changes you want to occur.

Ross Craft is a real estate investor whose health caused him to retire. He has recovered from blindness, cardiomyopathy, and Wegener's disease using the Law of Attraction and visualization. He has written a book titled *Learning to Dance in the Rain,* which tells the story of his ordeal. For more information, visit his Web site at *www.learningtodanceintherain.com* or contact him by e-mail at *craft@learningtodanceintherain.com.*

LIVING WITH HOPE AND VICTORY

By Patty Skinger

If you think you can win, you can. Faith is necessary to victory.
—William Hazlitt

I was born Patricia Ruth Rehfeld in Salt Lake City, Utah. I lived there the first two and a half years of my life. Then my family moved to Naperville, Illinois, a suburb of Chicago. When I was thirteen, we moved to Greeley, Colorado. Most kids wouldn't have liked moving when first starting high school, but I didn't mind it. I made some wonderful friends that first summer at a local swimming pool, which helped me adjust.

After graduating in June 1976 from Greeley Central High School, I attended the University of Northern Colorado in Greeley. In December 1981 I graduated with a degree in elementary education/early childhood education. I have used my degree off and on over the last twenty-six years.

During college, I spent several summers working in Yellowstone National Park for TW Services. I worked as a clerk at Bridge Bay Marina and Old Faithful Inn. It was a wonderful place to spend an extended period of time. I met people from all over the world while working and playing in the park. I absolutely love the outdoors, wild animals, mountains, and nature. What a wonderful place to experience all of that in one package! I still long to spend time there each time June rolls around. I met my husband, Paul, in Yellowstone National Park on July 4, 1981.

I still call Greeley home. Life is looking up daily now, but that has not always been the case over the past twenty-some years.

I experienced many health issues over the last twenty-two years of my life. I started dealing with cardiac problems when I was pregnant with my son, Ben. I had a condition called WPW syndrome. It affects the electrical part of the human heart. The heart is beating along normally, and then for whatever reason, it

9

would start beating so fast that a person could not count the beats per minute. You could see my sweater bouncing because the rhythm was so fast! The only way I could get it to stop was to lie down horizontally. My son used to like to mimic me when he was young. He would lie down and then get up and laugh repeatedly, which actually helped me out a lot!

As time went on, the episodes became more frequent. I had to lie down in the middle of restaurants, grocery stores, or pull the car over while I was driving and have Ben hop into the back seat so I could stretch out horizontally. The most difficult time was when my family was flying to my brother's wedding in Dallas, Texas. My heart rhythm started up and I had to lie down in the aisle of the airplane. They finally gave me an ultimatum to get back into my seat or they were going to taxi back to the terminal and force me to see a strange doctor. I didn't want to do that, but I also couldn't get relaxed enough to get the rhythm to stop. Finally, they rearranged a few passengers so I could stretch out on several seats and the plane could take off. When we arrived in Dallas, I called my husband to pick me up because I was not going to attempt another flight anytime soon.

I was fed up with the whole nonsense of living with this. That is when I chose to go through a new procedure I had been told about the previous year, a catheter ablation. I had the catheter ablation done in January 1992 at University Hospital in Denver. This is a procedure that cauterizes an extra electrical circuit in the heart to block the electrical pathway. I was one of the first to go through the procedure in this region of the country. I felt like I could live again! For the first time in a long time, I felt like I could get out, dream, and function as a normal person. What a wonderful concept. This procedure is now routinely done in the cardiac medical field.

I thought life would be absolutely wonderful now. I thought my heart problems were all dealt with, or so I had hoped. I started to work for Eaton Elementary School in August 1992, in Eaton, Colorado, as the librarian. That was great fun. I love children and books. What a wonderful way to experience both at the same time! Everything was fine for a year and a half.

Then I was diagnosed with fibromyalgia, an autoimmune disease, in the spring of 1993. A person with this is in constant pain that floats throughout the body, has difficulty sleeping, and many other lousy symptoms. I began the cycle of pain medications, sleep medications, and anything else just to try to function. I had my son to think about, and I continued on as the librarian for almost five years.

I then worked at a local plant nursery for almost a year, but I finally had to leave the job when it became too painful to lift the hose to water the plants. I think one of the hardest things I have ever had to do was tell them in the fall of 1998 that I could not continue working at Eaton Grove Nursery. You see, I also love plants, flowers, and vegetable gardening. It is an adult playground of sorts. And who wants to leave a place where you enjoy spending time?

Then, in April 2000, the heart problems began again. It all came to a head when I went into heart failure in June 2003. One day I was fine and the next it was like a very large man was constantly stepping on my chest. The pain was so severe I had to seek medical attention immediately. By October 29, 2003, I had an ICD, implantable cardioverter defibrillator, implanted in my chest to control and regulate my heart rhythm and issue a shock if I went into ventricular tachycardia or fibrillation. Both are lethal rhythms. An ICD is a pacemaker with a defibrillator built right into it.

I never thought my heart would go into this deadly rhythm, but it did. On March 22, 2005, I received two shocks in one day. I was asleep the first time, and the second shock came a couple hours later while I was sitting at the kitchen table. I was writing a to-do list and getting ready to do some errands when all of a sudden the room started to fade away and spin. I had to hold onto the table for dear life! My heart had gone into ventricular tachycardia. I felt the surprising jolt from the defibrillator which made me jump up out of my chair. I grabbed my chest because it really hurt. Then I realized I had been shocked and started crying because suddenly fear came over me. I thought, "I need to call Paul!" He works in the cardiac catheterization lab in the Cardiovascular Institute of Northern Colorado at North Colorado Medical Center in Greeley. I knew I needed to get there to be examined.

My body went into a tailspin of poor health for months after that, and there didn't seem to be any end in sight. I wasn't sure if I had the energy to start building my strength back up. I had finally worked myself up to walking a mile and a half at a time before this happened. This was a frightening experience. Now I was being told to limit my activity such as not lifting more than twenty pounds and being very cautious while doing any gardening. Even the cold weather would bother me.

During the summer of 2005 I went through heart transplant evaluation at University Hospital in Denver. The doctors actually said I was too healthy for a heart transplant but could be a candidate down the road. At that point, I had decided I would not go through with it because of all the medications I would be required to take for the rest of my life. It felt like my options in life were just hopeless at this point, and I had basically given up on life and living.

In September 2005 I decided to start walking again, bit by bit. It was a struggle to walk around just one block. I would have to stop several times and catch my breath. Even the dog thought it was a bit much, I believe.

One day, I was out walking when Dale, a neighbor from down the street, came out to say hello. I was feeling pretty worthless at this point, not being able to go very far and not being able to catch my breath. I couldn't understand why this person was bothering to say anything to me. Our paths crossed several more times over the next month or so. We talked about possibly walking together regularly.

Soon, Dale and I began walking together daily. He was healing from surgery, and I was just getting by. He started to challenge me to live a bit more every day—stand tall, take deep breaths, go a little farther, laugh, feel good about myself, etc. For several months, he was sharing the Law of Attraction's principles with me without my realizing what he was doing. When he told me where the principles came from, I began to read and study as much as I could. I could hardly get enough! It felt so wonderful to be excited about something great again. It had felt like such a long time since I had hope and a body that was responding in a positive way.

I began to change for the better. With the help of Dale's daily words of encouragement, I began to improve, but we could not figure out exactly why.

With these constant words of encouragement and following the Law of Attraction principles, I stopped talking about my health issues. I began to wean myself off pain medications. There were fewer days of pain and inability to sleep and function. Then I realized months had gone by and the fibromyalgia had disappeared. My body was pain-free! Without realizing it, I had learned not to give any energy to the fibromyalgia.

By this time, Dale and I were walking over three miles a day. I was also practicing yoga regularly. In March 2006 I even started ice skating for the first time since I was five years old. I absolutely fell in love with it! In September 2006 I attracted into my life a job at the Greeley Ice Haus, the local ice skating rink. I went from deathbed to life again in four months.

In July 2006 the movie, *The Secret,* was attracted into my life, and finally I began to really understand what a change in thinking and attitude had done in my life. In December 2006 I began the coaching/consulting program offered by Bob Proctor. I am truly beginning to realize what has taken place in my life over the last year and a half. I am continuing to grow on a daily basis through the Law of Attraction and all the concepts that Bob Proctor's program has opened up to me. As I study, work, and apply all the wonderful concepts that are in the Goal

Achiever program, I feel myself stretching and growing like nothing I have ever experienced. My life has absolutely done an "about face" from sitting on the couch full of pain two years ago to having excitement, energy, and goals and seeing what is next for me.

My focus has changed by making the Law of Attraction an important part of my life. I feel a strong desire to share with other people the idea that positive change is truly possible with a change in one's attitude. Learning and understanding how we can control the direction of our own lives is so important. We have to shift our focus away from the negatives like fibromyalgia, and focus instead on the positive experiences we want to attract into our lives.

Message: Learning to live with the Law of Attraction in a positive manner is life-changing. It is very important to continually be grateful for all the good that flows into our lives. I have learned to look at the major hurdles I have overcome in my life as victories. These victories come from taking steps forward, whether they are baby steps or giant steps. It is also important to realize that failure is feedback we can learn from.

Patty Skinger is a licensed and certified LifeSuccess consultant. She is also a coauthor of the book, *Magic of Winning*, one of seven people who contributed a chapter. She is enjoying growing her business as a life coach and seminar presenter. She can be contacted by e-mail at *PattySkinger@LifeSuccessConsultants.com*.

HERE IN VITALITY

By Jason Stephenson

A bird doesn't sing because it has an answer; it sings because it has a song …
—Maya Angelou

My name is Jason Stephenson. I am forty years of age, and life has truly just begun! I work as a vocalist/performer and have also spent the past fifteen years working with people with disabilities. Very soon, I am about to embark on my long-term dream of speaking and singing at seminars to assist others to make more of themselves, specifically, to love themselves and learn to master their thoughts.

But first, I want to take you back to my "past life"—the past ten years....

My life was all over the place. My thoughts were erratic, and along with that, so too was my life. I said yes to all demands placed upon me, making sure I pleased people along the way—*all* people. If I couldn't please, I felt a sadness. I felt alone. I felt a failure. In short, I believed I was useless and worthless if I could not please.

To assist and ease this process, I began to drink, take drugs, and have many casual sexual partners. I needed to fill a void. You see, if I was not happy with myself, I wanted to please others in any way I could. If they wanted sex, I had to obey. Even if I hated it, I went along for the ride and put it down to a bad experience. Anyway, it was a form of love—at least so I thought. I did not realise at the time that this was a process of stealing from each other—one of abusing our bodies, our emotions, and our souls. I took drugs of all kinds, ecstasy, amyl nitrates, marijuana, MDNA, and crystal meth. These helped to give me some short term "joy" and assist me to enjoy the sex that I so much despised.

A concerned friend once said to me, "Jason, what are you doing? You're going downhill. Be careful!" I told him not to worry. It's only a phase, and it will all pass. Something inside me knew that I could not keep up this life—that this was not the life for me.

The day was Remembrance Day 2005. I was to pick up the results of a test from the sexual health clinic—apparently I had given a friend an STD—at least that's what he thought. I had a bit of a sore throat, so I thought he could be right. I was not prepared for what was about to hit me. All results come back clear—except the HIV test the doctor had decided to throw in at the last moment. The doctor announced that I was HIV positive. Everything stopped. I felt myself sink into some deep, deep despair. Tears rolled down my face as I thought of my parents and the love they had given me all my life. And now I may in fact leave this world before them and break their hearts. I howled.

I drove home, and upon getting home, I sang. The first song I picked out was called "Stand Tall." In front of my audience (my dog, Dharma), I sang probably the most passionate performance I had ever sung in my life. I felt a twinge of joy! I could still sing!

Within three weeks of the diagnosis, my CD4 count (an indicator of how well the immune system is) went from a fairly healthy 590, to 300. The average/normal range is between 500–1200. To this day, I know it was the fear I felt that dragged my body into total shock and despair. My health declined over the next twelve months as I fought against this so-called "deficiency virus."

I battled during those twelve months living in total fear, guilt, shame, sickness, shock, anger, and sadness. I was fighting against the disease. I believed if I fought it, I would be okay. I read books on it. I focused on it. I wrote about it and joined groups associated with it. Yet, the very acts of fighting the disease and concentrating on it were wasting my energy and beginning to take their toll on my life. Toward the end of 2006, I became sick and had to go on medications—something again that I was fighting against. So finally, I let go.

I decided I was not going to live with a negative title—HIV—the human immunodeficiency virus. I was no longer going to be *deficient* in anything. That was my past. So I changed HIV to "Here In Vitality!" I said it over and over again. It was also at this time that a dear friend gave me *The Secret* to watch. But I still had to battle the demons inside my head.

Yet, something inside me knew I would make it through. Sometimes I would lie in bed and watch *The Secret*. Just the music alone inspired me! But the presenters and the pictures were awesome! My spirit welled up and gave me hope and joy. I would cry at times with happiness even though I may not have been too well. I decided that 2007 was going to be *my* year. I was going to put the Law of Attraction to work. And so I did.

Not even two years down the track since the initial diagnosis, I have love, a supportive and loving family, and beautiful friends. And the most important thing—I am living with good health and much joy! My mind has turned my previous erratic lifestyle into a heaven on earth! I now face my future with more optimism than I have ever mustered in all of my life.

I no longer take drugs; I no longer have sex with partners I barely know; and I am living my life based on the Law of Attraction, love, and *joy*. My life is blessed. I never thought it could be this good. I have turned a huge negative into the biggest positive of my life!

I have been booked to speak and sing at my first seminar based on living for the moment and the Law of Attraction. I will be linking the speaking with songs that inspire people to move forward in life. I have dreamed of doing this for over ten years—but have never followed through—until now.

One of the songs I sing states: "Love is in the air, everywhere I look around." Only now do I realise the true meaning of this, after ten years of performing this song!

Message: It's how you perceive things. It's how you think. Change your thoughts. If you don't like a label, toss it in the trash! Make your own label and live—Here In Vitality!

Jason Stephenson is a life coach, motivational presenter, and vocalist living on the south coast of New South Wales, Australia. His goal is to inspire all those he connects with and to give people encouragement to let their inner light shine. He can be contacted by e-mail at *beginitnow2020@gmail.com* or by visiting his Web site at *www.myspace.com/jayfordstephenson*.

WINNING THINKING

By Michael Cortson

*The basic fact is that all sentient beings, particularly human beings, want happiness
and do not want pain and suffering.*
—Dalai Lama

I had a terrible time controlling my thinking. I was a successful lawyer for nearly
twenty years when on April 1, 2003, I collapsed and was rushed to the hospital. I
had an emergency colonoscopy; died twice during the surgery; had five cancerous
polyps removed; underwent further testing; and discovered I was dying from
pancreas, liver, and colon cancers. Nice. I was *not* a candidate for treatment or
further surgery and was sent home to die.

I was depressed and my family was sure I was suicidal. I had lost sixty pounds
and was withering away fast. My family had me arrested, imposed a conservator-
ship on me, and I was thrown into the "looney bin." I managed to talk my way
out of there after a few days and was released. By then my digestive system was
shot. My body was completely jaundiced, and the whites of my eyes were orange.
The pain was horrific. I got home and finally realized that I was indeed going to
die. I called hospice. They were shocked since the patient rarely makes that call
himself. I then made my funeral arrangements on July 16, 2003.

I continued to get worse and was finally facing the end. By October, hospice
had brought out the "comfort pack" which is the final stage where you get the
maximum morphine until you expire. I got as much as I wanted whenever I
wanted it. I still felt the pain. Nothing would help. The pastor had prepared my
funeral service. My funeral would be a simple affair. The funeral director asked
me what I wanted to do. I told him "roast and toast." He laughed and then
immediately apologized. I told him it was no big deal and that I had come to
grips with what was happening and where I was going. He could laugh all he
wanted. I would take no offense. My sister, Kim, was there and tried to fight back
her tears. I think she felt that somehow she had let me down. The funeral planning took less than an hour. It seemed so ironic that I had fought like hell to stay

alive and the end was going to be over in a few moments. I couldn't wait to have everything stop. The fear was gone. The pain was horrific. No pain and peace sounded just fine to me.

Just when everyone was slowly starting to accept the facts, things took a turn for the worse. On October 16, 2003, I had a massive stroke that left me in a coma for several weeks. When I woke up, I was not lucid and I was paralyzed. Oh, lucky me!

The hospice volunteer found me lying on the upstairs bathroom floor. He told me later that I said "I fall down go boom." I have no recollection of what happened that day. Kim said that the fateful morning was nothing out of the ordinary. She came by and gave me my medication. She was in a real hurry that morning. She slammed my medication down my throat and said that I was "out of it."

My next recollection is waking up in a stupor. I didn't recognize anything. I didn't have any presence of being. I just was. It is difficult to explain. I didn't have a concept of being anything. I could have been a rock, an animal, a piece of fruit, or even a vegetable. I now know what the term "vegetable" meant. I was one and didn't care. My eyes saw but I didn't see. Nothing made sense. I had no concept of sound or touch. All I could do was blink. Blinking is what I treasure most to this day.

I was extremely confused, and there were only bits and pieces of recollection following the stroke. I was not in pain. I was nothing but a blob—silly putty. There was no feeling. If there was pain, I didn't consciously feel it. Kim took me to my niece's home for Thanksgiving. I was totally paralyzed on my entire right side. I didn't know it. They showed me photographs of the dinner, and I was there with long greasy hair and a scraggly beard. I don't have any recollection of it at all. There is nothing. Kim said my dad was so upset at the sight of me, he couldn't stand it and left. I didn't know it and it didn't matter if I did. I know this sounds like crazy talk. But I am trying to be as accurate as I can. It might scare the hell out of you. It should. It is no laughing matter. I'm not laughing. I am also not dead.

The road back was arduous. I was in three different nursing homes. I was cast aside and left in the hands of strangers that hopefully had the skill and training to keep me alive. I had to relearn everything from scratch. I was like a newborn baby. I had no concept of reality or the skills I had once possessed. I was no more than a slug oozing down the sidewalk. I had to learn to talk. I slurred like an insane person. I learned how to press my feet against the foot board in an effort to strengthen my legs. My right side was shot. I worked like a dog, so I'm told. I have little or no recollection of the process I went through. I don't remember Christmas. I totally missed New Year's though I have some recollection of seeing the Rose Parade on television.

I do recall at some point in January 2004 the blood clot in my brain worked itself loose. It felt like a comet zipped above my left eyebrow. In a split second I could remember pretty much everything. My motor skills improved slightly. As the days wore on, I could remember case law and the cases I had. I could remember my daughter, Allison, and the things that we had done when she was growing up. It was amazing. I could remember. I was overjoyed!

I had a problem walking and especially using my right side. I now had some hope which sparked my tenacity. I was not going to give up. My blood panels were still bad. I was still dying. It was depressing. I was determined to get past the cancer at any cost. My ability to pray came back. I had continuous conversations with God. I didn't try to make a deal with him. I only asked for strength. I made no promises. I knew that I couldn't keep them anyway, so why lie? There was no positive benefit to lying.

In February, the social worker unexpectedly appeared in my room. She had given me a tablet and pencil so I could practice writing again. She was very supportive. She had this big grin on her face. She was holding a piece of paper. I was playing with the computer. She finally spoke. She told me my tests had just come back from the lab. I thought it was a bit strange for her to be smiling when I knew she was going to be delivering more bad news. She simply said, "You're clean!" I looked at her with a perplexed look. I didn't know what she meant. She explained to me that the tests showed the cancer was gone.

After that, I started really pouring on the steam to get my ass in gear. I would walk every chance I got. I started being a contributor and stopped sucking off the system. It gave me a sense of being needed as well as a sense of giving. I made sure that I participated in activities. I would get up each morning and dress myself. I would clean up after myself and even make my bed. I bought a new electric razor online. I was turning into a far better person than I had been at any time before. I walked and worked. I did everything I could. I would go down to the activity department each morning, sweep the floor, and make coffee for the girls. It felt wonderful to have a completely new appreciation for life itself.

In May 2004 I was told that the State of Michigan had approved my release from the nursing home. I still had problems walking and using my hands. I had to struggle to sign my name and write checks. I had to learn everything again about shopping and managing my finances which are meager and virtually non-existent. I am permanently and totally disabled. No one would ever consider hiring me for a regular job. I can't get health insurance and will never get any. I am just far too high of a risk. The little cancer guys could go back to work at any time.

To everyone's amazement, on June 11, 2004, I was able to walk out of the nursing home on my own two feet. It was a joyous and sad day wrapped into one. This all became a reality with one simple step—a resolve to be happy no matter what and then just living that way. My doctors have no explanation. The hospice people can't believe I didn't die. I became determined to walk again and made my goal to leave the nursing home and return to a "normal" life. It was *work!* But my determination never faltered. Each step was agony, but every one was a win.

Message: No matter how horrible your situation, a bright spot is waiting to be found if you just look for it and then embrace it. You have every right to be happy. You choose your reality. Choose to be happy and smile! Being happy in the moment, no matter what, turns you into this wonderful receptacle for more happiness. It just grows and grows. Remember, the most important thing a human can do is … *smile!*

Michael Cortson is the author of the book, *Winning Thinking: How to Be Happy Almost All of the Time*. In this book he shares the techniques you can use immediately to take total control of your thinking. He is living proof of the power of the mind. For more information, please visit his Web site at *michaelcortson.com/winningthinking*.

OUR GREAT HEALING

By Jessica Levesque

There are two ways to live your life. One is as though nothing is a miracle.
The other is as though everything is a miracle.
—Albert Einstein

My son, Kaden Reece, was gently born into my hands on April 14, 2006. He was born at our home, full-term and healthy. When Kaden was three and a half months old, he suddenly became ill. He was in severe respiratory distress and had a fast heart rate. His chest was retracting and he was breathing between eighty and ninety breaths per minute. We were sent to a cardiologist to rule out a heart condition. Kaden's blood oxygen levels were in the eighties but they sent us home with no answers. I did not know at the time that the blood oxygen level should be ninety-eight when awake.

Over the next eight months, Kaden and I went from hospital stay to hospital stay, test after test, trying to find out what was wrong with him. The doctors could not pinpoint exactly what the problem was. He seemed perfect except for his persistent rapid breathing and retracting, requiring oxygen 24/7. I brought him for second, third, and fourth opinions, all over the state of Florida. Over eight cardiologists, six pulmonologists, and all the other pediatric specialists that exist saw him. Kaden is such a happy spirit, and anyone who examined him would tell us how great he looked despite his obvious distress. They were all amazed by his strength and would comment on his deep brown eyes and bright smile. Kaden underwent lots of testing, and every test came back normal except his lung CT scans. His first showed a ground glass appearance which usually means interstitial lung disease, for which the only result is death.

We were under lots of other life stresses as well. Our children are fifteen months apart. I had severe postpartum depression after my pregnancy. Our house was almost foreclosed on (we sold it on the day it was set to be auctioned), and our marriage was suffering. Things were spiraling down faster and faster. I had already worked with affirmations for many years prior to our lives becoming so disastrous, and I was telling my son Kaden that he was healthy. But I was feeling and believing otherwise because none of the doctors could figure out what was wrong with him, and his breathing was getting worse. Taking care of two babies with one on oxygen is very difficult.

After we sold the house, we moved to a nicer city. Things started to look up. I was so excited to be finished with the house problems and felt like this was a new beginning for our family. We watched *The Secret* a few weeks after we moved in, and it reminded us deeply of what we had forgotten. I decided it was time for Kaden to heal and come off the oxygen.

I set the intention that he would be off by his first birthday. As I put him to bed, I told him he was completely healed. His lungs were healed, and he was all better. I told him over and over again and imagined the healing on his lungs taking place. I gave him Reiki and poured my heart and soul into his healing. I told him I believed in him and that I always have and always will. He was breathing at one hundred breaths a minute and was on two liters of oxygen. I imagined his cute little face without a nasal cannula (a plastic tube which connects to the oxygen tank), something I hadn't seen in eight months. I pictured his breathing soft and steady and how happy it would make him to just be free of that long cord.

The next morning, he kept disconnecting his oxygen, which he had never done before. He pulled it off his face and his breathing was perfectly normal. I was so excited! I didn't want to put too much stress on his lungs, so after half an hour, I put him on half a liter. He then ripped it off, and I shut off the machine. I said, "Okay, buddy, you did it!" His sister, Jeweliana, was so happy. I kept checking his oxygen saturation levels and his heart rate all day, and he was perfect—he had healed his lungs! I got them dressed and ran outside to show anyone and everyone that he was free. I was so proud of him and so grateful. I cried so many happy tears. That was April 2, 2007. He also started walking that day and hasn't slowed down since.

I should add that Kaden was also on three medicines through a nebulizer three times a day, antibiotics three days a week, along with Prevacid and a lot of steroids. It would take over half an hour to administer the three medicines and much longer if I had to chase after him. He has had no medicine at all since that day.

He is an amazing spirit. No matter what tests he would endure, he would be back to smiling and laughing in no time. He is a very loving child, and I am so grateful to have him. He has taught me so much about the power within us all. Our lovely daughter, Jeweliana, amazes us each day. They are best friends and bring each other so much joy and laughter. Kaden wakes up each day smiling and is quite the comedian. He is a very sweet, loving boy who loves to cuddle. He is also a big risk taker; he has no fear and loves a challenge. I am so lucky to have such a miracle take place right before my eyes. It's been seven months since his healing and our healing as a family. Our lives have changed so much in the past seven months. We are very happy, we are financially secure, and we have our health and our family. I now experience each day as the best day of my life. I have so much to appreciate.

Life is amazing, and this is just the beginning of our journey. I now know that no matter what I choose to experience in life, I will continue on. And if I don't like the outcome I created, I can choose something else. It doesn't have to take a long time for that change to occur because I believe in miracles. Kaden is my miracle.

Message: Stop limiting yourself. Take responsibility for every area of your life and take action. When you let your heart and spirit triumph over your limiting beliefs, miracles happen. Believing is seeing the invisible.

Jessica Levesque is a wife, mother, Reiki Master/teacher, doula, real estate investor, author, natural childbirth advocate, and future president of Birth House—Birth Centers. She can be contacted through her Web site at *www.embracingbirthbook.com*, by e-mail at *TrueEssenceReiki@aol.com*, or on MySpace at *www.myspace.com/JewelKaden*.

STORIES OF TRIUMPH OVER PAIN AND DEPRESSION

MY JOURNEY TO HEALTH

By Jennifer Mannion

When you dance, your purpose is not to get to a certain place on the floor.
It's to enjoy each step along the way.
—Dr. Wayne Dyer

By the age of thirty-five, I had been diagnosed with two painful chronic illnesses as well as one genetic blood disorder. I felt like life as I knew it was over and I would spend the rest of my life in pain. Through my personal journey with the Law of Attraction, I realized I did not need painkillers or to be in constant pain. These days, I have very little pain and take *no* painkillers. The only medication I am on is Coumadin to regulate the thickness of my blood. *The Secret* was the most integral part in my healing and has allowed me to be free of medications and free of pain.

It took years to be diagnosed properly with even one of my illnesses. On the way, they found lots of "little problems" that accounted for a few of my symptoms and caused minor surgeries and more tests. The final diagnoses required many embarrassing and uncomfortable tests, blood being drawn weekly, the stress of waiting in doctors' offices and hospitals, and waiting for results. The first diagnosis was for fibromyalgia; the second, a year later for benign hypermobility syndrome (HMS); and the third was the blood disorder factor V Leiden. Once diagnosed with factor V Leiden, I realized I was fortunate to have been able to have two healthy children and that the disorder had probably been the cause of my daughter being born nine weeks prematurely. Factor V Leiden is the lack of a protein in the blood that helps keep the blood thin, so I am prone to clots. I had a deep vein thrombosis (DVT) in 2005 that caused me excruciating pain in my leg, hospitalization, and a very slow recovery.

Fibromyalgia and HMS have extreme pain symptoms. Often, on a bad day, I felt like an eighty-six-year-old when I attempted to get out of bed in the morning.

Everything ached. The pain was everywhere. I have two young children, and it used to make me very sad when they saw me almost crawling in the morning as I got my six-year-old son ready for school and my three-year-old ready for the day with me. These diseases have no real "cures," and the treatment is usually heavy doses of painkillers, a low dose anti-depressant (to help with sleep), and staying as active as possible. I fought taking painkillers for a long time having always been afraid of any kind of dependency, and I was adamant about not being on anti-depressants. I was on the sleep/pain cycle that accompanies so many chronic illnesses. I couldn't sleep because I was in so much pain, and the lack of sleep didn't give my body a chance to heal itself which made the pain worse.

Eventually, I gave in to taking pain pills hoping if I started to get some things done on my daily list, I would at least feel happier mentally. I was very down on myself for taking them, and while the pain pills gave me a few hours of relief, when they wore off, the pain would return with a vengeance. Considering I was thirty-five and the prognosis was for me to have these conditions for the rest of my life—I did not like the prospect of needing more painkillers as time went on. I didn't want to show my kids that Mommy needed pills all the time. I tried many different treatments including several natural remedies. Some things helped a bit, but nothing made me feel like my old self.

There were a few things that were making my life more bearable, such as a new close friend and reading inspirational books. I felt I was on the path to healing but could never make that final leap. I usually wound up more frustrated and in more pain than before. Then a good friend told me about a movie I "had to see" called *The Secret*. For Christmas 2006 my husband got it for us to watch. That was the beginning of the most dramatic change in my life.

The Law of Attraction is *The Secret*'s main principle, and it helped me tremendously. It made so much sense—that if you are positive and grateful, you will receive more things that are positive and to be grateful for. If you are negative and worry all the time, you will receive more that is negative and more to worry about. I was so preoccupied with my constant pain and what it was costing me that I was not taking the time to be grateful for all that I had. This led to the next *Secret* theme that helped me—living with an "attitude of gratitude." I have so many things to be grateful for: healthy kids, a good husband, and family and friends who are supportive and filled with life and love. I have a house that will truly be my dream house when it is fixed up, and I have the ability to look out of any window of my house and see the mountains. I started to focus on these things every morning as I got ready for my day and any time during the night that I awoke in pain.

The Secret also helped me by how it touched on illness. It said your body is constantly creating new cells, and every few years you have a totally new body. By focusing on the negative and how "sick" you are, your body will create "sick cells." Immediately, I began to lie in bed for a few minutes when I awoke being thankful for my health. After all, I could go for walks, I am average weight, I could get around the house, and I had parts of me that were not in pain. All my concentration shifted, and within a few days I was a different person. Now, months later, I am on *no* pain pills and am in minimal pain. I still go to the chiropractor and am on Coumadin for my blood, but that is all.

Another way *The Secret* has changed my life was to teach me to ask for what I want. If anyone had asked me what I wanted before I saw the movie, I would have said, "To not hurt so much, to be financially sound, and to be happy." That's all good, but there was no way to achieve those things without elaborating on them. I sat down and wrote out my goals and imagined myself feeling those things and how happy I would be. I am now physically 100 percent better. My relationships with others have improved because of my health, and my relationship with myself has improved as well. I have seen the Law of Attraction change my physical and spiritual self. I am now focusing on it changing my financial well-being, which I have no doubt it will. I am already seeing the signs. I am so grateful for *The Secret* and truly feel it came into my life at exactly the right time.

Message: As the great Dr. Wayne Dyer has said, "When you change the way you look at things, the things you look at change." If you concentrate on how bad you feel and the negative things in your life, you will attract more of the same. Instead, think about what you are grateful for—things will get better and you will find even more to be grateful for.

Jennifer Mannion lives in upstate New York with her husband and two children. She has a bachelor's degree in psychology, attended graduate school in forensic psychology, and taught computers to kids in New York City. She also ran her own desktop publishing/word processing home business. She enjoys dancing, walking, and cross-country skiing. She loves learning about the Law of Attraction and the mind/body connection and hopes to inspire others to take control of their health and limit their dependency on pain medications. She maintains several Web sites and blogs on healing pain naturally: *heal-pain.blogspot.com* and *www.thankfulformyhealing.com*. She has also written an eBook about her healing. To purchase Jennifer's eBook, please visit *www.thank-fulformyhealing.com/e-book.htm*.

I FOUND THE
ANSWERS
BY LIVING THE
EXPERIENCES

By Julie Donnelly

All fears, worries, and doubts ... all feelings of lack, scarcity, and need come from thinking about yourself. Forget yourself and focus on helping others. Only then can you truly make a difference. Only then will you truly know love, happiness, and abundance.
—Rich German

I had been living the Law of Attraction long before I knew it had a name. I was always saying that I could manifest what I wanted faster than anyone I'd ever met. My life's goal has always been to make the world a better place because I lived here. I was accomplishing that with my work as a deep-muscle sports massage therapist. It was fulfilling to have people come to me in pain and leave my office pain-free. I knew I'd found my calling, and I was satisfied that life would only get better for me. Then, in 1996, I began to have severe wrist pain that felt like someone was pushing a hot spike into my wrist. It got worse and worse. The pain spread, and my fingers became so numb that eventually I couldn't hold a glass or even wash my hair.

I tried everything I knew that had worked at manifesting my goals in the past ... visualization, meditation, and speaking to "the Universe" to clarify my wants. Nothing worked! I was devastated when I had to close down my practice, knowing I was going to have to go on welfare while I learned a new career that didn't require the use of my left hand. The night before going to the welfare office, I cried and shouted out to the Universe, "Why did this happen? All I wanted was to help others ... and I was. Now this! If you want me helping others in a different way, that's fine, but you'd better let me know quickly because I can't pay the rent." When I calmed down, I said, "All I want to do is help people. There must be another way, and I just want to know what it is." Then I went to sleep.

The next morning, I awoke from a dream with my mouth saying out loud, "The problem is the muscles that cross over the median nerve." I repeated it slowly, trying to make sense of what I'd just heard, and then it hit me what I was saying. I jumped up and shouted, "Thank you, thank you, thank you!" I studied the anatomy and research books in my office. I pressed on the trigger points that have been documented through years of medical and clinical research. And within three hours, my pain and numbness were completely gone. I was thrilled! I also realized that I'd asked for and I'd received the answer to carpal tunnel syndrome. Plus, I had treated myself so I could teach other people how to treat themselves. The thought of "Give a man a fish and you feed him for the day; teach him how to fish and you feed him for his life" entered my head, and I knew this was the reason I'd suffered for so many months. I needed to be open to creative thought to receive this understanding and then bring it to others.

Immediately, I put out a call to anyone who had wrist pain, numb fingers, or carpal tunnel syndrome. And they came, in droves. It amazed me as each person was able to self-treat and get relief, often total release, from pain.

There was Carl, a man who was paralyzed on his left side from a stroke and was diagnosed with carpal tunnel syndrome in his right hand because of the pressure of using a cane to assist his walking. He was terrified of surgery because he knew if there was a mistake, he'd have no hands and would be totally dependent on others for the most basic of needs. At first, I had to teach his wife to treat Carl, and then it occurred to me how to have Carl work on his own muscles with a plastic tool I'd devised. It worked perfectly, and he was now able to self-treat even though he only had one working hand. And there was Mary, an eighty-seven-year-old lady who couldn't lift a teacup or even cook for herself. She was unhappy when she had to give up her independence and move in with her son's family. She was thrilled when she was once again able to use her hand normally, even returning to crocheting which she loved to do for relaxation. Also, there was Jim, a thirty-two-year-old professional classical guitarist whose career was ending because he couldn't use his right hand. Jim didn't want to live when he found he couldn't play any longer. He told me that I'd saved his life when I showed him how to get the feeling back in his hands.

My work with athletes, and my goal to help them continue their sport, led to my having sciatica, frozen shoulder, whiplash, and a serious knee injury—each forcing me to figure out how to self-treat the injury. Now I knew to ask, and then wait for the answer to come to me. It always came, and it came quickly. I could then translate that self-treatment I'd discovered to teach others how to release their pain. It was amazing how I'd have a run of clients with the same injury each time I'd worked out a new self-treatment. They were asking for answers, and I wanted to share what I'd found. We were a perfect match. The Law of Attraction was, and still is, working in each of our lives.

I made the decision that I wanted to help as many people as I could before I died, and I attracted the right people to move my practice into a wider venue. Associations have members that do repetitive movements as a part of their careers, and corporations are having serious problems with repetitive strain injuries undermining their productivity and financial stability. In each case, simply teaching the individuals how to self-treat the tense muscles changes the lives of the workers. And, by lowering the amount of sick leave and medical claims, it is beneficial to the business. This is a "win-win-win" situation: the worker is out of pain, the company is saving money, and I'm fulfilling my goal of making the world a better place because I was here.

It was exciting to me when I learned that there was actually a Universal law bringing me my goals. I found that with focused attention on my goals, I was actually able to deliberately create my day-to-day life. Blame is no longer a part of my life. Even when something negative is happening to me, I can say with strong conviction, "I created that." And then I focus on what I want to bring into my experience. It's also wonderful to know that I am not a victim of anything; I create all of it. I know that by the Law of Attraction, everyone who comes into my life has been brought here by my thoughts, and I'm happy to say that I'm now surrounded by people who want to benefit mankind and bring joy to the world.

The Law of Attraction continues to work in my life, and I can see it clearly in the lives of those with whom I interact.

Message: It's good to look at today's challenges as the fuel that will give tomorrow's answers. Often what looks negative is actually lining up circumstances so you'll receive exactly what you've been asking for—never quit!

Julie Donnelly is an internationally-respected expert on repetitive strain injuries, including carpal tunnel syndrome. She specializes in teaching self-treatments for chronic joint pain and sports injuries. She may be contacted through her Web site at *www.aboutcts.com* or by e-mail at *jd@juliedonnelly.com*.

THE SPRAINED WRIST

By Michael Skowronski

Love is the great miracle cure. Loving ourselves works miracles in our lives.
—Louise L. Hay

It had been a very satisfying day. I worked for the first time in five weeks; a sprained wrist had been preventing me. Still the wrist had not fully healed and there was pain. I was very careful of the way I used that hand when I gave my two clients their massages that day. I do mostly deep tissue therapeutic work which is taxing enough on a healthy therapist's body. So I had to find a way to work without reinjuring my wrist. Mostly I was successful, but giving the massages did make my wrist hurt just a little worse. I knew I would easily recover. At least I had money … $120 for two hours of work. Not bad!

At this time, I was so financially broke I could barely feed myself. I am an American who was living in Australia without a job, without any savings, and without any social services available. I had borrowed all I could from everyone I could ask, and I was again at the end of my rope. I had to go back to work doing the only thing I knew I could do to make money on such short notice. I had decided to work through the pain.

I had just spent my last $30 on some food and a one-day advertisement for my massage services. The ad had to pay off. I did not want to face the prospect of borrowing money again just to advertise, nor did I want to face starvation. Sometimes, I would advertise and get no clients. Thank God it worked out today. Now I had enough money to advertise for the next week and eat for the next three or four days.

I was in the midst of one of the most difficult times of my life. Just fourteen months earlier, I had lost my job at Compaq Corporation which was the source of my working visa. I was unable to find another employer in the computer software industry in Australia. Writing software was the reason the government of Australia permitted me to remain for the nearly five years I had been there. I had also tried establishing my own business over the Internet, but lack of proper funding and inexperience was killing me. Financially, I was facing a pretty dreary picture.

Emotionally, it had been no bed of roses either. At the same time I lost my job, I also lost my Australian fiancée. I was still very much in love and attached to her. Even at this time, I held out hope that she would change her mind and invite me back into her life. Needless to say, it was a very stressful time in my life.

Fortunately for me, I had my spiritual experience and awareness. I had been studying intently for sixteen years with many different enlightened masters. Abraham, channeled through Esther Hicks, was my current teacher. I had been applying the principles of all I had learned in my life on a regular basis and I was getting profound results. It was these experiences, coincidences, and miracles that gave me the strength and faith to get me through this difficult time of my life.

So I was feeling very happy to receive $120 that day and to know that I was once again healthy enough to work. I could at least feed myself and pay the current bills. That was a step in the right direction.

I lived on the Isle of Capri just outside of Surfers Paradise on the Gold Coast of Australia. One of the things I loved to do was to go out rollerblading with my dog, Sasha. All of the streets were smooth and flat. We would skate over our half of the island, stopping at the various waterfront parks and vacant lots to enjoy the beauty, and for Sasha to have a swim. There was a wide open parking lot right next to a soccer field where I would skate around like a figure skater. I loved the feeling of such fluid motion.

Want to guess how I sprained my wrist? Yep, I sprained it figure skating in that parking lot just five weeks earlier. I had a wrist guard which I stopped wearing because my wrists and hands would get hot, sweaty, and itchy. Besides, I hardly ever fell, and when I did, I was usually able to recover without damage. But, after I sprained my wrist, I was pretty careful to wear the wrist guards every time I went skating … except on that particular day when I just forgot to put them on.

So once again, I went down, pretty near the same spot as the last time. I fell on the same side of my body, while skating backwards, and automatically caught my fall with the same hand. I sprained the same wrist all over again, but this time it was much worse. It swelled up immediately and turned black and blue in a surprisingly short amount of time.

I got right up and skated away in total embarrassment. I felt like someone was watching me, and I had just done something very stupid. Soon, I realized no one was around, and I just stopped in the middle of the street. I became lost in my thoughts, "*It's your first day back at work and you injure yourselves worse than the last time. What kind of idiot are you? No one is going to have any sympathy for you at all. Your father will tell you to come home to the United States. Your friends will have some excuse, but they will never talk to you again if you ask for more money."*

Then I caught myself in my destructive thinking and realized I needed to stop. But even in the midst of that realization, my mind was flooded with fear. *How will I eat in a few days? I only bought enough food for three or four days. I just spent most of my money on massage ads. No. Stop thinking like that! I have got to get a grip on my mind. Okay, I have had healing miracles in the past ... that is what I need right now ... a healing miracle. I won't focus on my wrist at all. I won't tell anyone what I did. I will just take the most care possible and continue on with my life as if this never happened.*

That is exactly what I did. I went home and made my dinner, sat down in front of the TV with a glass of wine, ate my meal, and enjoyed my evening. And I did not tell a soul. At one point while I was cooking, I instinctively grabbed the pan with my injured wrist and twisted slightly. The pain nearly sent me through the roof. For a moment I started to worry. *How am I going to give a massage tomorrow with my wrist like this?* I felt like I wanted to cry. But I quickly gained my composure and reminded myself that I have experienced healing miracles before, I have seen them occur for others, and there was no room for any other possibility in this situation. I went on with the rest of my evening and enjoyed it thoroughly.

I awoke abruptly with pain a few times in the night. Then the worry would kick in, which I quickly caught. Every time I would worry, I would consciously spend a little time recalling and reliving past experiences of healing miracles. This would calm my mind. The next day, my wrist was still swollen and still black and blue in spots. I had lots of phone calls for massage. I figured if I could get through two of them, I would be doing well.

My first client showed up at 11:00 AM. I was very good about protecting my wrist; my focus was strong. I was not going to forget and accidently use my hand or wrist incorrectly. Afterwards, I felt a little bit of extra soreness, and as soon as the client was out the door I iced my wrist for about thirty minutes.

It was during my second massage, which began at two in the afternoon, that I let my focus drift. I was doing well, feeling confident, and getting lost in the music. I get very artistic and dance with my hands, arms, and elbows on the body of my client when I give a massage; this time was no different. Then it happened. At one point, while I was totally lost in what I was doing, I realized I was using the hand of my sprained wrist as if it were not injured. I caught myself doing really strong petrissage on my client's leg. Petrissage is a Swedish kneading technique that entails gripping and twisting and flexing of the wrist. That is what I was doing when I realized … *What am I doing?*

I stopped immediately in a state of shock. At first I was just waiting for the pain to come shooting through, but there was no pain. I stood there and stared in amazement at my wrist, which appeared to be completely normal—no swelling and no black and blue color. There was no pain, none at all. Not even the little leftover pain from the sprain of five weeks ago. My hand and wrist felt absolutely fine. Then I realized the client might notice an abrupt absence of touch, and I continued giving him his massage. My mind was stunned at the realization of what had just happened, and like a mantra I just kept repeating, *Thank you, God. Thank you, God. Thank you, God.* Tears of joy were streaming down my face, which I had to keep wiping away so they wouldn't drip on my client.

When my client left, he thanked me and said, "Without a doubt, that was the best massage I have ever had in my entire life." I had other clients try to book appointments that day, but I turned them down. I was happy to have another $120 in my pocket and I could wait until the next day to work again. I celebrated this magical miracle by going out rollerblading with Sasha. This time I wore my wrist guards.

Message: I cannot emphasize enough the power we hold in our minds. When we learn to use our minds correctly, nothing is impossible. We start by first trying out new ideas and being open to experiencing the results. We advance with practice and diligence. Slowly our inner programming changes; our new ways of thinking replace the old and become automatic. Life responds by delivering different experiences to us. Our successes give us strength and vision to stretch our minds further and create even grander life experiences.

Michael Skowronski is the author of the book, *Unforgettable: A Love and Spiritual Growth Story*, which demonstrates the Law of Attraction at work through equally amazing true life experiences. For more information on his book, please visit his Web site at *UnforgettableBook.com*. You can contact him by e-mail at *Michael@gr8Wisdom.com*.

OUT OF THE DARKNESS: DEPRESSION IS A CHOICE

By Julie Ann Connelly

Emancipate yourself from mental slavery ... none but ourselves can free our minds.
—from "Redemption Song" by Bob Marley

The Secret

Although my outward appearance may look the same, I am no longer the person I once was. I have known despair. I have known heartache. I know what it is like to be at death's door, knocking, wanting to be let in, not wanting to stay alive because the pain inside was too great to endure. My despair has dissipated. My depression has faded. I am no longer angry. My heart is now open to give and receive love. I am happy and content. The abundance I now have in my life is difficult to put into words, but it is obviously there and it is overflowing.

Through some miracle, God sent me to find this small little book that I can hold in my hands. This powerful book of wisdom has changed my life in a way that before reading it, I never thought was possible. I am so grateful that someone was able to put into words, information that finally broke through my sick and unhealthy way of thinking. I am so thankful that a book, a small tiny book packed with invaluable information, somehow had the power to allow me to finally break through this concrete barrier I had enclosed around myself. The concrete is gone. It is now mere dust. I am free.

My life before *The Secret*

I don't really remember the exact date this illness began. The illness was very slow and methodical. It took its time. It was calculating. It was cunning. It did not appear all at once. One day I felt fine and the next, an explosive panic attack that would leave me exhausted in its wake would occur.

My mind, not my physical body, was not healthy; it was not generating healthy thoughts. The inconsistencies with the anxiety and panic attacks left me vulnerable, fearful that another attack would occur at any place and time. I was embarrassed. I was confused. I began to live in fear. Fear of the unknown. Fear of not understanding why this was happening to me. Angry that it was happening at all. My life, as I knew it, was being taken away from me, and I did not understand why.

I can now see the truth. The truth is that I, Julie Ann, who was experiencing anxiety and panic attacks, who would eventually embrace major depression with open arms, was ill and out of balance. There was something gravely wrong, but it was not at the physical level as most would have you believe. It was greater. It was my mind, my thoughts. It was the way I looked at the world. It was the negative energy I was putting into the Universe. It was the constant worrying thoughts of, *why me?* What have I done to deserve this? Why is this happening to me? Why am I sick? Why am I so angry with God for doing this to me?

For over four years, I lived in this manner. I could no longer work, let alone leave my home. I could not function. I required assistance with daily living tasks. I was alive, but I was not living. I know what it feels like to live in hell on a daily basis.

I could write about the illness and the symptoms that consumed me. However, they are now forgotten, and I no longer wish to live my life in the past. I wish to live in the present where my life is now so incredible that I wake up every morning and thank God for allowing me to have another glorious day.

There are many individuals who do not understand anxiety, panic attacks, or depression. I will provide an analogy of what my life was like on a daily basis. Perhaps this will help you understand the absolute madness that surrounds this disease:

Morning was slowly approaching. The beautiful yellow sun was beginning to peek through the clouds. I took a deep breath and slowly exhaled. A slight breeze was gently filtering the room, and the smell of salt water permeated my senses. I could hear the sound of seagulls and the hypnotic melody of ocean waves. It was pure bliss.

I opened my eyes and found that I was trapped in a large hole dug in the sand. As I lay on the floor of the hole looking upward, I realized that the hole was deep, and it was impossible for me to climb out of it. I could hear people playing volleyball on the beach, jet skiing, talking to their children, and enjoying the day. I screamed and I screamed. "Can anybody hear me? I am trapped in this nightmare of a hole. Help me! God, please help me!"

A volleyball teetered on the edge of the hole. "Oh God, please let the ball fall into this hole so someone will see that I am trapped down here." An individual grabbed the volleyball and looked in my direction, but I appeared to be invisible. "No one can see me. I do not matter."

I decide to climb out of this hell, and I put one foot into the side of the wall of sand. I dig my hands in the sand above my head. I hold on tightly. I insert my other foot only to fall farther down than when I started. I try again and yet, nothing. I cannot escape my torturous surroundings.

I give up. I tell myself that tomorrow will be a better day. Tomorrow, someone will finally notice me and will send help. Tomorrow, I will be rescued. The truth is that no one will rescue me, and I know this. I am tired. I decide to go back to sleep, for in sleep is where I find my only source of solace. As I drift off to sleep, I pray to God to take my life for this is not a life worth living. I pray that I will not wake up and will stop living this unworthy existence.

My life transformed after introduction to *The Secret*

One night, like many, I was unable to sleep. I was tired of tossing and turning in my bed and decided to watch television. I live in the Chicago area, and *The Oprah Winfrey Show* is always televised a second time in the late evenings. I viewed the end of a show in which a panel of guests was talking about a book titled *The Secret*. The guests were so excited, jubilant, and passionate about the information they were sharing. One guest began discussing her "vision board" and the positive influence it had on her life. I had heard about a vision board before but never gave it much thought. To be fairly honest, I listened to what these individuals were saying but never gave it much further thought. I was too wrapped up in my own little world of misery.

The information regarding *The Secret* instantly became explosive. It seemed as if everyone was talking about this book and the Law of Attraction. My thoughts initially were, "Whatever! Just another book solicited on *The Oprah Winfrey Show* that will be forgotten within a couple of months."

On another sleepless night, I could find nothing on television that warranted my attention. I decided to log on to my computer, and for some unknown reason I went to *The Oprah Show* Web site. I was immediately drawn to the past show archives and opened the transcripts for the show on *The Secret*. As I started to read, I became interested in the information. I quickly printed the pages and sat in my bed and read them over and over again.

I believe that our souls have the innate ability to know truths. At that very moment, while reading the transcripts, my soul instantly knew that what I held in my hand was absolute, pure, and perfect truth. I sat reading and crying as tears of emotion flowed down my face. These emotions were, without any doubt, locked up inside me for many years. These pages of typed information were breaking through this concrete barrier I had enclosed around myself. The concrete was fracturing and falling in little pieces, one by one, to the ground. As the concrete hit the ground, it became mere dust.

I am free. I am finally free.

My life after embracing *The Secret*

The morning after I read the transcripts, I awoke to watch the sun rise. I sat on the grass in my backyard and allowed myself to breathe in the true beauty of the Universe. It was peaceful and quiet, and I could hear the sweet sound of the birds singing. I closed my eyes and said to God:

"Thank you. I am happy and content. I am a beautiful and precious human being. I am part of a delightful, outstanding family. I have good, courageous, and caring friends. I have a home to live in, a bed to sleep in, blankets to keep me warm, running water, electricity, heat and air conditioning, and I live in a town that is friendly and peaceful. I am surrounded by abundance. There is abundance in every avenue of my life. I am so incredibly blessed. Thank you, God, for allowing me to finally see the joy that has always been in my life."

This particular morning was the day I allowed myself to come out of the darkness. I knew my current state of depression and fear was my choice. I knew, as I never knew before, that I alone could cure myself of this disease by making a conscious choice to alter my thought process. From this day forward, I told myself I was healthy. If a family member or friend would say they were sorry I had endured a long-term illness, I would immediately correct them and say, "I am healthy. I am happy. I am whole."

I believe when we have predominant, recurring thoughts, whether negative or positive, these thoughts create crevices in our brain that allow for the ease of negativity or positivity to prevail in our mind. My challenge was to create new crevices for positive thoughts to flow while minimizing the large crevices where negativity flowed easily and freely. It was as if I was blazing a new trail to walk where I had never walked before. I knew there would be fresh grass to walk on, branches to move out of the way, and trees to duck under, but it would be my new, exquisite, and strong trail.

I would like to tell you that my journey from illness to optimal health was easy, but I cannot. Every day, every second, when I start to slip into old habits, I must stop myself and reprogram my thoughts into my new way of thinking. I must walk on my new trail. Some days it is reasonably challenging. Other days, it is fairly easy.

Regardless of the ease or difficulty, the change I have experienced is immeasurable. I glow. I radiate from the inside out. I smile and I laugh. I am in complete happiness. Bliss. Sheer and absolute bliss. I feel comfortable with people. All people. Family, friends, and perfect strangers. I no longer hide in my house. I no longer hide from myself. Fear no longer controls me. That word is no longer in my vocabulary.

The only thing that stands between us and what we want in life is the will to try it and the faith to believe it is possible. The Law of Attraction is not only possible; it is more correctly stated as complete truth. Our words move us, and we are responsible for our words. This seemingly simple law will make such a tremendous difference in your life that you will be in complete amazement. Believe in the Law of Attraction and move forward. Be as God has intended for you to be.

Every day I wake up early to watch the sunrise, and I thank God for blessing me with another day of life. If you knew me, you would know I am truly honored that you are reading my story and are trying to understand how the Law of Attraction can change your life. More than likely, I have never met you face to face, but if I could have one wish, it would be for you to experience nothing but good health, happiness, prosperity, and a life surrounded by those who love you. May you be blessed in ways you never thought possible.

Message: In the United States of America, depression has become an epidemic. Anti-depressant drugs are being prescribed in record levels, and nevertheless, individuals are still living in a depressed state. Stop. Change your thought process and change your life. The change is not always easy. It requires work, but the abundance and goodness that will flow into your life is miraculous!

Julie Ann Connelly lives in Ottawa, Illinois, a very small town west of Chicago. In January 2008 she began pursuing her master's degree in speech-language pathology at Northern Illinois University. She loves photography, gardening, reading, and dedicating one weekend of every month to some sort of volunteer work. She also absolutely loves to perform random acts of kindness. But more than anything, she enjoys spending time with her family and friends. Julie Ann can be contacted through MySpace at *www.myspace.com/stoneandsand* or by e-mail at *julacon13@aol.com*.

IT'S MY TIME TO SHINE

By Donna Webster

When you forgive, you love. And when you love, God's light shines upon you.
—from *Into the Wild* by Jon Krakauer

Being diagnosed with a chronic illness was not what I had in mind for my life. One illness would be enough for most to handle, but for some reason unknown to me at the time, I was given two. Somehow I was chosen to spend the rest of my life living with fibromyalgia and interstitial cystitis. The good news was that I could take a variety of pills each day to manage the symptoms. The bad news was these little pills could not guarantee I would be symptom-free each day. I spent many nights crying myself to sleep and praying that when I woke up in the morning this would all be a bad dream. Unfortunately, it was not a dream at all, and I knew I had to figure out a way to accept this part of my life.

I was angry, mad, frustrated, and depressed about having to deal with this. After all, this was not what I signed up for, and I couldn't understand why it happened to me. I wondered to myself each day if I did something so bad that I was being punished for it now. To make matters worse, I didn't look sick, so I was treated badly and almost lost my job in the process. I was never one to complain, but it really hurt me to think that anyone thought I was making this up. After I got over being hurt, I got angry. But as time went by, my anger, frustration, and depression somehow faded away, and I started accepting this new part of my life. Knowing I could not control what happened to me and knowing I couldn't change it left me no alternative but to accept it—and that's exactly what I did.

The funny thing is, once I started accepting it, some amazing things started happening for me. I found out millions of women just like me lived with chronic illness every day, and I decided to start reaching out to them. I knew first hand how it felt to feel alone and how frustrating it can be to deal with an illness that most people had never even heard of. I wanted to find a way to help other women. I wanted to find a special poem to send out to them. I searched for the perfect poem for several weeks but had no luck in finding one. Then I had what

Oprah calls an "Ah ha!" moment. I remembered that I used to write poetry many years ago and decided I would write this poem myself.

When I sat down to write that first poem, I ended up writing over twenty poems in a matter of hours. I took my poems to a printer, had little cards made, and started sending them out to support groups, hospitals, and anywhere else I could think of. Over the next few years, I sent out thousands of my "Secret Angel" poems and several other poems as well. I was also lucky enough to have my story featured in newspapers and magazines, and my poems were featured in newsletters as well. I ran a support group for fibromyalgia for awhile, and I even received a proclamation from the mayor of my city. I set a big goal for myself during all this: to inspire women all over the world with my writing. I didn't know it at the time, but I was using the Law of Attraction to attract women to inspire as well as everything else that came into my life.

It was a big goal to set, especially since I had never figured out what I wanted to do with my life. But I felt I was given this gift of writing for a reason, and I knew I had to use it the best way I could. For many years I had no idea what my purpose in life was, and searched in all the wrong places only to discover the answer was inside me all along. It certainly would have made it easier to know earlier in life that I needed to look within for all the answers. But, maybe earlier in my life, I would not have been ready to receive the answers or the gifts I possess.

I have received many gifts since that day, and these gifts have taken me on the most amazing journey of my life. Over the past several years, I have gotten to know the real me and learned many lessons along the way. I have been tested many times, and the greatest thing is knowing I can survive whatever life throws at me. I've been out of work, had multiple surgeries, was carless at one point, and dealt with a disk problem in my back that caused me excruciating pain.

Life had been going great for me. I took my love of writing and put it together with a bath and body business on the Internet and was having the time of my life. I was interviewing women for my site and taking my goal of inspiring women to a new level. But, as most of you know, it's usually when life is going great that you receive a new challenge. My back problem took me back to a place I thought I wouldn't ever have to visit again. My world turned very dark as the pain consumed every hour of the day. All of a sudden, I found myself wondering once again, "Why me? What did I do to deserve this?"

I had found my gifts and purpose and thought I was using them to the best of my ability and couldn't understand why this would happen to me again. As far as I was concerned, two chronic illnesses were enough for me to handle; I certainly didn't need or want any more pain in my life. I found myself crying myself to sleep once again and asking God why he did this to me. What did he want from me? Honestly, I felt like giving up all my dreams and settling into a life of pain. I couldn't stand for more than a minute or two. I couldn't sleep. I couldn't walk for more than a minute. I was in horrible pain twenty-four hours a day and popping pain pills like they were candy. I wondered if this was how the rest of my life was going to be. What about my dreams and my goal of touching lives? I wondered if this was the end to all those dreams. If it was the end to my dreams, what would I do with the rest of my life? I don't give up easily, but I was very close to giving up all my dreams and it was a terrible feeling.

I racked my brain trying to figure out what to do, and then I remembered a friend had told me about some shots she received in her hip from a pain specialist. After hearing about the success she had, I decided to check into it. I asked my doctor, and she referred me to the same doctor my friend had seen. The doctor explained she could not guarantee these injections in my spine would work, but she also told me there was a good chance they would work. So I started receiving my series of three spinal injections at my first visit.

I am excited to say the treatment did work for me, although we don't know for how long. I might have to get more injections in time, but today I am pain-free. It's strange to live with pain for so long and to finally be free of the pain. When I find myself getting nervous that the pain will return, I focus on the feeling of gratitude that the pain is gone. I believe God wanted to get my attention because he had more gifts to give to me and wanted me to do more with my life. He wanted me to reach out to more women, and a seed was planted within me to start a new organization to help support abused women.

I didn't waste any time getting started, but I also learned that this was not all God had planned for me. Knowing that I love to talk, a little too much at times, he also put the seed in my heart of doing a radio show. Knowing that I could not do it alone, I have attracted some amazing women into my life, and recently, Divine Diva Inspiration was born. I had a goal in my heart many years ago of wanting to inspire women all over the world, and what better way to do that than with a radio show. Interviewing women on my radio show has been a dream come true for me. Meeting women who help me inspire other women around the world is the most wonderful gift!

I can tell you first hand that the Law of Attraction works when you use it and allow it to work. There have been times in my life when I wasn't using it as much as I could have, and it was apparent in my life. I am now living the life of my dreams and using the Law of Attraction to bring everything I dream of into my life, and it is truly amazing.

I believe we all have amazing gifts and talents we are given, and it's our job to discover them and share them with the world. Sometimes those gifts are not easy to find, but if you look within yourself, they will be revealed to you. It has been a long journey for me to get to this place in my life, and at forty-one years young, I want to tell the world—it's finally my time to shine!

Message: Overcoming hardships, adversity, and reaching out to touch lives, I am using the Law of Attraction to live the life of my dreams.

Donna Webster is an inspirational writer whose goal is to empower, inspire, motivate, and build self-esteem in women and girls all over the world. She does it with her writing, her inspirational bath and body site, *www.divinedivadelights.com*, as well as through her organization which supports abused women, *www.divineseedsofhope.com*. She also works one-on-one with young girls dealing with abuse, depression, and self-injury. Donna can be contacted by e-mail at *donna@divinedivadelights.com*.

STORIES OF
WEIGHT-LOSS
SUCCESS

WEIGHT LOSS AND THE LAW OF ATTRACTION

By Sierra Goodman

You and I are not what we eat; we are what we think.
—Walter Anderson

I first learned about the Law of Attraction in 1992, from an incredible woman named Marilyn Umbach. Marilyn taught me about manifesting all the things I wanted in my life by using my divine power and the Law of Attraction. And manifest I did! I created new homes, jobs, relationships, cars, boats, money, and eventually, the life of my dreams, owning oceanfront property in the rainforest of Costa Rica, surrounded by monkeys, toucans, macaws, dolphins, and whales. I created a very successful eco lodge specializing in dolphin and whale tours, and I also founded a non-profit foundation, Vida Marina, working to create a protected marine sanctuary in the area. I did it all with conscious co-creating, using the Law of Attraction.

I know with 100 percent certainty that the Law of Attraction is real and that it works. If you practice the steps to manifesting your true divine path and use the divine power that we all have because the Law of Attraction is a Universal law, magic and miracles truly do happen. I was able to manifest everything I wanted in my life—except for my perfect weight.

I am one of the millions of people who have struggled my entire life with weight loss. I have yo-yo'd up and down all through my life—sometimes chubby, sometimes obese, and occasionally thin. I cannot remember a time in my life, since childhood, when I was completely happy and satisfied with my weight. Every time I got near my goal, my bad eating habits and negative thoughts would creep back in, and I would find myself *fat again!* I now know I believed that I didn't deserve to be rich *and* thin. And I also didn't want to give up the security and other advantages that being fat gave me, at least not on a deeper level. I know that now.

I was always looking for the magic pill, the diet breakthrough, the one "outside" thing that would let the thin me, the *real me,* come out. I was starting to give up and give in to being fat for the rest of my life. I was up to over 300 pounds! I was a fat mermaid, always in a bathing suit, swimming in the ocean, hanging out with dolphins and whales, and extremely obese.

We see a lot of really successful people who are still overweight. Weight loss is very different from making money and using the Law of Attraction to manifest material things. Weight loss is very personally about *you* and *your body*. It takes different and really concentrated work to get thin for good. For me, making money is easy compared to losing weight!

I know what it is like to be overweight and all the feelings of failure, embarrassment, and insecurity that come along with it. I have been there! And I finally made it to the other side, using the incredible tools we all have within ourselves and co-creating my life with God or Source Energy, whatever you call the divine power that we are all an extension of. Now I really want to share my story with others so that they, too, can lose weight and live the life of their dreams.

Thanks to a dangerous fall in my bathroom and hitting my face hard on the cold tile floor, I was reminded that I already had everything I needed inside me and that I have the divine power to have whatever I want, including my dream body. I had already used the Law of Attraction and my divine power for many years to manifest other incredible things in my life—real miracles—why not use it for my body? By applying these incredible tools of manifestation, I finally found the way to permanent and healthy weight loss. I finally applied the Law of Attraction to my body in a very conscious and concentrated way.

I began my manifestation process for weight loss. Among other things, I wrote in my journal: *I have the divine right to be healthy, happy, prosperous, and thin. It is my birthright and within my divine power to have everything I desire. I am thin, I am happy, I am healthy! I am! I am! I am!*

You see, Marilyn taught me that it is more than just the Universal Law of Attraction that everyone is talking about right now. The Law of Attraction works because it is your divine right to live the life of your dreams. God created the Universal Law of Attraction to give you the power within yourself to manifest that life. You are attracting things to you because they are already yours by divine right. You are just saying yes to them! When you are on your divine path, your vibration matches the vibration of those things that are yours, and they come to you in the most miraculous and mysterious ways!

Using visualizations, affirmations, manifestation wheels (now known as "vision boards"), and thought training games that I made up to keep my thoughts and feelings positive and happy, I shed 170 pounds in a little over a year without surgery, pills, or excessive exercise, and have now kept it off for more than a year.

One of the games I played with my mind was to picture myself as Barbara Eden's character in *I Dream of Jeannie.* When I found my thoughts wandering to things that were not part of creating my divine path, I crossed my arms, blinked my eyes, and made it go away. I became my own *Jeannie*, master of my thoughts! Games like this can really help you to keep your thoughts on your dreams and not on mind chatter that can be destructive to your success.

Now my path is to help others learn about the divine power we all have inside us and how to apply that power to weight loss and creating the perfect body for each of us. We are all a physical extension of Source Energy. It is my desire to show people they really can be thin and stay that way once they decide that is what they really want. That is the biggest step, making up your mind you are ready to give up all the reasons why you stay overweight. Then it is just up to you and God to re-create your life in the thin body you desire. And I can promise you, if you do this work, if you consciously create your life using the Universal laws that are there for each and every one of us, you can have the body you desire, and so much more!

I have written a book called *From Paralegal to Paradise* which tells my story of learning about, and using, the Law of Attraction to create the life of my dreams, what happened when I stopped consciously creating my life, and finally using it to lose the weight I had been fighting my whole life. I have also developed an interactive Web site at *www.iam-iam-iam.com* where you can learn more about the Law of Attraction, share your divine moments with others, get helpful suggestions for your manifestation lists, inspiring affirmations, and much more.

My book and Web site give people all the tools they need to not only lose weight, but to create the life of their dreams. No one wants to be just rich or just thin; we all want it all, and we can have it. It is already divinely ours!

Message: The Law of Attraction can also be applied to your body to lose weight!

Sierra Goodman is originally from California where she worked as an independent paralegal for many years before her heart and her dreams led her to create a company called The Divine Dolphin, running dolphin swims in the Bahamas. This quickly led her to Costa Rica where she purchased ten acres of oceanfront/

rainforest property, first creating a successful eco lodge and now a marine conservation and research center for her non-profit foundation, Vida Marina. Sierra now runs the center and inspires others through her writing and Web sites. For more information, please visit her Web site at *www.iam-iam-iam.com*.

THIN FROM WITHIN

By Marna Goldstein

One way to get thin is to re-establish a purpose in life.
—Cyril Connolly

What did I, as an eighteen-year-old, know about the Law of Attraction? Apparently, I knew enough, because what I learned transformed my body from a size 14/16 down to a size 6/8, easily and effortlessly in a matter of months.

I was twelve years old when my mother was in a car accident and my dad fell from a ladder. I had always been an active and athletic child, but now I needed to be there for my mother, my father, and my little six-year-old sister. I'm not sure if I was really there for them, but somewhere in my twelve-year-old mind, I felt I was the Greek deity, Atlas, taking on the world. Due to my anger and frustration regarding not being able to be what I perceived as a "normal kid," I would come home after school and eat while doing laundry, cleaning, playing with my sister, and working on my homework. Slowly, I began to gain more and more weight.

Barely squeezing into a size 12/14 a year and a half later, I found myself astonished at my weight gain. My pediatrician at the time was also thrown back. How did this athletic kid gain so much weight in such a short period of time? Well, it doesn't really matter the "whys" or the "woes" of my life; the reality was that I needed to lose weight.

I began working out. I was even employed at an athletic club, but no matter what diet plan or exercise program I tried, I was unable to lose more than a few pounds. I scoured the library shelves looking for any morsel of hope and information I could get my hands on. I knew there was something I just hadn't figured out.

Have you ever had that feeling? That feeling that lies deep in your soul that tells you there's an easier way. That there's something you just haven't figured out and once you do, the money, the clients, and the relationships or, in my case the weight, would just roll off. Well that's exactly the place I was in from the time I was twelve up to age eighteen.

In college, I continued researching various diets and exercise programs. I was majoring in psychology, so now I had a more sophisticated library with loads of research and journal articles to enjoy and wrap my mind around. I was desperate. I was sick and tired of having big legs rubbing together, feeling fat, ugly, and out of shape.

I was obsessed. I had to find the answers, not to mention that my boyfriend at the time, upon my asking, honestly told me that he thought I could lose weight in my legs. *Yikes!* I had to find a way to slim down, so I asked professors, doctors, psychologists, nutritionists, and kinesiologists about permanent weight loss. I learned about food chemistry and how our bodies assimilate food. I asked and asked and asked, and guess what? For every person I asked, I received a different answer. Literally, no two answers were the same. Some professionals said to eat mainly carbohydrates, and others said protein, while others felt increasing my fruit and vegetable intake would be the long-term answer. They told me when to eat, what pills and/or supplements to take, when to take them, and how to take them. It was crazy!

One day in my dorm room in Boulder, Colorado, some of my skinny friends were hanging out and talking about how they could eat whatever they wanted and never gain weight. They didn't understand the concept of dieting and had no idea about nutrition. The light immediately went on! Why had I been spending all this time and energy talking to overweight people and compulsive dieters?

Without knowing I was using the Law of Attraction, I began interviewing successful, naturally thin individuals. When I say naturally thin, I mean those people who never diet, never watch their calories, or measure food. Those individuals who maintain naturally thin bodies over the course of their lives. I began watching, talking to, and researching these thin individuals. In fact, I became obsessed with them. I wanted to know what their secrets were and if I would be able to mimic their ways of eating and living. I researched hundreds of thin individuals on campus, in formal settings, in relaxed settings, downtown, in schools, at grocery stores, and in malls. I just had to know! I conducted market research and statistical analysis, all to see the differences between thin and overweight people.

I learned everything I could possibly learn about naturally thin individuals. I compared these new tips and naturally thin ways of living to the diets and the methods of losing weight that I had tried in the past. Once I began thinking like a naturally thin individual, I lost weight faster and more naturally than ever before. It was amazing! I was shrinking right before my eyes. I could hardly believe it, and neither could my college friends. They couldn't understand how I could be losing weight while eating everything I wanted. Once I began living and thinking like a thin person, the extra weight had to come off.

Now that I understand the Law of Attraction, I clearly understand how I transformed my body. First, I began to think and feel thin. I walked the walk and talked the talk. Without a reservation in my mind, I began feeling thin and acting as though I had the body I desired. I walked like a thin person, shared food like a thin person, ate ice cream like a thin person, said "No, thank you" to food like a thin person, and I even worked out like a thin person. Before I knew it, *I was a thin person!* It didn't take long either, only a few months of harnessing the Law of Attraction, and I went from a size 14/16 to a size 6/8.

Currently, I am a size 6/8 and I have maintained this size for over fourteen years. I am comfortable in the body I have. I no longer binge, exercise compulsively, or diet. Through the Law of Attraction, I have learned that weight was never the problem, for if it was, I would have lost the weight once and would have never had to think about it again. Weight was the symptom of my "fat" thoughts and my "fat" mind. It was the symptom of my boredom, my procrastination, my anger, my Atlas complex, and my stress.

Message: You, too, can transform your body by harnessing this incredible law. Understanding and utilizing the tools and principles in this book is your magical key.

Marna Goldstein founded *ThinWithin.com* to inspire people to transform their bodies by understanding how to think, live, and feel thin. She is the author of *Naturally Thin Secrets* and is featured in the 2008 documentary *Facing the Fat*. You can learn more about Marna at *www.ThinWithin.com* or contact her by e-mail at *Marna@ThinWithin.com*.

I FINALLY UNDERSTAND

By Deb Micinski

You're getting exactly what you're feeling about,
not so much what you're thinking about.
—Bob Doyle

My story begins twenty-seven years ago when I was twenty years old and started dieting to lose about ten pounds. Six years later ... those ten pounds had soared to over forty!

My life during that time was best described as pure chaos! I was on and off diet after diet without success. In fact, I usually ended up gaining more weight. I was attending college full time and working part time. I was financially broke and physically exhausted most of the time trying to keep up with school, work, and my social life. My relationship ended with my boyfriend of over four years after he confessed he'd become romantically involved with a female co-worker. A married friend, unhappy in his marriage, expressed a romantic interest in me that soon became an obsessive, stalking situation. My car was vandalized four times. My younger sister and brother were both planning their weddings, while my life consisted of partying, bar hopping, and bad dates. I was very depressed and my self-worth was in the toilet.

The turning point came after I started dating a guy I'd casually known since I was sixteen years old. I'd dated a few other guys (some good, some bad) but he was different. We really felt "connected" right from the start. I loved spending time with him. I was happy and for the first time in years, I didn't feel consumed with issues and anxiety about my weight. I was actually *living* and *loving* life for a change. The funny thing was, this renewed *"zest for life"* had nothing to do with losing any weight because my weight hadn't changed.

However, several months later, I was pleasantly surprised to discover I had lost weight. I think it was only about five or six pounds, but the point was … I had not been trying to lose weight!

That's when the "lights" finally came on!

Why was I able to lose weight now without even trying? Priding myself on self-discipline, I felt I should have been able to get this weight thing under control a long time ago. So what was different now? What was I doing wrong before? Curious, I had to dig deeper to find some answers.

I began reviewing the past events of my life, making comparisons of my life then versus today. Surprisingly, it honestly didn't take too long to discover what the source of the problem was. It was the way I *felt* (emotionally) about myself and my life at that time. I suddenly realized just how truly unhappy and discontent I had been at different times in my life. The fact is my spirit was broken. The question was why. I've always been blessed with a wonderful, supportive family and fantastic friends, so what caused me to feel this way, and why wasn't I able to get control of it and "fix it"?

Well, I gave this a lot of thought and I came to a conclusion. I thought I was trying to "fix it" each and every time I started a new diet! You see, I was so convinced my weight was the sole reason for my unhappiness, I virtually ignored other issues going on in my life at the time and the effect they were having on me. I honestly believed if I could just lose weight, it would fix everything. I'd have everything I wanted and finally be free to be happy. Since I repeatedly failed to do that, I didn't feel *worthy* of happiness because I hadn't *earned* that right yet.

While there were other contributing factors, the constant failure to lose weight perpetuated a very poor self-image and lack of self-respect. The lack of self-respect triggered binge eating. The binge eating caused me to gain even more weight. Gaining more weight deepened my feelings of worthlessness and depression.

Wow! What a self-destructive cycle. Needless to say, I was an emotional mess.

Time for a fresh start!

After dating ten months or so, I felt happier and better about myself than I had in years. I decided to go back to the gym and start working out again. This time, however, my goals were going to be different. This time my intention was to create a healthy new *lifestyle*.

I vowed to never go on another restrictive diet again! I was going to respect my body and make a commitment to eat healthy and treat my body, mind, and soul right from now on.

Less than five months later, I painlessly dropped thirty-five pounds and weighed 113 pounds. I finally learned what worked ... and I've kept the weight off for over twenty years now.

About four years ago, a friend and I were having a discussion about losing weight and I mentioned how often I have people ask me how I stay so thin. He told me maybe I should write a book. I chuckled and replied, "Yeah right!" and basically forgot about it. After all, I'm no writer!

Well, time passed, but for some reason this crazy idea of writing a book never left me. It's sort of hard to explain, but "situations" seemed to periodically pop up in my daily life "reminding" me in some strange way that I needed to write this book ... *"signs"* perhaps?

I contemplated the idea for well over a year until finally deciding one day to just do it! The book (guide) is called, *I Finally Understand!* I briefly share my story and experiences with traditional diets, exercise, etc., but mainly focus on the realistic, common-sense approach that finally worked for me, as well as the tips, tricks, and philosophies I learned along the way. I also discuss the importance of developing a healthy mind and spirit and their vital role in achieving life-long success.

It took me over three years to write it, but I have to say I've been most impressed (and surprised) by my persistence to stick with it until it was finished. I could have quit at any time. I always had a good excuse. Plus, I never told anyone I was writing it so no one was even holding me accountable. But, for some inexplicable reason, I felt it was important in some way that I finish it. So I did!

In early 2007, I was home from work one day and decided to watch *The Oprah Show*. The topic was *The Secret*. I must say, I was literally *blown away!* I even yelled out at one point, "Oh my gosh! I know what they are talking about! I understand this! This is the same kind of thing I wrote about in my book!" As strange as it may sound, I felt as though I finally had some confirmation of what I already knew was true.

I found I had unknowingly used the Law of Attraction principles before, during, and after my weight loss and even wrote about it!

Here are a few examples:

- Prior to losing weight, all I thought about was how overweight I was. Being fat was constantly on my mind.—*"You become and attract what you think about most."*

- I had nothing but negative thoughts and feelings about my body and my life.— *"Our thoughts and feelings create our life."*

- I felt trapped in a cycle of physical and psychological self-destructive behavior. My life felt out of control.—*"You manifest exactly what you are feeling because of your thoughts."*

- Once my negative thoughts and feelings were replaced with thoughts of laughter, fun, happiness, and gratitude, I began attracting more happiness in my life, and weight loss unexpectedly followed.—*"Happy thoughts, confident thoughts, produce feelings which attract happy circumstances.—Like attracts like."*

- I visualized my life in a whole new positive way, one with meaning, purpose, and direction. I opened my eyes and saw the bounty that life holds when we focus our attention on it.—*"Life is meant to be abundant."*

- I committed to change and shifted my focus from negative thoughts and feelings about my body to positive ones and improving my overall health. I focused on creating a healthy new lifestyle.—*"Energy flows where attention goes."*

- I learned the importance of having a positive attitude and being grateful for the things I have in my life and the things yet to come.—*"You create your Universe as you go along."*

- When I talk about *"my crazy idea of writing a book and the 'situations' that seemed to periodically pop up in my daily life 'reminding' me in some strange way that I needed to write this book … 'signs' perhaps?"* I now understand that I attracted those situations into my life through my subconscious thoughts and feelings about writing this book.

Learning about the Law of Attraction has only improved the way I live my life today and is proof positive to me of the power of the mind and the Universe. I view life as a wonderful gift … and I'm grateful to be here enjoying every minute of it.

Message: Change your thoughts … change your life!

Deb Micinski has worked in the information technology field for the last twenty-one years and is currently employed as an information technology support supervisor at a mid-sized Northern Indiana bank. She lives in the South Bend area (home of Notre Dame) with her husband and two daughters. She loves spending time with family and friends, traveling, working out, and visiting the beaches and wineries of Southwestern Michigan. If you would like a copy of her book, *I Finally Understand!*, please visit her Web site at *www.Ifinallyunderstand.com* or contact her by e-mail at *deb@Ifinallyunderstand.com*.

STORIES OF
SUCCESS IN SPORTS
AND FITNESS

ROCK AND ROLLING
WITH THE LAW OF
ATTRACTION

By Bonnie D. Stroir

Live with passion!
—Tony Robbins

When I first read about the Law of Attraction a few years ago in Lynn Grabhorn's *Excuse Me, Your Life Is Waiting*, I felt like I'd hit a goldmine! I was already an ambitious goal-setter, but I wondered why I was achieving *some* of my goals right away and others either *very* slowly or not at all. Learning about the Law of Attraction was like finding the missing link! Previously I'd been writing down what I wanted and thinking about it, but I hadn't been *feeling* it.

It felt like a brand-new world at that point, and I became a prolific visualizer. This proved to be very effective when I set the intention to start a roller derby league in San Diego.

I'd been commuting from North San Diego County to Los Angeles to play roller derby with the L.A. Derby Dolls for about two years and the traffic was getting seriously old! I contacted the founders of the L.A. league and asked them if they'd mind if I started a sister league in San Diego. They said, "Go for it!" So I got straight to visualizing. I imagined all of the same awesomeness in San Diego that I'd been experiencing in L.A.

This was in 2005, and at that time, no one I knew had ever heard of the Law of Attraction. In fact, very few people who knew me had any idea I even read books. I wasn't really sure how to explain the Law of Attraction to them. But I had seen it working for me on other goals I'd had: a free trip to Greece; a free bicycle; and once, I just focused on the fact that I wanted a white t-shirt and somebody gave me one. I didn't see how starting a roller derby league could be any different. So whenever somebody raised an eyebrow or asked me, "How are you going to do that?" I would just smile and say, "I have no idea!"

It's funny how little support I got back then. It's the first thing people brag about when they introduce me to others now. I don't think most people really *meant* to be dream killers, but darn if they weren't obvious skeptics! My own dad was the first person to say, "Roller derby? What a stupid waste of time. That'll never go anywhere."

To be fair though, I can't exactly blame people for looking at my current situation and doubting me. On the surface, I didn't exactly appear to be in a position to be creating any empires. At the time, I was over $25,000 in debt, two months behind on my rent, and my truck had just been repossessed. I'm a barber by trade, and I had walked away from a very successful barbershop with a lousy environment to work at a brand-new barbershop with literally no clientele, but a great environment. On top of that, I didn't even live in or know any part of the actual city of San Diego. I lived in Oceanside, a town thirty minutes north of San Diego, in the North County. (A heck of a lot closer than L.A., though!)

But I've always had somewhat of a "*kiss my ass, I'll do what I want*" attitude, and this was one time that it came in especially handy. I wasn't about to let anyone's lack of confidence in me, or the apparent negativity of my current situation, stop me from creating something amazing. If anything, having all the odds stacked against me and a total lack of support only fueled my fire. I had more reason than ever to test these new ideas I'd read about, and see if they really worked.

I decided step one was to find some skaters. So I put daily posts on craigslist.org and got a huge response. Every day I imagined getting dozens of e-mails, and every day they arrived in my in-box. I didn't even have a computer at the time; I used to skateboard to the library's computer center every day to do my business. I was so excited to check my e-mail and find so many enthusiastic women ready to get the crap beat out of them, that I was like a walking ray of sunshine at all times! Feeling good is the main priority when you're setting big intentions, so I literally started tossing my bothersome bills in the trash. It felt so free and liberating! I had no time for anything that brought me down; I was just feeling good, good, good all the time. I even bought myself some new skates!

Okay ... skaters: check. Now I needed a place for us to skate....

Once I figured out which skating rink was the most centrally located in San Diego, I knew I'd found my practice space. I called to find out when the rink owner would be there, grabbed my shiny new skates, and Mapquested my way to Skateworld in Linda Vista.

When I got there and told the DJ/rink manager, Monty, what my intentions were, he told me there was no way it would ever happen and that the rink owner, Gary, had already turned down two other people who wanted to hold roller derby practices there. "Well," I said, "he hasn't met *me* yet!" I skated the session while I waited for Gary to arrive and imagined the floor full of excited Derby Dolls practicing their skills and doing drills. The session ended with still no sign of Gary, so I offered to help clean up the rink between sessions if they'd let me stay and wait for him.

I picked up abandoned water bottles and slushy cups, imagining I was duti-fully picking up after forgetful Derby Dolls at the end of practice. Occasionally, I'd stop and drink at the water fountain, scolding myself for not remembering to bring a bottle of water to my imaginary roller derby practice. I felt great! In my mind, the Derby Dolls were already there.

Five hours from the time I got there, Gary finally showed up. By the time I sat down with him in his office, I knew it was a done deal. He was skeptical and leery of having a dangerous liability like roller derby in his rink, but I assured him that the Derby Dolls' intention was to create a legitimate sport of it and that there would be strict rules and regulations.

Two weeks later, on June 13, 2005, the San Diego Derby Dolls had their very first practice. My friend and fellow former commuter to L.A., Ruthless Killa, who also lived in San Diego County, saw all the brand-new Dolls showing up to prac-tice and whispered nervously to me, "Is there anything you want me to do?" I said, "Just be excited with me," and we were! I had never coached anything before, but I visualized myself being the best coach ever, and my actions reflected my visions!

It was so overwhelmingly awesome that I cried. *Twice!*

Now I was a firm and absolute believer in the Law of Attraction. Everything I had needed to get this going came to me, and quickly, as long as I kept feeling good and visualizing rad outcomes. Then I had a thought.... If I can attract this much radness and rad people on my own, imagine what amazing results would come about if *all* of the San Diego Derby Dolls put it to practice!

Keep in mind that I raised myself on punk rock and a kind of "screw ideolo-gies" attitude. So despite all these rad results, I still wasn't ready to come out and preach this "Law of Attraction" to people, because if they were anything like me, they might reject the idea on principle alone. So instead, I started out with subtle ways to sneak it into practice, giving random pep talks to generate excitement (excitement is the number one factor in making the Law of Attraction work for you, hands down); creating goal sheets; and encouraging skaters to write their biggest and best case scenarios, feeling them like they're real, and reading them to the group. I started coaching visualization techniques and reading scientific studies that backed up their efficacy to the group from Dan Millman's *Body Mind Mastery*.

Eventually, they got used to my talking like this, and I started talking more openly about these concepts. I reminded the skaters not to use defeating words like "I can't," but to say things that made them feel empowered and in a constant state of progression. We started setting our league goals together, and we adopted the slogan "America's Finest Roller Derby." (San Diego's slogan is "America's Finest City.") Their success has been evident in the level of skating ability our league generates and the mind-blowing rate at which they learn. The San Diego Derby Dolls literally learned their skills in one-third the time it took me to learn things, and I attribute 50 percent of that to our visualization practices and the other 50 percent to how incredibly rad these women are! Derby Dolls attract the most amazing women ever!

When the movie, *The Secret,* came out, I went crazy! Here was the Law of Attraction, neatly packaged for the world to see. I bought multiple copies to loan to people and held a special viewing for the San Diego Derby Dolls. We filled in blank checks to the Derby Dolls and wrote more new goals.

We've already accomplished so many of our goals! These include the purchase of a $15,000 banked track which we intended from day one despite the fact that at the time we didn't know of any in existence. And, wouldn't you know, just when we had enough money to buy one, a former L.A. T-Bird (1970s and '80s school roller derby) had one for sale. She had several leagues interested in purchasing it, but we had so many Derby Dolls visualizing it as ours, there was no way anyone else was getting that track! We even named her "Greenie," and put a picture of her on our Yahoo! Newsgroup so we could see her every day.

The San Diego Derby Dolls still have about a million goals we've yet to accomplish (do ambitious people ever run out of goals?), but we know now that it's only a matter of time before this grass roots effort becomes a professional sport. We look forward and *feel* the abundance, gratification, and success that come with providing positive female role models for kids nationwide (and eventually worldwide). Only two years old, with a world of possibilities at our wheels, the San Diego Derby Dolls can thank the Law of Attraction for truly making us America's Finest Roller Derby!

Message: Passion is highly attractive.

Bonnie D. Stroir is the founder of the San Diego Derby Dolls and a two-year veteran skater of the Los Angeles Derby Dolls. She is also a writer, barber, and spiritual counselor in San Diego, California. Bonnie can be contacted by e-mail at *bonniedstroir@gmail.com.*

THE MARATHON

By Trish Kapinos

You will recognize your own path when you come upon it, because you will suddenly have all the energy and imagination you will ever need.
—Jerry Gillies

It was May 2006 when I decided to take some things off of my "I'll do someday list" and put them onto my "doing now list." I have always wanted to run and finish a marathon before I died. So I figured since I wasn't getting any younger, *now* would be the best time to start. I announced my plan to several friends and family members.

Two weeks later, one of my dear friends, Richard Moxley, called. He said registration for the Marine Corps Marathon was opening in an hour and asked if I would like for him to register me. I panicked, because saying yes meant I had to do it. Then I remembered my commitment—to finish a marathon before I died—so I told him yes.

Now, what is important to note here is that I am a non-runner. I'd never run farther than three miles … ever. I had no idea how I was going to do it—just that I was committed to completing a marathon. I began running and discovered that running was clearly the hardest thing I'd ever done. I ran on my own for about four weeks and honestly was ready to throw in the towel, when one night my friend, Richard, the same one who got me into this mess, asked me how it was going.

I told him how hard it was and how much I doubted being able to do it. He looked me straight in the eye and said "Trish, running a marathon is 80 percent mental and 20 percent training. What you need is a running buddy." That sounded really good. Then, out of nowhere, his wife volunteered to be my running buddy. I play "The Perfect Game," so of course, I said yes. We had exactly sixteen weeks to train before the race. She helped me plan runs, nutrition, sent me to the right running store for equipment, and off we went. I met Cheryl each Saturday morning for our long runs. Every Friday I had trouble sleeping, because the next day meant that I would run farther than I'd ever run before. The really cool part about running your first marathon is that each week you are literally running farther than you've ever gone in your life. We'd run six miles, then eight miles, then ten miles … until, ultimately … 26.2 miles! My husband was concerned in the beginning, and he actually tried to talk me out of it because he knows how hard it is for me to breathe. The doctors call it asthma—but I never bought into it. I control my mind, and my mind controls my body. No asthma here. So clearly, I had no need for an inhaler, either.

There were many challenges along the way. Running was absolutely the hardest thing I'd ever taken on, and now I was committed to a marathon. Wow! I had no idea how I would do it; I just knew that I wanted to complete a marathon. So I began to visualize. I would see the crowd cheering me on, and at the end, I saw the Marines clapping and cheering me on to the finish line. I could literally hear the cheering in my head, the clapping and roaring—it felt so real that it brought tears to my eyes imagining what it was going to feel like to cross that finish line. To do the impossible! To run a marathon!

There was a song by Kelly Clarkson, "A Moment Like This." I put it on my iPod, and when it would come on during my runs, it would move me to tears. Can I really do this? Can I run a marathon? I began to hear that song as I crossed the finish line. "… a moment like this … some people wait a lifetime for a moment like this." It was the hardest thing I'd ever set out to do, and all I could think about was how amazing it was going to be to cross the finish line.

Race Day: I was nervous. I cried during the national anthem. I cried walking to the starting line. Just the thought of crossing the finish line moved me to tears. The gun went off. I crossed the starting line, and all I knew was the next rest stop was 26.2 miles away. It was amazing. You couldn't have prepared me for running in a pack of people like that. People wrote funny sayings on their clothes. Some people were running for lost soldiers; others were running for fun. I was running to the finish line.

It was fun. At the five-mile mark, I announced to my running buddy, "I can't wait to run my next marathon." By mile ten, I was recanting that statement. Miles seventeen to twenty were lonely miles. The course looped out by the water, and few spectators were there. It was windy, and my legs were beginning to feel the soreness of the previous miles. I kept thinking about the finish line—and how amazing it was going to feel when I crossed it. I even imagined a tape line for me to run through. Now, I run fairly slowly, so there would be no tape for me, but it was fun to imagine.

All I really cared about was getting past the twenty-mile mark where, if you were too slow, they would pull you from the course and your race was over. I got to twenty miles and made the cut. I was going to complete my marathon! All I had to do was keep moving forward. My commitment to finish carried me through those last 6.2 miles of the race. The finish line! That was all I had to think about to keep my tired body moving. Those last six miles are permanently etched in my mind.

My running buddy, Cheryl, was a godsend. You never met a girl like this one. She is the most positive person I know, and there is literally no room in her to listen to whining, complaining, or any self-indulgent, negative emotion whatsoever. We got to the last .2 miles of the race. (Holy rollers—it was up a flipping hill! Who are the sadists who designed this course?) We began up the hill, Cheryl motoring up the hill like she had wings, me struggling like I was carrying an anvil behind me. Halfway up, I stopped to walk. She got ten steps beyond me and turned to see where I was. She put her hands on her hips and looked at me like, "What happened?" She took two steps toward me, and I couldn't let her come any closer. I began to run again. (Man, did I mention how much I hate hills?) We got up the hill, and I thought for sure I was going to die … but I kept going, of course!

The Finish Line: About twenty seconds later, there it was, lined in balloons with the soldiers cheering. It was exactly like I had pictured. Only now my body disappeared, the aches, the discomfort, the wheezing was gone, and the lungs no longer burned. The excitement of actually seeing the finish line had me. I was really going to do it … my God, it was really happening!

Just thinking about it now, I am instantly transported back to that magical moment of crossing the finish line. I could see the finish line now, and it was calling me exactly like I'd imagined it would. The Marines were cheering. My running buddy wrapped her arm in mine as we charged the finish line together. In that moment, it was true. I could do *anything* I set my mind to, and now I had proof. Now I *knew* it too. I am powerful beyond measure, and in that moment and many moments since, I know life is calling me forth to be great. I now know that I can do anything I'm willing to commit to … *anything!* And by the way … so can you!

Message: You can do anything you set your mind to.

Trish Kapinos is a life coach in Virginia. She can be contacted through her Web site at *www.Bridges4You.com* or by e-mail at *Kapinos@hotmail.com.*

KEEP YOUR CHIN UP

By Jan Graham

*Our doubts are traitors and make us lose the good we oft might win,
by fearing to attempt.*
—William Shakespeare

About six months ago, I joined a gym. Every morning, there is one personal trainer there who works out at the same time that my little group does our workout. He does his routine with such a quiet determination that he makes it all look very easy, although I know all too well how hard he is working. When I am tempted to whine and quit, I watch him push himself to his own limits, and I find myself motivated to work as hard and without complaint.

One day, I was watching him do chin-ups. He made them look effortless. I broke away from my group and asked him if I could try a chin-up. I had never tried before, but he just made it look so easy. He eagerly stepped aside and encouraged me to step up to the bar. I pulled myself up without thinking ... once ... then twice. That was all I had in me; I had no strength left. I told him that was all I had, so he stepped up behind me and pushed me up for a third and fourth "pull." It felt so good. I felt strong, and I smiled from ear to ear.

The next day, when I was done with my workout, I asked him to spot me again. Again, I did two. I did the same on day three and so on. I thought it was pathetic that I could only do two, but when I came to the gym at the end of the week, he was standing there just shaking his head. When I asked him what was up, he said he was impressed with my chin-ups. He told me that when they are training firefighters, the men are required to do five chin-ups, and women are required to do one or two. He explained that most people can't do them at all and that he was impressed that I could. He further told me that if I practiced every day, I would be doing five or six in no time. At this point, I should probably add that I am fifty years old ... and female.

The moral of this story ... because I didn't know any better, because he told me I could, I saw no reason to doubt. I just jumped in and gave it a try—and I did it! I didn't see it as a great accomplishment because I didn't realize that it was difficult, and it became my goal to get stronger. No one told me I couldn't do it. In fact, I was encouraged to try. Had he told me initially how difficult it was, I more than likely would not have tried at all. Or, I might have tried but given it only half an effort, because failure would have been the expectation. I applaud him for letting me believe that for me, it was not only a possibility, but that success was a realistic expectation.

How many times have we decided not to try at all because we were told that we couldn't, that we shouldn't, that we had expectations that were too ambitious? How many times have we told our children, our friends, and our co-workers that they couldn't do something, that their ideas were impossible or beyond reach? How many times have we told ourselves that we would fail before we even started?

I started to ponder examples that I had witnessed and this came to mind: I recalled a conversation a friend of mine had with his daughter just prior to her heading off to university. He spoke to her (with good intentions) of how hard she would have to work in order to succeed. University wasn't like high school—this was the real world, and now she would have to grow up. This child quit after two years. Another friend spoke to her daughter of the adventure she was embarking on and how proud she was. I remember how we laughed because the mother already had her outfit picked out for convocation day! This child just graduated with her degree in physiology. Looking back, neither daughter was more intelligent than the other. Was it the silent expectations (or lack thereof) that predicted the outcome?

I have a new approach now. I have experienced first hand how good it feels to rush in so innocently, to believe that we *can* do it, and go on to accomplish exactly what we set out to do, because no one told us we couldn't. I've learned how important it is to support others (and ourselves) in their endeavors and to let them know that we believe they can do it rather than telling them we think they can't.

I personally want to be like my trainer, standing there behind the people I love, encouraging them, believing in them, and being ready to catch them when they get tired. I will be the one who is there on the second and third day making sure they try again, because I know they *can*.

What a powerful lesson this has been for me. I'll be doing five in no time at all. Because I was told I *can*.

Message: Believe you *can* and you *will*.

Jan Graham is a full-time Realtor in Calgary, Alberta. She is a single mom to three amazing young women who make her proud every day. Feel free to e-mail your thoughts on her story to *jan.graham@telus.net* or visit her Web site at *www.jangraham.ca*.

BUSINESS AND CAREER

STORIES OF
SUCCESS IN
BUSINESS

9/11 EMERGENCY WAKE-UP CALL

By Carole Baskin

Today a new sun rises for me; everything lives, everything is animated, everything seems to speak to me of my passion, everything invites me to cherish it.
—Anne de Lenclos

Big Cat Rescue is the world's largest accredited rescue facility for big cats such as lions, tigers, bobcats, and sixteen species of wildcats. The sanctuary had never come close to being able to support itself, and for the first eleven years, it relied heavily on me. I had lost my husband four years prior, and our assets were tied up in court. During that time, even though I had built our real estate business from the time I was nineteen, I was restricted to only being able to use $125,000 per year for the cats. The cost of running the sanctuary was several times that much. I had sold off my personal effects to feed the cats. I was near the end of my rope in 2001 when 9/11 rocked the world.

Donations and tourism stopped. Just stopped. The money over and above what I was able to provide was not coming in, and I wondered how I would feed more than a hundred big cats. As the weeks turned into months and 2002 rolled around, there seemed to be no hope of the economy turning around. I used the last $20,000 I had in a last ditch effort to find some way to turn this all around. I could feed the cats for a few more weeks, or I could take this gamble and hopefully find a way to ensure the cats' future. It was *not* an easy decision.

I hired a team to look at the situation and advise me on what to do to turn this dire situation around. I had never employed consultants before, but I was out of ideas. I had never heard of *The Secret* or the Law of Attraction. I had no idea that I could change my world by changing my focus. The consultants put me through a visual process that is commonly called a S.W.O.T. analysis. That is where you list your Strengths, Weaknesses, Opportunities, and Threats and try to come up with a game plan.

We didn't come up with a game plan, but they were well worth the $20,000 invested because they got me thinking about something other than what I was seeing. As I wrote down all of my strengths and opportunities, I found myself focusing on them. I would hardly even think of a reason why I couldn't succeed, because failing was not an option. I just kept thinking about all of the strong points that I and the sanctuary had. I kept thinking about all of the opportunities that were available, and believed that we deserved all the good I was picturing.

In November of 2002, I met my future husband, Howard Baskin. I brought him out to meet the cats, and when we approached our west fence, tears welled up in my eyes as I saw the condos being built next door. Developers wanted my land and were threatening to have me shut down if I didn't sell. But I couldn't sell. The money the land was worth was not enough to start over again. I explained the threats I had been dealing with and the belief that I could not get the zoning I needed to stay.

Howard set off on a mission to find out what needed to be done to secure the zoning. He immediately attracted into our lives people in all the fields we needed … and they were donating their time to help. As part of the process, the Genesis Group asked us to draw a huge map of the forty-two acres and think about everything we would ever want to have for the animals and for the furtherance of our mission.

To be dreaming up multi-million dollar buildings, cat hospitals, snack bars, education centers, and the like seemed ridiculous when I didn't even know how I was going to feed the cats. But I dared not show my negativity in the presence of so many gracious people who were trying to help. So I dreamed. Just like with our 100+ volunteers, I tried not to ever let them know how desperate things were. I didn't want them to despair and give up.

Whenever I dreamed small, I was encouraged to make it bigger, better, all I would ever want because we had to get the zoning approvals now for everything the sanctuary might ever be. So I dreamed big.

I thought about all the wonderful things we could do for the cats and how we could create a better world by reaching all of these people who weren't there, but who I was sure would be coming. I could see a wonderful future. I believed it was in the making. I did everything I could every day to bring it into reality, and before I knew it, things were turning around.

The right people were showing up. The donations began increasing. The message was being spread, and laws were being changed to protect the animals. I didn't do this by myself. I saw what I wanted, and some of the most wonderful people in the world showed up to make it so. I didn't have to see the whole plan.

I just believed that it would work out, and I took small steps in faith toward the goal.

Since 2005, the sanctuary has actually been able to support itself and is doing so in a time when others are folding due to lack of funds. Better laws are being signed into effect each year, and those laws are helping us stop the over-breeding, exploitation, abuse, and abandonment of big cats. I have learned to stay focused on the end result—on what I want—and not on what is wrong with the current system.

I am so happy and grateful that the right people came along and showed me how to use the Law of Attraction. This is why I want to share our story with everyone who will read it. We all want to live in a world where life is cherished and respected. Those who understand the Law of Attraction will make that world our reality.

Message: The Law of Attraction is always working whether we understand it or not. Knowing this empowers us to create the world we want to live in.

Carole Baskin, after unwittingly using the Law of Attraction to build a multi-million dollar real estate business, found her life's passion in establishing the world's finest sanctuary for lions, tigers, and other exotic cats. It was through this rescue mission she discovered that we are all one. To learn more about Big Cat Rescue or to make a donation, please visit *www.BigCatRescue.org*. Carole can be contacted by e-mail at *MakeADifference@BigCatRescue.org*.

ALL I HAD TO DO WAS ASK

By Laura Treonze

Freedom lies in being bold.
—Robert Frost

I was always optimistic, but I let things happen to me because I felt everything happened for a reason. Then I saw *The Secret*. I am no longer willing to allow things to happen—I want to make them happen. There have been many small miracles since I first watched *The Secret*, but during the past two months, everything I have requested has simply appeared.

I am a Realtor, and my experience in real estate had been pretty negative. I worked for a money-hungry broker, I wasted time with prospects who never bought anything, and I couldn't get listings. Although the clients I did close deals with were great, I had a hard time getting new clients to meet with me because people don't trust real estate agents. I attribute the lack of trust to a lack of professional respect among Realtors. I felt that the agents' feelings toward dealing with each other transcended to clients. At the time, I didn't realize my past negative experiences were controlling my current reality. When I watched *The Secret*, it was easy to see I was getting exactly what I asked for … clients who don't trust Realtors.

Since I had had trouble getting clients during the past eighteen months, I desperately needed a sale. I wrote a description of my ideal client, made my request, and within two weeks I was given a referral from a friend. The prospects hired my partner and me. They agreed to our commission, they let the market determine the sale price, and they took our advice and properly prepared the home for sale. In addition, they put the house on the market earlier than originally planned. In this "buyer's market," the house had six offers in six days and sold for $17,000 more than the list price. During the following two weeks, I found a home for my sellers which would result in another closing in the same month. Through the original listing, I met a wonderful young couple who would also be buying a home through us.

By the way, here's how I described my ideal clients: "People who are eager to sell their home; who recognize the importance of preparing a home for sale; are willing to pay a 6% commission for the service they know I provide; who let the market determine the sale price; who value real estate professionals; and who are decisive and eager to refer me to friends, family, and colleagues." It blew me away to reread the order I placed and to see the results I received.

My intended life had just begun. In the meantime, I received free tickets to a real estate investment conference but had no intention of attending until my mom expressed some interest in going. The day before we went to the conference, I listened to a Jack Canfield podcast. I realized I worked hard, but I didn't know if I was spending my time working toward my core genius. That night I prayed for guidance. The next day, at the conference, it came to me—my core genius is helping people realize their dream of home-ownership through non-traditional real estate methods.

During an intermission, I asked one of the speakers his advice for "beginner" investors, and he said, "Find a mentor." I had been searching for a mentor for the past three years but hadn't met anyone who was financially successful, spiritual, and dedicated to making home-ownership a reality for everyone. Within the hour, I met a gentleman who was doing what I defined as my core genius. He was financially successful, spiritual, and was helping people of all walks of life own their first home. As I drove home from training, I felt like I was breathing in a new life. I was overwhelmed with emotion.

I attended a subsequent training conference, and next week will make an offer on my first non-traditional real estate investment. In addition, I will be working with an investor coach/mentor for the next twelve weeks. This is only the beginning.

The night before the conference, I saw some local investors on a national television show. I decided to call them and request an interview. I met one of their staff members during lunch. It just so happened they were looking for a local Realtor to help them get their message out to other real estate agents. As a result, I will be helping them promote their program in the fall.

The training I received at the conference gave me a chance to help a client obtain a fabulous property through non-traditional methods, while he helped a former client prevent foreclosure. These have been the most professionally rewarding months I have had since I started in real estate. All I had to do was ask!

My success with the Law of Attraction is a result of my faith in God. Some send their requests to the Universe. God is my Universe, and therefore, my gratitude and my requests are made to him. Before *The Secret*, I felt unworthy of his attention. I already had a blessed life. I have wonderful parents; I had a great childhood; I was successful in school; I had a fulfilling career; I married a terrific man; I have two healthy, beautiful, smart children; and we live a very comfortable life. How could I possibly be worthy of more? Before *The Secret*, I thought I shouldn't ask for more, but thinking that way prevented me from living my potential.

As a way to show my gratitude to God, I started to attend regular Mass again. The Sunday following my training, I went to church. During the drive, I said to myself, "Today is the first day of my new life. Everything is going to change today." Ironically (or maybe not so ironically), it was the official end of the Church's Easter season, and that Sunday's sermon was about new beginnings. I started to cry. I think we all look for signs that we are doing the right thing. This was my sign. I was literally breathing this new life, and God was affirming it through the reading and priest's message.

The possibilities are endless when you believe in the Law of Attraction. Your thoughts get your mind on the right track. Your willingness to work keeps the engine moving forward, and as long as you are moving forward, your dreams get closer to reality. We should all dream bigger!

Message: Don't be afraid to ask for what you want … dream big!

Laura Treonze currently serves as president of her own investment firm, the Newport Holding Group, LLC and is a Realtor with Keller Williams Realty in Trumbull, Connecticut. Laura spends her spare time with her husband and two wonderful children. You can visit her Web site at *www.DHomeA.com* or contact her by e-mail at *Laura@DHomeA.com*.

ONE DAY THE LIGHT BULB LIT UP

By Kristen Marie Schuerlein

Your world is as big as you make it.
—Georgia Douglas Johnson

Goal setting has always come easy to me. At age thirteen, I saw myself owning a 1965 Mustang. On my sixteenth birthday, I was so proud to sit in my vintage burgundy hardtop with its beautiful white leatherette interior. At eighteen, I thought I'd like to start a graphic design company. At twenty-five, I was living that dream and loving every minute of it.

I've always enjoyed that time of year when the cool weather comes and the bright shiny New Year is right around the corner. This is when I begin the process of reflection on the past, and I start crafting big, bold goals for the future. Each fall as I would review the sheet with "My Goals" so beautifully typeset at the top, I'd find that some I achieved, while others I did not. I never really knew why; I just kept writing goals year after year. But it wasn't until I started creating visual versions of my dreams that my life started to shift in a powerful way. Once I could see my goals and imagine what it would feel like to achieve them, the Law of Attraction would invite fabulous results.

After eleven years at the helm of my graphic design company, a new idea came that would transform my life and business. The idea was to silkscreen positive affirmations about love, joy, abundance, courage, and serenity onto personal-sized fleece blankets so people could wrap up the ones they love in those big ideas. And the intention was to weave charitable giving into the fabric of the company by giving to causes that make a difference in the world.

I knew it was a good idea with the potential to touch thousands—if not millions—of lives. The key was delivering the message around the nation with heart and impact. Earning favorable placements in the local and national media was the path I chose to achieve that goal. That meant setting big and very specific intentions to get coverage in the magazines that had the influence to carry my message to the right people who could give my dream wings to fly.

About this time, I met a business owner named Janet. She and I became fast friends who helped inspire each other to dream big. We carved out time to set goals with gusto. Our "Vision Days," as we call them, became a quarterly event. Soon, my written goals transformed into a vision book that represented powerful and specific images of all the things I wanted most in my personal life. An abundance of travel, friends, love, money, time, health, and spirit were all represented. What delight I took in finding new images, adding and subtracting visuals, as my view of my extraordinary life took very specific shape!

Then one day a light bulb lit up. Why not create a vision board for my company? I could instantly see a whole wall in my office dedicated to my intentions and dreams for the business, the lives we would touch, and the difference we would make by both doing well *and* doing good.

In as much time as it took to get excited, I wondered, who makes a vision board for their company? Who was I to think so big? What if my results fell short of my goals? What would people think about my seeking publicity in magazines and newspapers? How could I create a nationally-recognized brand from my desk in Seattle? This mind trash was really clogging up my thinking.

Finally, I shook loose and remembered my commitment to playing full out. After all, I sold my house to start this venture; I wasn't going to let fear, insecurity, and small thinking get in my way. So the fun began. I imagined what magazines and newspapers were going to feature our company and products. I considered what companies with which we would partner. I scoured the Internet to identify magazines, companies, and organizations that were in alignment with our big vision. Everyone who saw my wall of possibility would just stop, take it in, and encourage me.

If ever I wondered if something I wanted was too big, too out of reach, I made it a habit to post it to the vision board right away. It's my way of getting past limited thinking. I remember the day I put a *PINK* magazine cover on my vision board, and I caught myself thinking, "That'll never happen." It's a magazine that's dedicated to professional women and the only magazine I read cover to cover the very same week it arrives. I love this publication, and thought, gosh, if they would feature us, it would illustrate just how powerful our ability to intend and attract really is.

Long before I created my vision board, I'd retained the services of a publicist who believed in our company with all her heart. Among other excellent introductions and recommendations, she suggested I get re-involved with the local chapter of a national networking group for women business owners and professionals. I had stopped attending years ago, yet she was confident that this group would offer opportunities to bring great results to life for me and my company. She just had a feeling I should start attending again, so I did. Eighteen months later, the founder came to Seattle and inspired me to attend the organization's annual conference in Dallas later that summer.

Whenever I attend events like these, I chart a course for myself, reviewing the program to make sure I use my time wisely and attend those sessions that speak to my passions and interests. As I read the agenda, I remember my heart skipping a beat. The program featured a panel discussion on how to connect with the media that included none other than the founding publisher of *PINK* magazine! The moderator was a freelance writer who regularly contributed to the magazine.

I've always been a believer in the power of relationships. I love getting to shake someone's hand and find out how I can be of service to them. Now I was in a room at a hotel in Dallas on a Saturday afternoon with the publisher and a freelance writer for the prestigious publication I had highlighted on my vision board!

I introduced myself to the writer and made the most compelling story pitch of my life. I captured her interest, and the editors agreed that our story belonged within the pages of their magazine. About sixty days later, I received a call checking the facts about the blanket they were including in their holiday guide. As I hung up the phone, I felt tingles shoot through my body.

Different versions of this magical scenario have played themselves out over the last year, and it's been amazing. The "big ink" just keeps coming. The power of the Universe to deliver on our visions and dreams through the Law of Attraction is exciting and humbling at the same time.

Today I delight in knowing that the Universe is cooking up wonderful ways for all our vision board intentions to come into reality. Some happen really fast; some take time. Some come to life in ways that are better than I could have ever imagined.

All I know is the Law of Attraction works. The wall in my office proves it.

Message: Our job is to dream. Listen to your heart's desire, and focus on that. You never know when one step one way is actually a step directly toward your vision. Trust the Universe and know that a grand plan for the things you desire is in the works.

Kristen Marie Schuerlein is committed to living intentionally by harnessing the power of affirmations. She is the founder of Affirmagy, a company that creates inspirational products that people love to give—to themselves and the people they adore! Kristen's positive life force inspires others to design—and live—a life they love. Learn more at *www.affirmagy.com.*

THE POWER OF SINCERE CONTRIBUTION

By Elizabeth Callaway and Sally Schoeffel

The fragrance always remains on the hand that gives the rose.
—Gandhi

By applying the Law of Attraction over the last two years, we have taken our already "great" family real estate practice to a whole new level! This learning process has been wonderful and inspiring, and we have had the privilege of meeting so many amazing people. The "magic" occurring daily in our lives is thrilling, and we see it happening for our families, friends, and clients too. We are now living in a way that is truly "full out," with more joy, more love, more energy, and bliss than ever. The boundaries between work and play have blurred … and we are having a wonderful time doing what we love and achieving spectacular results!

We recognize and appreciate how blessed we are to be supported by a wonderful group of people, including our families, mentors, coaches, support staff, clients, friends, and also the community in which we live, work, and play. There is so much positive energy and a true team spirit. We share in this commitment to create an extended community that goes beyond geographic boundaries.

We have refined our business practices to work with the clients who recognize and appreciate our dedication to truly be "of service." We genuinely enjoy our profession and are privileged to work with an extraordinary group of people. The commitment to our clients is simple: to provide the best service possible and to embody an "it's our pleasure" attitude. Working with appreciative, happy clients is a joy whether closing on a first home, purchasing or selling an estate property, or creating a real estate portfolio of investment properties. We consider it an honor to work with our clients. Whether buying or selling properties, our clients know they can count on us to oversee complex transactions with finesse. We are passionate about our work and have a track record that we are very proud of. We also enjoy investing in our own real estate portfolios and sharing our knowledge!

Key factors in achieving and amplifying our success have been a combination of determination, "right focus," gratitude, and paying attention to the details, both large and small. Additionally, we take the time to know our market inside-out and enjoy using innovative ideas to achieve dramatic results.

We have created very specific systems that have all been developed to focus on the desired outcome while also being diligent, proactive, and positive. We also remain conscious of what is important to each client and serves their best interests. It is our belief that we have created an optimum environment for successful results.

Overall, the combination of these simple principles has translated into more peace, joy, and harmony in our lives and a very successful real estate practice.

Each day is a gift ... it sounds like a cliché, but it really is true. We look forward to each day whether it is smooth and easy-flowing or holds challenges ... we will enjoy making the most of it. We have also learned to go with the flow, and sometimes, what seems like the wrong direction, ends up being more perfect than we could have ever imagined. Be open! Through our travels, we have realized that the more we experience, the greater our own perspective ... and perspective is a wonderful gift.

For years, we have intuitively been applying the Law of Attraction ... without being truly conscious of its power. When we learned more about this Universal energy ... we realized how amazing and wonderful it truly is!

Being aware of the power our feelings and thoughts can have on our lives, families, and business has changed the way we live our lives. The effect has been that miracles are happening every day. We notice an amazing synchronicity, and the people, opportunities, and connections are truly amazing.

We invite you to join us in making the world a better place. Give from the heart, be true to yourself, treat others how you would love to be treated, surprise someone with something wonderful and unexpected, and let people know you care.

Life just keeps getting better and more inspiring. We believe the only limits, for all of us, as a people ... are our own beliefs.

Message: If you can dream it and pursue that dream ... anything really *is* possible!

Elizabeth Callaway and **Sally Schoeffel** are a highly successful mother-daughter real estate team specializing in San Diego's "metro" and coastal communities. In addition to working with both buyers and sellers, they enjoy restoring historic properties, real estate development, and investing in real estate. Together they have earned a reputation as dedicated, experienced professionals with a warmth and integrity unique to being part of a family business. For more information, please visit their Web site at *www.RBVrealestate.com* or contact them by e-mail at *info@RBVrealestate.com*.

BUILDING A COMMUNITY

By Brad Axelrad

Dedicate your life to a cause greater than yourself, and your life will become a glorious romance and adventure.
—Mack Douglas

As my mother spoke, I knew immediately that something was wrong. Normally upbeat and confident, she spoke with bewildered hesitation as she told me my father had some trouble finding his way home. My heart dropped into my stomach. My father, the man whom I have always looked up to for strength, does not get lost in the small community he knows so well.

We both agreed that she had to get him to the doctor immediately to see what was wrong. After a few days of tests, we found out he had a golf ball-sized tumor in his brain. It was malignant and had to be surgically removed immediately. After the surgery came chemotherapy and radiation. He was given one year to live. He slipped away in four short months.... I watched my father take his last breath on October 19, 2005.

As I held my father's hand in the ICU, I watched his spirit lift from his body. It truly was the most difficult, yet amazing experience to see his transition into the spiritual realm. I am grateful to have been at his side during those last moments. To see my father at peace helped me find the strength to cope with my loss and to make a transition into a deeper, more spiritual life.

Less than two days later, I found myself again in the most loving place I have ever experienced—The Hoffman Institute in St. Helena, California. Seven months earlier I had enrolled in their three-day workshop. The timing was magical as I needed a place to grieve and reconnect with my spiritual self. After I completed the healing workshop, I drove two hours south to the Bay Area for my father's life celebration. I was petrified to face the reality that my father was no longer with us. Once I arrived, that all changed as it became a joyous celebration of life as I witnessed how much this man had impacted others.

After a few days of decompression, I drove home to Orange County down lonesome Highway 5. I realized it was up to me to leave a legacy as my father did. As my awareness of this purpose opened up, I simultaneously went into the darkest months of my life. I had never felt so alone, so scared, and so raw. I was regularly overcome with sudden outbursts of crying. I missed my father very much.

During my dark days and nights, alone and hibernating, I could feel the heavy burden and guilt from many years of not being around my father. I ran from my family and myself to Orange County from the San Francisco Bay Area. Geographic healing was something I knew well; I was an expert at it. As angry and resentful as I was at my father for not being perfect, I had never missed him more. Even with people around me, supporting me, loving me, I still felt very alone. Emotional pain was now part of my everyday life. Tears rolled down my face as I was beaten into submission. Begging the Universe for relief, I realized I had nothing left and had no choice but to surrender. Mortality—my father's and my own—woke me up! It made me suddenly conscious of how precious every moment is.

I found my purpose when I realized I had nothing left but to use my body as a vessel of service to humanity. My entire life of self-indulgence had left me feeling empty. Only this time, it was a mirror held up to my face. In that moment of self-realization, I finally realized my powerful abilities of manifestation. I am a natural-born leader, just as my father was, and I had to use my knowledge and passion to create a better life for myself and others around me. I immediately embraced this role and sought out a way to be of service.

To initiate my higher purpose and to give back to humanity, I decided to host monthly Hoffman graduate gatherings in my home. I met many powerful, positive people through Hoffman, and I wanted to continue the energy. By leading these meetings, I was inspired to host a book study group on quantum physics. I had been studying this material for the last few years, and it resonated with my core beliefs. A short time later, I read *Ask and It Is Given* by Esther and Jerry Hicks. From that moment forward, I knew my life would never be the same. By embracing this deep, truth-filled material, I realized that my desires were obtainable.

Two weeks later, I hosted our first book study group where I led a small group through *Ask and It Is Given* and *The Secret*. By the second week, people were driving from a hundred miles away to attend the meetings! Within four weeks, we doubled in size. Within eight weeks, we were visited by *NBC Nightly News*, and

The Law of Attraction Center was on the map! USC's *News21* later did a piece on us as well as the *Orange County Register*, *Los Angeles Times*, and a local PBS affiliate television station.

Today, the center is growing exponentially each week. We have had numerous keynote speakers including Rich German (the coauthor of this book), Pat Finn (the host of the California Lottery's *Big Spin* TV show and founder of the Rubicon Results Institute), and Audrey Cavenecia (a consultant to Anthony Robbins). The platform in the community I created and the growing number of awakened people that show up week after week is truly profound.

As I host weekly gatherings that are filled with up to 150 awake co-creators, I infiltrate the Universe with expansion and love of self and humanity. As the community grows, so does my humility and gratitude. To expand our message, we will soon be hosting weekly tele-seminars with well-known speakers, coaches, authors, and experts on the Law of Attraction and other related topics. Our collaborative model has been incredibly conducive to long-term relationships with key people in the Orange County area and beyond.

I feel my whole self being guided and living connected to the Universal energy. There is a knowingness now that we are ever-expanding beings with infinite creating potential. I am tapped into the flow and am using it to benefit others locally and globally. As our membership base grows, we are spreading our message around the world. My life is flourishing and expanding. I am joyous and experience bliss on a regular basis. People around me are feeling and experiencing it, too. I have become a servant of the flow!

As I surrender to being an instrument of the Universal Law of Attraction, I watch my life and legacy unfold. I am forever grateful for the pain of my father's passing and the wonderful character he instilled in me. I allow him to guide me on a regular basis and watch my dreams manifest. I am honored to be on the leading edge of this movement as humanity wakes up to this new paradigm.

Message: From the darkness to the light. Sometimes we have to break down to break through.

Brad Axelrad, founder of The Law of Attraction Center in Orange County, California, is considered to be a leading expert on the Law of Attraction. Brad currently resides in Costa Mesa, California, where he dedicates himself full time to serving and growing the community of like-minded individuals he has manifested through the center. For more information, visit his Web site at *www.theLOAcenter.com*. For meeting information, visit *www.lawofattractionRSVP.com*.

HEAR WHAT THEY AREN'T SAYING

By Greg Harrelson

*You can't live a perfect day without doing something for someone
who will never be able to repay you.*
—John Wooden

During a routine meeting with a former high school friend, he happened to mention to me that his mother owned a property that may be desirable for development. As he described the land to me, I quickly discovered that it was one of the few large tracts of unimproved land still available within the city limits of Myrtle Beach, South Carolina.

I immediately started to see dollar signs as we discussed further how much money we could potentially make. He then proceeded to tell me the biggest problem was that his mother would not sell the property for fear the kids would take the money and blow it on things that do not matter and eventually be broke once again. As a woman who was raised on this land and in turn raised her children on the land, she would not tolerate that type of activity, so selling was not an option.

Months went by, and he kept telling me that his mother would not do anything and to just forget about it. He and his brothers were upset about the fact that their mom would not sell. The family has no money, and they are barely able to pay the yearly property taxes.

I soon forgot about the property and was introduced to an amazing coaching company that started teaching me about the Law of Attraction. A few weeks into the class, we were asked to set an intention as to what we hoped to attract within the six-month course. They asked us to think big, so after much challenge, I set my intention to attract $20 million in six months. Keep in mind that I had never made more then $1.2 million in any given year so this was surely out-of-the-box thinking.

For about thirty days straight, I continued to visualize my intentions and discuss the vision with many people in my life. Unexpectedly, I received a phone call from my friend wanting to discuss his mother's property again. This time I was in a different space, so I told him I thought it would be good if I had a chance to speak to her myself in person. He said okay and called me a week later with a time they could come into my office. Before the meeting, he mentioned again that she was worried about the family squandering the money away. I just listened without judgment.

I greeted the family as they entered the office, and we proceeded to go into the conference room. I could feel a little tension from the mother probably because she felt as if she had been forced to meet. In the beginning, it was my intention to have a conversation with her and the family to understand exactly what she was going through. She was concerned about the family getting so much money and what they might do. All the while I just listened. I spoke a little about estate planning, explaining to her how she could remain in complete control of the money and only drip the amounts that she felt were needed at the time. Based on the information provided by the family, I would have thought this would provide her with some relief. She acted as if she already knew she could control the money, so it was obvious at that moment that was not the issue holding her back.

Before I was in the Law of Attraction class, I would have likely just thrown my hands in the air and given up and declared that she was not going to do anything. I did the exact opposite. I remained calm and continued to have a good conversation. We talked about how long they had owned the property, who originally purchased the property, what they did with the land, and so on and so on....

It became very clear that she was deeply rooted in this land, and at one point, she said to me, "I can never imagine seeing someone else on my land." That was the beginning of a miracle.

All of a sudden, words started pouring from my mouth as if someone else was speaking through me. It was as if I was an observer to a conversation versus actually having the conversation. I related to her and the fact that her family worked so hard. I was present to the blood, sweat, and tears they must have put into the land. We were connecting. I felt as if she felt that I understood, and more importantly, that I respected her for all that she had been through.

I said to her, "I once thought that maybe we could develop the land and place your family name on the street signs. Yet, now that I have talked to you face-to-face, I feel that is the last thing you are concerned about. You do not strike me as a person who cares if your name is on street signs. That would mean nothing to you." She immediately agreed. Then I said, "How about this? What if we take three to four acres of land and subdivide it and donate it to the City of Myrtle Beach? We will donate it for public park use only. We will donate it in honor of your grandfather who was the first person in your family to work this land. Once we build and donate the park to the city, no one will ever be able to take it away. Then you could take the rest of the land and develop it. Think about this. Sixty years from now, this will be a place where your great-great grandchildren can go and push their kids on the swings. As they enjoy the park, they can talk about all of the blood, sweat, and tears that your family went through in order to create that park."

As I was speaking, it looked as if she had some interest in what I was saying, like she had never thought of that idea before. She looked down at the conference table for a moment and said, "Let's do it. Let's make this happen. I'm ready." That was the miracle. I found myself listening to her in a way that nobody had listened to her. Many developers, investors, Realtors, attorneys, and others had tried for years to get her property, and it was me who she said yes to. She said yes to the solution that I presented her.

Looking back over the past few months, I learned something. Prior to understanding the Law of Attraction, I knew about this property and failed in all attempts to develop it. After learning about the Law of Attraction, I created an intention, I attracted them calling me, and I set a time to speak with her. Because my intention was to serve others, I listened for a solution versus listening for an opportunity. The answer appeared without effort, and now we are on our way to building a wonderful community with that special park that her family will enjoy for many years to come.

And by the way, this was one transaction I attracted that eventually helped me reach my goal of $20 million.

Message: Too often we only hear the words that come out of others' mouths. True conversation is more than words—it is emotion. When you are really being with someone, you will hear their emotions. It will touch your heart, and the true message will be heard.

Greg Harrelson has been in real estate sales and development for over fifteen years. While owning multiple Century 21 franchises, Greg has been successful at closing over three hundred real estate transactions per year. At the same time, he coached his agents to outperform the average agents in his market by five times their production. Greg is a past chairman of the Boys & Girls Club of Myrtle

Beach and has recently co-founded the Feed-A-Family non-profit program. He can be contacted through his Web site at *www.gregharrelson.com*.

GRATITUDE BRACELETS

By Cheri Haug

Let us be grateful to people who make us happy;
they are the charming gardeners who make our souls blossom.
—Marcel Proust

When I watched the teachers of *The Secret* being interviewed on TV, I was inspired. I immediately went out and bought the DVD. The next morning, I woke up with the idea of making gratitude charm bracelets.

My gratitude bracelet reminds me to be grateful for all the good things that are, or will be, in my life. I'm grateful for my Yorkie, Chloe. I'm grateful for my house, for my good health, for my bead store, and for my EZ Bracelet™ bracelet sizer. My bead store is represented by a little word charm that says "beading." When I see and touch it, I remember to be grateful for my store and all the good things it has brought me. I have a Yorkie charm, a charm to represent my house, one for my health, and other charms representing my good friends and family.

But there are other things I would like to have in my life. I have a heart problem, and I want to manifest a healthy heart. So I added a heart charm to my bracelet. Every time I touch my bracelet, I visualize my healthy heart. I would also like to lose some weight. So every day I'm grateful for my beautiful, healthy, slim body.

I know this technique works because I've used it so many times in my life.

A long time ago, I was living with a boyfriend who didn't want to celebrate Christmas because he said we couldn't afford to spend a hundred dollars on each other. No matter how much we argued, I couldn't change his mind. So one morning I left the house to go to a cafe and thought, "If only I could find ten bucks, I could buy him a gift. If only I could…" A block from my home, there it was! A ten dollar bill was lying on the ground. I don't know why I didn't think to ask for more. But the next day, it happened again. I swear! Anyway, living with that fool was always a struggle when it came to financial matters, and I used the Law of Attraction to bring me money whenever things were rough. I found $50 on the floor at a store when I really needed some spending money. Another time I found $300 when I was having a hard time paying for my tuition.

Well, that was in the 1980s. Since then, when I want something, I just start looking for it. Somehow, things always find *me!* It's weird. I have a reputation for having good luck, for having good things come to me, and for leading a charmed life. Whenever I am undertaking a new project, like opening my bead store, for example, I just tell people, "Whatever I need will find me!"

Soon after I opened Gossamer Wings Bead Store, I was pretty low on money, having spent a fortune on beads, carpeting, and displays. My store is furnished with white plaster pillars and glass table tops. I had one pillar left over and just couldn't afford $50 for another round glass table top. The next morning, on my way to work, I was driving out of my trailer park past the dumpster. Someone had thrown out a sofa next to the dumpster. I drove past the sofa, and in my rear view mirror, there it was—my round glass table top sitting on the sofa! It wasn't even chipped, and it was exactly the same size as the others!

Last year, I wanted to buy a house and made a list of all the things I wanted. I wanted a kitchen that is open to the dining and living area so when I have guests, I can interact with them while I'm cooking. I wanted a sunny yoga room, wood floors, a fenced yard for Chloe, and among other things, I wanted it to be within walking distance of my store. I carried the list with me for months. On my first (and only) day of house hunting, there were thirteen houses in the paper in my price range. The fifth one I looked at was the one! *Everything* on my list was in this house, and it was in my price range and only twelve blocks from my store.

I called my cousin Greg, a real estate agent, to help me with the paperwork. During the thirty days it took to close on the house, he expressed concern that everything was going *too* smoothly. He was worried that something was going to go wrong and prevent me from closing on the house. I told him, "Don't you know? I lead a charmed life! That's just the way things go for me." He said he'd never sold a house where there were no complications. But, of course, the closing went smoothly as I had predicted.

I think one reason I lead a charmed life is that I am always grateful for what I have. I stand in the shower in the morning thinking how great it is that I can just stand there, with my eyes closed, leaning against the wall, and enjoying the hot water on my body. So many people in the world don't have hot water, or running water, or a shower of their own, or a home of their own in which to shower. Why am I so lucky?

When I'm feeling bad, it seems that someone always comes into view to let me know I should be grateful for what I have. It could be a person in a wheelchair at the grocery store or someone who is obviously in poor health. It brings me back to reality. It reminds me that even though I have a cold, or cut my finger and had to go to the doctor, that I should just quit obsessing about it and be happy that I'm not in worse shape. I would never trade my problems for someone else's problems!

It's not that nothing ever goes wrong in my life. It's just that I have an attitude of being happy with what I have. I appreciate the fact that things could be a whole lot worse. I know that no matter what awful things could happen to me, there would always be someone worse off than me. I'm actually grateful for my problems!

I'm living proof that if you focus on what you *do* want and are grateful for what you *do* have, good things will continue to come into your life, and your little problems will always be little.

Message: There are two steps to leading a charmed life. First, be grateful for what you have. Second, make sure others are grateful for having you in their lives.

Cheri Haug lives in La Crosse, Wisconsin, and owns Gossamer Wings Bead Store. She is a life-long positive thinker. She has a BS in philosophy from the University of Wisconsin at Madison and a juris doctor degree from the University of San Francisco School of Law. She practiced law for ten years before turning to more creative endeavors. She taught business law at the Minnesota School of Business and at the University of Southern Illinois. She is a self-taught artist specializing in pastels, India ink, and acrylics. She opened Gossamer Wings Bead Store in 2002 and employs nine people who share her passion for beads. She also does business consulting and business coaching for craft-oriented retail stores. Gratitude Bracelets can be purchased on her Web site at *www.GratitudeBracelet.com*.

FINDING MY CALLING

By Sharon Schmitt

Anything is possible. You can be told that you have a 90 percent chance or a 50 percent chance or a 1 percent chance, but you have to believe.
—Lance Armstrong

I was first introduced to *The Secret* through *The Oprah Show*. But, as I look back at the circumstances in my life, I realize I had frequently applied the Law of Attraction and didn't even know it. I watched the DVD many times with amazement and wonder.

Years ago, I read a book by Louise Hay called *You Can Heal Your Life*. I needed guidance on changing my life, and she made excellent suggestions in her book. She had had terminal cancer and cured herself by positive thinking (applying the Law of Attraction). We have so many years of built up "dis-ease," it's no wonder we manifest illnesses in our bodies. We were told in our younger years, don't think this, don't do that, why are you doing that, money doesn't grow on trees, kids are to be seen and not heard, quit daydreaming. And later on, your spouse says the same things or worse. I could go on and on, but the point is our lives are based on what our parents and others told us and not how we think or feel. So we keep our frustrations deep inside and *presto*, we have "dis-ease." It's very hard to stay positive with all the negativity around us. But according to *The Secret,* the power lies in believing in yourself, truly loving yourself, and being happy in the moment, no matter what. The mind is a very powerful tool.

With the Law of Attraction, you can manifest anything you want by thinking, feeling, believing, being grateful, and letting it go to the Universe and/or God. Before I even knew about the Law of Attraction, my life's dream was to own a Corvette. I would think about it, feel it, see the color, and imagine myself in one, but I thought it was just a far-fetched dream. People would tell me they are expensive, the insurance is high, and it's a gas guzzler; but I didn't care ... I wanted one. I was out with relatives one day when my husband called. "Are you sitting down? I got a deal on a Corvette, and I'm going to buy it for you." I couldn't believe my ears. I was afraid to get too excited because the dream may disappear. When I arrived home, I saw the car and thought, "Shoot!" I wanted a white one, and it was black. Boy, did I sound ungrateful! A few weeks later, another one came along … a deal we couldn't refuse. Would you believe, it was white! A few weeks later, another deal came along, and that one was white too. Good lord … now I had three, what *heaven!* Now I am down to one, and every time I drive it I am so happy for the joy it brings me; I feel young again! By the way, gas and insurance for the Corvette are cheaper than for our Durango. Who knew?

In 2000, I went for a yearly mammogram and learned I had breast cancer. Once the doctor told me the awful news, I didn't hear another word. My husband and I were walking to the car, and I burst into tears stating, "I'm going to die." He hugged me and said, "You didn't hear what the doctor said. It's curable!" I had surgery, a lumpectomy. Unfortunately, the cancer traveled to a lymph node, so chemotherapy and radiation were on the agenda for me.

While I lay on the couch having a pity party, a thought came to me. Either I could wallow in this or get up and enjoy life! I was up late one night after chemo and decided to surf the Internet for wig stores. That was when I had a "light bulb" moment … I decided to open one. I had some inheritance money I was saving and wanted to do something worthwhile with it. And since I was a hairdresser, I had a lot of experience with hair!

Ever since I made that decision, everything just fell into place. One day, I was cutting a client's hair. I knew he owned business rental property, and I approached him with my idea. He loved it so much he gave me a deal on the rent that I couldn't refuse. This was in November of 2000, and the rental would be ready January 1, 2001. My husband remodeled the store with the help of plumbers, electricians, etc., who he knew. I found the distributor I wanted to purchase the wigs from. I opened on May 5, 2001, selling quite a few wigs that day.

Unfortunately 9/11 happened, and all of a sudden no one was buying. The world was scared and devastated, including me. I was nervous since sales were way down. But I knew in my heart this was what I was supposed to do. After all, I attracted cancer for a reason; this was my calling.

After some time, business did pick up. Since the day I opened, I have not regretted a single day. I am grateful for the opportunity to help others in the same situation, to ease the unknown, and make them feel better about themselves. It is a wonderful and satisfying occupation. There is life after cancer!

Right now I'm manifesting my big, beautiful new home and being able to enjoy it with family and friends. I know I will receive it because I believe, I believe, I believe!

Message: Believe in yourself, and anything is possible.

Sharon Schmitt was born in Kentucky and now lives in Massachusetts. She was married for seventeen years and divorced in 1988. Sharon has two children and five grandchildren and is remarried to a wonderful man. She is a licensed hairdresser and opened a wig store after battling breast cancer in 2000. For more information, please visit her Web site at *www.sharonswiggallery.com.*

ANSWERING YOUR INNER VOICE

By Bethany St. Clair

Let the beauty of what you love be what you do.
—Rumi

While working for a start-up for an entertainment company in the late '90s at the apex of the "dot com" boom, my personal life was spinning out of control. My sons were twelve and fourteen, my husband at the time traveled a great deal, and I realized I didn't know the people I lived with and loved the most. My sons were, for the most part, largely unsupervised—a dangerous notion for teenaged boys. I recall one day while outside gardening, my oldest son casually walked past me and said he was "going out for a while." Something compelled me to follow him. Waiting at the end of the driveway was a white BMW with three unfamiliar faces inside. My son opened the car door, hopped in, and away they drove. "Oh, boy," I thought, "we are entering a whole new territory in parental supervision and family values." And what happened to those values I tried so hard to instill when my sons were younger? My family and I were going in four different directions; it felt like we were all roommates.

Crestfallen, I walked back inside my house. Looking around, I scanned the piles of partially read books and magazines, the video games and toys tossed carelessly, and unfinished projects laying about everywhere. My home felt chaotic and sluggish—like me. How did life get so out of control? How was it that I could successfully hire nine hundred employees in less than five months and lead a staff of eight, but I couldn't manage a 1,600 square foot household? Life seemed upside down.

On Mother's Day 1999, I had my "Ah ha!" moment, as Oprah would call it. Each year on Mother's Day, I decided how we would spend the day—our family tradition. This year, we all went hiking in the foothills of Northern California. It was a spectacular day, the air was still, the skies were blue, and the sunshine played on the trees and grass. As we walked up a narrow path enjoying Mother Nature's simple show, I looked upward toward the top of the hill watching my boys ahead of me jostling each other with sticks and twigs while absorbing the beauty of the moment, and suddenly felt gratitude beyond anything I ever felt before. In a gesture of appreciation, I began reciting the Lord's Prayer and recall saying, "Thy will be done on earth as it is in heaven." At this point something came over me I'll never forget. Not certain of this feeling, I recited the prayer about three more times until knowingness for what the feeling was engulfed me—illumination and clarity. Right then and there, I made a commitment to myself that I would *live each day for the rest of my life here on earth as though I were creating my own heaven on earth.* "Was it really that simple?" I asked myself.

Within weeks, I booked a ten-day mother-daughter trip to Eastern Europe. My mother and I had fun rediscovering our heritage and one another. I fell in love with Vienna and Salzburg, and I was stunned by the architecture and earthiness of Prague and the majestic beauty of the ever-efficient Munich. When I returned to work, I gave my boss a six-week notice and resigned from my position. For the first time in thirty years, I was taking responsibility for my own healing, to get back in touch with myself and reconnect with my family. My husband was agitated when I told him of my decision. I had always been the main "breadwinner" in our household, and he wasn't eager to embrace a lifestyle that differed from the one he was comfortable and secure in. Hesitatingly, he acquiesced.

I gave myself one year to find my passion and get back to my authentic self. It wasn't long before I realized our marriage had run its course, and it wasn't possible for me to manifest the newness and life purpose I was destined to create until I first emptied out all that was presently toxic and unhealthy for me. After making the decision to move forward, deeper insights and clarity came to me, and along with them, synchronistic opportunities and people to help me achieve my life's purpose. It was about this time I found a book called *Discover Your Genius* by Michael J. Gelb. In his book was an exercise—as quickly as possible write down fifty things you love to do. That simple exercise gave me the vision for where I was to go next in my life.

In 2002 I created a company called St. Clair Organize and Design, offering services in feng shui (a talent I was born with), professional home and office organization, staging for real estate, and interior arranging. One of my missions in creating my company was to help people clear their exterior environment of clutter, and in doing so, enable clarity of the inner path where the magic really happens. In order to do this, leading by example is crucial; hence, my spiritual path was born again. I began to meditate, feng shui my own life, and live with "light in my soul," as I did when I was a young girl growing up in the Midwest. Soon, clients were calling, and I hadn't even advertised!

One day, I was moving a desk for a client. I opened the top drawer to get a better grip, and inside was a large photo of a beautiful man's face. With his penetrating eyes and brotherly features, I could tell he was a special human being. Looking into the eyes of the man in the photo, a subtle vibration came over me especially in my hands, arms, and shoulders; it was like getting a big hug. I showed my client the picture and asked her who he was. She replied, "That's my meditation teacher." Amazingly, the past six months had been spent earnestly looking for a new meditation teacher. Soon, my introduction to Steven S. Sadleir and the Self Awareness Institute was made. Now, several years later as a graduate student of the program, teaching high school students how to meditate and interestingly, attracting clients who enjoy meditation, has resulted in a new service to my design business—creating rooms for meditation.

There is an old adage, "When the student is ready, the teacher will appear." Being a student of life is remarkable. For me, leaving everything I ever knew behind and living a life filled with positive thoughts, positive people, and positive energy was unimaginable until walking up the foothills on Mother's Day in 1999. My sons are now nineteen and twenty-one. We're closer than we have ever been, and I'm so proud to be their mom and watch them figure out how they are going to contribute back to society. Being here creating and living a passionate life enables me to share my light and educate others to freely express their talents and abilities in a loving and harmonious way.

Message: Every morning upon waking we have a choice: we can open our arms to the Universe allowing new people, new ideas, and new experiences to come into our lives, and if the feeling is good, bring us closer to our life's purpose and authentic self, or we can plod through the days asleep. Choose to wake up with open arms and an open heart!

Bethany St. Clair was born with the ability to walk into a room and determine if it is functional, efficient, and has good energy. When a room or office space has good furniture placement, the occupants are more efficient and can accomplish more. Prior to owning St. Clair Organize and Design, Bethany worked for more than thirteen years in human resources for several large companies. She is currently working on a book about the spirit of de-cluttering. She lives in Northern

California with her two sons. You can contact Bethany through her Web site at *www.stclairorganizedesign.com* or by e-mail at *info@stclairorganizedesign.com*.

WHO ARE YOU BEING?

By Michael Morawski

All thoughts are seeds planted in your subconscious mind. Those thoughts are BEING choices disguised to look like attitudes, opinions, and points of view. With each thought, you are choosing who you will BE under the circumstances.
—Darel Rutherford

I was first exposed to the concept and ideas around the Law of Attraction about six years ago. I thought it was too "way out there" for me, and I did not want to believe it or even look at the process. I just wasn't ready at that time in my life. They say when the student is ready, the teacher will appear—and then it happened.

In August 2005, at the Success Summit put on by my long-time business coach Tom Ferry, I was wondering where my life and business were and where they were going. It had been a challenging few months prior to the event. I felt lost and afraid. I was searching for new ideas and a new direction for myself and my business. I was speaking with a friend about my situation when he made a profound statement to me. He said that it was about "who I was being." I did not understand it. This concept was new and foreign to me. He invited me to join a new group that was forming, and soon my eyes and ears would be opened to what was going to be an incredible journey. It has already proven to be quite a ride, and I have not even scratched the surface. I have been involved in several other self-help groups and personal growth coaching for many years, but this has been different … this really works.

After getting involved in this new coaching program, "The Being," I developed some incredible new relationships and entered into a small accountability group with Rich German. We have since developed a strong friendship and a relationship that will last forever.

In November of that same year, at another Tom Ferry workshop, Rich talked to me about how I could adopt even more new ideas and principles into my life. He introduced me to the *10–10 Exercise* and has been my incredible accountability partner ever since that eye-opening day. Each day, as part of my morning ritual, I type a list on my computer of ten things I am grateful for, like my wife and kids, Jesus, my friends and family, and all the abundance in my life. I take the opportunity to start my day in complete love and joy and feeling really good.

Then I type a list of ten things I want, like to feel good, to live with passion, and to make a million dollars per year. But then it gets even better. I set my intentions for the day: to have health and safety; to be a great husband, father, leader, and visionary; and to build a billion dollar company by 2017.

Next, I delegate to the Universe to bring me serious sellers and investors for our investments, renters for our rental properties, and for all our rents to be paid on time. I intend that my life will be simple, effortless, and easy all the time. Every day, when I'm finished, I e-mail my lists to Rich, and he e-mails his to me. We have been doing this for the past two years. That's true accountability.

When I first started business coaching, my goal was to build a team and sell five hundred houses per year and to open a couple of Keller Williams offices. I found that I did not really have the burning desire or passion for that—it just wasn't "sexy" enough for me, and it didn't get me out of bed in the morning.

Things certainly have changed. My life has become easier, and I love what I am doing. I am finally following my passion. Today, I have a new company and two life goals that are exciting enough to get me out of bed in the morning:

1. To pay our investors in our syndication offerings over one million dollars per year in returns on their investments every year.

2. To give away over one million dollars per year to kids who are much less fortunate than mine.

The assets of our company today are quite large. I attribute this and all we have to the life changes that have taken place from the tools I have received from using the Law of Attraction and being committed to the process.

Now, I constantly look for more ways I can grow and how I can climb to the next level. Today, I believe more and attract more into my life than ever before. I am truly powerful and fearless. My business is growing, and I love my life.

More importantly, my relationship with my wife and children is awesome. I am able to take time off and have a business that runs smoothly even when I am not there. I have attracted great investors and team members to help our company grow and help me to have a life worth living. Today it is truly about what we as a company can do for others. Today it is truly sexy.

Message: Start your day in gratitude, focus on what you want, and then take inspired action all day long. Allow the Law of Attraction to work for you both personally and professionally.

Michael Morawski has been self-employed for over thirty years with seventeen years of real estate experience. Prior to that, he spent seventeen years in the general contracting business. Real estate syndications have always been a goal, and the power of the Law of Attraction has enabled his company to flourish. His partner, **Frank Constant**, has twenty-five years of business management and turnaround experience. Frank's accounting and management background helps protect investors' returns and stimulate company growth. They can be contacted through their Web site at *www.michaelfranksllc.com.*

STORIES OF CAREER
SUCCESS

LETTING LIFE HAPPEN

By Elizabeth A. Grant

Between the wish and the thing, life lies waiting.
—unknown

In February 2006 I was laid off from my job as marketing director for a TV station, a position I loathed. In fact, like a square peg being pounded into a round hole, I had spent my entire seventeen-year career dreading going to work each day. While the shock of this event threw me off for a couple of days, I quickly embraced it. I was fully aware that I was in my defining moment. It was time to finally leave the corporate world behind and launch my dream career as a freelance writer. Even though this had been my wish for many years, I had only a meager portfolio, no savings, and no clients.

Still, I declared it!

Without the energy-drain of a job I dreaded, I found that my years of meditation paid off in droves. I quickly reached a state of inner happiness I'd never experienced before and had my first glimpse into spiritual bliss. At first, it was just a day here and a day there. External circumstances no longer had any effect on my well-being; I could be flush with money and blissful or penniless and blissful. Life was no longer a practice in reacting to events.

I diligently looked for writing gigs—anything—each morning on the Internet. It was slow-going. After a couple of months, I had picked up my first B-level journalism gig, for which I would be paid $650, and had another in the hopper. Financially, I was teetering on the edge, and I caught my ego saying to me a few times, "If you don't make it big soon, you're going to have to go look for a corporate job." While my ego probably saw this as a clever tactic to keep me from changing and growing, it backfired. (Evidently my ego didn't know that I would have done virtually *anything* not to have to go back to corporate America.)

One night, I was having dinner with a friend. She asked me how things were going. "I am blissfully happy," I said. "I feel free, and for the first time in my life, I feel like I am living from an authentic place. But I'm starting to get nervous about money." I had enough money to pay bills about six weeks out, but I couldn't see beyond that.

"Why don't you get up tomorrow and act 'as if' you already have a full roster of clients, a literary agent, and everything else a successful writer has?" she said.

So I did.

I proceeded with an undying belief that everything would work out. I continued my practice of daily meditation and set to work on not just finding paid work but working on projects that I felt passionate about, like a fiction book. I simply gave no more thought to the "how" of my life. A few times doubt crept in and I remember saying to myself, "I trust that the Universe will bring me everything I need." These weren't empty words. I really believed it.

One of the things I did to reinforce my belief that I was a successful writer and journalist was to stay after concerts and ask the artist for an interview. "I'm a freelance writer, and I was wondering if I could interview you," I'd say. Sounds easy, doesn't it? It wasn't! I was very nervous, and a part of me felt like a phony. After all, if I'd never been published, could I call myself a real journalist? Sometimes, they would ask me what publication I was with, and I would just answer, "I'm freelance. I can't guarantee you I can get something published, but I love your music, and I'll see what I can come up with." Almost everyone I asked said yes.

One of the first people I interviewed was indie folk artist, Denison Witmer. It was a fascinating interview, and I marveled at his choice to follow his bliss at the age of twenty with no plan and no expectations.

Within a month after "acting as if," I effortlessly found a perfect part-time corporate writing job that would pay my bills while I pursued my writing passions. I had always heard freelancers issue two warnings: 1) Get ready for the dry spells, and 2) Your clients won't pay you on time. Well, maybe that was true for them, but I chose to believe something different. I really believed that after taking seventeen years to get up the courage to do this, it would work out beautifully for me. I have worked every day since on the projects of my choice, and all of my clients have paid me within ten days—allegedly "unheard of" for a writer.

Then I had an inspired idea: I would write a book featuring fifty people who got paid to do what they loved! Helping people find the freedom I had found became my absolute passion, and still is.

For the next couple months, I was consumed with the idea for this book. Every time I would meet someone who seemed passionate about what he or she did, I would whip out my business card and ask if they'd be interested in being in my book. Soon, the drummer for a Grammy-winning rock band and an internationally-renowned sculptor effortlessly came into my life, and both readily agreed to participate. Evidently, people were more than happy to help others find happiness.

I set an intention to make more money doing what I loved. Soon, I landed another part-time gig, and a third, and before long, I was turning away clients. It was all so effortless—so different from the feeling of swimming upstream that had become my way of life for seventeen years. It was my third writing project that made me realize there was something bigger going on—something beyond the physical realm. A man in Belgium found me on the Internet and asked if he could send me a $5,000 advance to edit his book for him. You have to realize I had no book-editing experience. There were thousands of other writers with lots of editing experience on the writers' site where he looked. Yet he chose *me*.

From a spiritual standpoint, what had started out as a glimpse into blissful happiness had gradually become my way of life. I felt light, free, and totally authentic.

My time and attention quickly turned to my paid projects instead of my own book. Several months went by. I had my paid gigs and the book-editing project wrapped up, and soon I realized those seven-day work weeks had taken their toll. And although I still felt passionate about my own book, it had virtually faded from my mind. I still believed, though. I had not yet learned about the Law of Attraction, or the law of gender, which says that everything has a unique gestation period. Everything happens in its own time.

Then one day in April, a co-worker said to me, "You've been working so hard. Why don't you take a vacation?" My ego quickly thought up fifty reasons why I couldn't do this, not the least of which was that I couldn't afford it. But a little seed was planted, and within a few weeks, I decided she was right. I decided I would take a trip for my fortieth birthday in June and began to search for the best destination. I decided on Ft. Lauderdale, Florida. It's not like I was dying to go to Ft. Lauderdale. It simply seemed like the right choice at the time.

In May I thought, "I'd like to take on a weekend gig. It can pay for my vacation." The next day, with that intention in the back of my mind, I went to a blog that lists freelance writing gigs, and boom! Like that, I found my perfect gig. It entailed writing an article to help people through the first thirty days of a life change—fulfilling and lucrative. Most writers spend weeks trolling the freelance sites to find scraps. But I had learned that things went differently for me than for other people. I understood what was going on in the unseen world around me. All I had to do was ask, believe, take inspired action, and receive.

As a part of this assignment, I had to interview three experts in the field of personal finance. When the editor sent me the list, I was shaking in my shoes! These were major well-known experts—contributors to *Oprah* and bestselling authors. Feeling a strange mix of terror and exhilaration, I forged ahead anyway. I called each person's publicist and was met with a resounding, "We'd be happy to be interviewed!" I breathed a sigh of relief, and my confidence grew just a little bit more.

Well, it turned out that the only time these folks were available for interviews would be during my vacation. Since writing isn't even like working to me, I was happy to oblige.

The first evening in my hotel, I considered ordering room service but instead decided to go down to the lobby bar to grab a bite to eat. A man came and sat down next to me, and we struck up a conversation. "Are you here on vacation?" I asked.

He told me his name was Richard. "No, I'm working. I'm a sea captain for a yacht owned by a billionaire. It's parked outside in the marina," he said. Now, being from the Midwest, this intrigued me. I mean, it's not every day in Chicago that one meets a sea captain.

Bing

At that moment, something clicked in my brain. My book, *Get Paid to Do What You Love*, came back into my mind. I was surprised when I realized how long it had been since I'd thought about that book—months.

"Would you consider being in my book?" I asked. I explained the concept. He agreed, and we exchanged business cards. A feeling of excitement came over me when I got back up to my room as I wondered if my book would ever get published. I didn't know how it would happen, but inside, I knew it would because it would bring a great deal of good to the world.

Two days later, I called one of the personal finance experts, Lynnette Khalfani, for our interview. As I listened to her talk (she was fresh off the heels of an *Oprah* appearance), I realized, "Wow, she is absolutely passionate about what she does. Plus, she is so *nice*." At the end of the interview, I mustered the courage and told her about my book idea.

There was a brief pause, and I wondered if I had overstepped my boundaries as an interviewer. "Not only will I be in your book," she said, "I'll help you get your book published!"

My body was filled with joy and exhilaration as I witnessed the Law of Attraction in action. By surrendering and embracing what life had brought me—the idea for a vacation, the destination that felt right, and the impromptu conversation with the sea captain—I had allowed the Universe to figure out the shortest path to my dream. When I got off the phone, I jumped up and down and was filled with an overwhelming sense of gratitude. "I love my life!" I thought. "I can't wait to see what happens next!"

I prepared a book proposal, and it was a couple months before our schedules meshed for a phone conference. Lynnette had reviewed my proposal in detail, and she spent three hours with me on the phone explaining what was good and what needed improvement. The greatest thing she stressed was that before a literary agent would be able to sell my book, I would need to establish a "platform" as an expert in this area, or at least prove I had a following.

This didn't discourage me because I knew it was possible—I knew *anything* was possible; but, it would just take some time. In the meantime, I had been mentoring several people in applying the Law of Attraction and other Universal laws, and it was becoming apparent that I should begin teaching and coaching people in this area. Not only would this prove rewarding, it would also provide a great opportunity for me to prove myself as an expert. I embraced it. I could begin holding workshops, offer to speak at events, and continue working on my book.

I knew it might be years before I would be able to make a name for myself. I would have to get an article published in a major magazine at a minimum. "What I really need is a publicist," I told a friend, "but they cost a fortune, and I simply don't have the money."

Two days later, I received an e-mail from a woman in New Jersey who I'd never met. Like my Belgian author, she'd found my profile on a writers' Web site and wondered if I would edit her book, a memoir of online dating. I asked her to send me a few chapters to review.

Part way through chapter one, I read the following sentence, and it stopped me in my tracks: "I think a lot of men are intimidated by me," it said, "because I own my own PR firm."

Although I have Law of Attraction experiences every day, when something like this happens, it always fills me with a sense of wonder, and it reinforces the idea that anything really is possible in life. Her name was Jane Coloccia, and I asked her if she would consider trading services. She told me she would be happy to and that she was going to ask me to anyway!

So I had my publicist, and it cost me nothing.

Lynnette Khalfani continues to work with me on getting my book published, Jane Coloccia helps me with my PR needs, and my practice as a personal growth advisor is thriving. This is how my life unfolds every day. I simply ask, believe, proceed "as if," let Universal energy take care of the details, and oh so gratefully receive.

Message: If you just let go and surrender to the moment—embrace it, in fact—Universal energy will take care of the rest. Let go entirely of the "how" of things. Instead, put all of your attention on your core passions. Then, go forth with absolute faith that your dreams will manifest.

Elizabeth A. Grant, a.k.a. The Quantum Coach, is an award-winning writer and personal growth advisor. She specializes in Law of Attraction coaching, teaching her clients specific techniques to help them live authentically and attract more of what they want into their lives. In 2007, she released her first spoken-word CD, entitled *Morning Commute*, to help people keep their attention on their intentions day to day. A native of Iowa, Elizabeth currently resides in Chicago. She can be contacted through her Web site at *www.thequantumcoach.net* or by e-mail at *Elizabeth@thequantumcoach.net*.

PICTURE ME SPEAKING

By John A. Williams

I advise you to say your dream is possible and then overcome all inconveniences, ignore all the hassles and take a running leap through the hoop, even if it is in flames.
—Les Brown

I have always been a person determined to get what I want out of life; however, I did not want much until I saw *The Secret*.

I was born in a low-income area of Brooklyn, New York. My father was in and out of jail, and my mother was a stay-at-home mom. When I was three, my parents separated. They used to fight often. My three brothers, my mother, and I then moved to my mother's hometown of Palatka, Florida. This is where I grew up and graduated from high school in 1988.

At the time, the most I wanted out of life was to be a U.S. Army sergeant. So I joined the Army and was promoted to the rank of sergeant three years later. After being a sergeant for a year, I wanted more. So I decided to leave the Army when my commitment ended and go to college; however, I could not decide on a major. After my first semester, I decided to major in psychology because I wanted to have a career helping others. Several years later, I finished my bachelor of psychology degree at Bethune-Cookman College in Daytona Beach, Florida. A few years after that, I finished my master's in counseling psychology at Howard University in Washington, D.C.

After finishing my master's, I moved to Atlanta, Georgia, and accepted a position as a foster care case manager for Dekalb County. It was while working for Dekalb County that I saw *The Secret* and learned about the Law of Attraction. Friends had been telling me to watch *The Secret* for months, but I thought it was just another self-help sermon. So I didn't. After all, I had read hundreds of books regarding psychology and had counseled hundreds of clients. I thought, "How is one more self-improvement sermon going to help me?"

I remember the night as if it were last night. It was a little over a year ago. I remember thinking to myself, with all the hype regarding this movie, I guess I'd better grab a pad and pen. So I did. While watching it, something came over me. I realized how I had never allowed myself to truly identify what I really wanted out of life. My previous career moves were loaded with fear … fear of failure and fear of rejection. Some of the notes I took read: *thoughts become things, control your thoughts, focus on what you want and not on what you don't want, feel good, be polite to attract positive people, and a positive thought is much more powerful than a negative one.*

Although I had always considered myself positive-minded, successful, and a "go-getter," I realized that I was not as positive as I thought I was, and that I was not successful. I also realized that I had always operated with a limited vision of myself and rarely controlled my thoughts. The Army and my mother made me good at controlling my behavior, but I had no idea that I could control my thoughts, until *The Secret*.

I realized that I had always been afraid to identify and pursue my dream job. Also, I never thought that by displaying a positive attitude, I could attract people who could boost my career. I quickly realized that every career I had ever chosen was a "sure-thing" career. In order to become a U.S. Army sergeant, all one has to do is stay out of trouble, exercise, and pass a few tests. In order to graduate from college, all one has to do is what the professors ask you to do. These were safe options for me … "sure-things."

While watching the movie, I kept picturing the motivational speaker, Les Brown. I envisioned him on stage over and over again. His career consisted largely of helping people, traveling, and getting paid—all of which are right up my alley. I also realized that I immensely wanted to become a college professor. *The Secret* led me to the realization that I never truly believed that these careers were possible for me. Although I had held several "good" jobs, I realized that these "good" jobs were safe jobs. My attitude about life, careers, relationships, and success changed. I thought to myself, "How can you really consider yourself successful when you hate your job?"

At that time, I was a foster care case manager for the Department of Family and Children's Services in Decatur, Georgia. Everyone I worked around was negative. *The Secret* allowed me to realize that the longer I stayed working for this company, the longer I would remain in my "safe job" and remain unsuccessful. So when I arrived at work on Friday morning, I looked at my co-workers to my right, then looked at my co-workers to my left, then started typing my resignation letter. I resigned from my "good" and "safe" job on that day. I was at work at 8:00 AM sharp, and my resignation letter was on my boss's desk by 8:30 AM sharp. She was astonished, but I knew exactly what I was doing.

I got home about 5:00 PM and began writing down everything I wanted: 1) a career as a college professor, 2) a career as a motivational speaker, and 3) to share the stage at a speaking engagement with Les Brown. I taped the list to my refrigerator door and went to sleep.

The next morning, when I went to prepare breakfast, I saw the list. While reading it, I realized that my dreams were possible. Knowing that one of the careers I wanted was that of a college professor, I called Atlanta Metropolitan College and got the name of the chairperson of the department in which I wanted to work. I immediately went to see him in my best suit with my résumé in hand. I met him in his office and we talked. I talked about my passion like I never had previously. I told him about myself and how much I wanted to teach in his department. Unfortunately, he informed me that there were no openings. I told him I would follow up in a few weeks. I went home and reviewed my notes from *The Secret*. I decided that I would commit to reading them on a regular basis.

The next day, I decided to get my career as a professional speaker going. I ordered a few tapes and videos of Les Brown's speeches and watched them daily. I also created a page on MySpace. After about two weeks of reviewing my notes, seeing my goals and dreams printed on my refrigerator, and watching the videos of Les Brown, I decided to begin speaking professionally.

The following day, I went to the library to work on a speech. As I walked inside, I noticed that there was a recreation center next door to the library. I had walked by this recreation center several times a week and never saw it as a way to assist me with achieving my goals. I went inside the center and inquired about using the venue for speaking engagements. I was quoted a price of $40 per event. Six weeks later, I was using it twice a month to speak to sixty people at each event.

About a week later, I received a phone call from Dr. Culpepper of Atlanta Metropolitan College. He is the department chair who interviewed me. He offered me a position to teach critical thinking and personal development in his department.

Three more months passed. I continued to read my notes from *The Secret* daily. I went to check my MySpace messages. I also went to Les Brown's MySpace page. I was in his "top friends." I could not believe it. Les has never met me and I was in his top friends. I think this lasted for about two weeks. Currently, I am in the top friends of his number one friend ... his daughter, Ona Brown, and I have never met her either.

About two months ago, I was speaking with one of my friends from graduate school about securing more speaking engagements. She told me about an event that was scheduled to take place in September in Sacramento, California. The event was a pilot recording for a future reality show titled *The Monstars of Motivation*. She also informed me that she knew the gentleman who was responsible for the entire event, Kevin Bracy. She called Kevin and informed him that I was interested in auditioning. Kevin listened to one of my motivational messages and invited me out to be part of his event.

I went out to California and participated in the event. That night, I went back to my room and visited Kevin's Web site, and I noticed a CD he had available for purchase. On the CD were Kevin Bracy and Les Brown. This was the Law of Attraction working! Two of the three goals that are on my refrigerator, I have already achieved: 1) becoming a college professor and 2) becoming a motivational speaker. There is one more goal unmet, and it is sharing the stage with Les Brown. However, I know that as long as I continue to live the Law of Attraction, this final goal will be met. Currently, I watch *The Secret* every other week to keep me focused. I love my life, enjoy pursuing my dreams, and look forward to sharing the stage with Les Brown while working in my new "sure-thing" career.

Message: Don't be afraid to ask for what you want. When you feel good, amazing things happen.

John A. Williams is a professional motivational speaker, college professor, experienced psychotherapist, and president of the John Williams Consulting Group, LLC of Decatur, Georgia. He received his master's degree in counseling psychology from Howard University in Washington, D.C. John can be contacted through his Web site at *www.johnawilliamsonline.com*.

FINDING THE PERFECT JOB

By W. Mason Preddy

The rainbow is more beautiful than the pot at the end if it, because the rainbow is now. And the pot never turns out to be quite what I expected.
—Hugh Prather

I worked as a healthcare recruiter for an awesome community hospital. In my time there, I was responsible for helping achieve record-low vacancy rates (there is a worldwide shortage of healthcare professionals) and increasing retention. I started new programs, and was responsible for applying for national and local awards, many of which we won. We then merged with a chain of hospitals in the area.

My position was eliminated, and I was devastated. I couldn't understand how they could do something so nasty to someone who had given them so much. I received a severance package and was able to use some of the money to work on a double master's certificate program from Tulane University. In looking back and examining what had happened, I realized that the work environment had really become miserable, and it was not a fun place to work anymore.

At first, I had my sights set on joining a consulting firm that did work in the healthcare industry. They were interested in me, and I went through a series of interviews. I was constantly writing affirmations that I got this job with "X" company, making "X" amount, etc. The job required constant travel—four or five days every week all over the country. While this was really not appealing to me, I told myself I would like it and it would be okay. Well, you can't "trick" the Universe!

It knows just by the way you feel. I didn't get the job. I was upset but knew that all the travel would have been a real drag. A series of other opportunities came along, and for various reasons, either I wasn't interested when I learned more or I didn't get the job. I continued to write affirmations with each position.

What I didn't realize is that you are not supposed to be telling the Universe "how" or "who," etc. You are supposed to let the Universe handle that for you. That is a very difficult thing to do.

I decided to quit writing so many affirmations and just start concentrating on the way I felt. Looking back at the other jobs, I knew they really weren't the best jobs for me, but I kept telling myself they would be great and everything would work out. Instead, I started talking about what I really wanted in a job. I would write an occasional affirmation, but rather than naming the company, I let the Universe work on what the organization would be. I just focused on what was important to me.

I wanted flexibility, to make a lot of money, to be happy at what I was doing, to like my co-workers and have them like me, to have the "perfect amount" of travel to pleasant places, and to be successful at what I was doing. Well, the Universe has presented me with an awesome new opportunity—with all of the above. I am very excited and start soon!

The major things I learned were: Don't worry about the "how." That is the job of the Universe. When something doesn't work out, know that something better will come along. The Universe had a plan for me, and even though I was disappointed along the way, it has all worked out perfectly. This opportunity will definitely make me the happiest and has all the things I wanted.

Message: Focus on what you want and let the Universe handle how to bring it to you.

JOURNEY TO AUTHENTIC TRUTH

By Jen Blackert

In every block of marble I see a statue as plain as though it stood before me, shaped and perfect in attitude and action. I have only to hew away the rough walls that imprison the lovely apparition to reveal it to the other eyes as mine see it.
—Michelangelo

I spent much of my late teens and early adulthood in a state of anxiety and depression. It seemed as if I was always chasing something, trying to get something, or being someone else or somewhere else. Eventually, I did get what I desired, whatever it was that I was chasing. Family members would point out that I was lucky, or that I could turn any bag of thorns into a bouquet of roses. Yet, I still wasn't happy. There were moments of exhilaration when I knew I was going to get what I had been working for, but there was little true happiness.

In 1997 I began to practice yoga regularly at a local gym. I started attending class during lunch breaks from work. Actually, I had used yoga mostly as a way to take longer lunch breaks and escape the daily grind. For me, the hardest part of yoga was final rest (savasana). Now I know it was difficult because on some level I feared knowing myself on a deeper level. The truth is I didn't really like myself.

Was I afraid of my other self? Who was this other self? I am just one person … aren't I?

I realized yoga had become an escape from my dual self. Or, should I say my dueling self? Yoga was the escape from this "other" voice, this negative, self-defeating voice in my head. While other people choose to use drugs or alcohol—not me—I chose yoga as my drug of choice. Thankfully, it has awakened me to a life of inspiration, consciousness, and flow.

By 2005 I chose to end my corporate career. By the time I left I was miserable, yet I still felt trapped by a high paying salary, although there was absolutely no respect. I was tortured with thoughts, "How could I possibly leave such a high paying job? I can't make this kind of money doing anything else." Boy, was I wrong! Who was I to tell myself this? I told myself, "I can't." No one who loved me would tell me such nonsense, whether they thought it or not. Where did I get such ideas? Maybe I didn't love myself. At a minimum, I was verbally abusive to myself. Who had I become? I, of course, didn't realize this until much later. And then magic started to happen.

One Saturday in March of 2005 I received a phone call from a man in Arizona. At the time, we didn't have a cable phone or caller ID, or who knows if I would have even answered the phone. My number was not available online or in the phone book. The man asked if there was a person who practiced transcendental meditation in our home. I said, "No, but I am very spiritual, and I practice and teach yoga." He then asked if it was Kundalini yoga and again I said, "No, I practice Vinyasa and Ashtanga yoga." I was starting to get a little defensive and agitated with his questions. Who was this guy, and why was he questioning me?

I began thinking it was some kind of joke, or perhaps he had found my name on some yoga list. Finally, I asked him who he was and why he was calling. He said he was a "TMer." At the time, I had no idea what a TMer was. He explained that TM stands for Transcendental Meditation. It's not a religion or philosophy, and it can be practiced by anyone looking to experience more mental clarity or reduce stress. I understood it as a form of meditation but nothing more. He told me that during meditation, he saw my number and had a strong sense that I needed to know that the Universe was in support of my new direction.

I spent the next week practicing yoga at a spiritual retreat center. After each day of practice, we journaled our experiences. After a few hours of intense yoga, we would journal about a given topic or our "after-yoga" thoughts. My journal entries included random statements such as ... *We die in the comfort zone. Step out of your comfort zone. There is peace with truth. There is no peace with self-doubt. Life is full of options. We must have the courage to face the truth.* I remember crying because at the time I wasn't following my true path, and I felt miserable because of it.

The Monday after the retreat, I wandered back into my corporate office feeling refreshed and relaxed. Then I thought, "What am I doing here? Is this just a pay check for me?" I knew a job like mine was a dream job for others, so why couldn't I just be thankful for what I had? I made it through the day and cried to my husband about my miserable job that night. He had some inspiring wisdom. He asked, "How will your life change if you leave this job? My job will support our current living patterns until you get up to speed with your own business. You will still have your computer, cable TV, and your car. Your life won't change. I want you to be happy." It seemed so simple to him, but to me it was huge.

By the end of the day on Tuesday, my computer's hard drive crashed. I would joke to co-workers, "Do you think God is telling me something?" Many would just giggle, but one man said very seriously, "Yes! You have all this talent waiting to be let out. Jen, what are you doing here? What are you waiting for?" Those words stuck with me. What was I waiting for? Why was I holding on to a job I disliked? Why was I torturing myself?

My new computer wasn't delivered until the following Friday. The computer company didn't even try to recover my hard drive. What had taken them so long? Those three days of workless suffering brought me to the conclusion that I had to quit. That day, on my new computer, I wrote my resignation letter.

I left with a determined intention in my head to build a coaching practice with thirty-five weekly coaching clients. I had also planned and designed this practice to be sold at some point. What I later realized was that what I really wanted was the compensation of thirty-five weekly clients.

Within eight months I had thirty-one weekly coaching clients and felt completely overwhelmed. By twelve months, I sold the business to a competitor. Now I teach Internet marketing and how to apply the Law of Attraction to small businesses.

Message: Uncover your hidden self and find your true path.

Jen Blackert is an intuitive, author, speaker, and coach. She has personally taught hundreds of individuals her unique principles and approach to success. Her principles are based on time-honored Universal wisdom. She has authored several articles, books, and programs, including *Seven Dragons: A Guide to a Limitless Mind* and *The Laws of Attraction Marketing.* She has a BS in nutritional science and is also a certified professional coach, NLP (Neuro-linguistic practitioner), and yoga instructor. Jen can be contacted through her Web site at *www.q2wealth.com* or by e-mail at *jen@q2wealth.com.*

HAPPINESS

STORIES OF LIVING
THE
LIFE OF YOUR
DREAMS

THE LIFE OF MY DREAMS

By Cindy Day

I liken the past to the wake of a boat. It does not drive the boat, nor does it determine the direction it's headed. It only shows where it's been.
—Dr. Wayne Dyer

Coming from an unhappy childhood, much of my adult life was lived with limiting beliefs, fear, low self-worth, and no spiritual grounding. Ten years ago, I was a single parent living in the Midwest. Not living, more like existing. Empty and depressed is how I would have described myself. I knew there was something missing, that I had something to offer, even though I grew up feeling worthless. I felt like my life was wasting away.

Not knowing about the Law of Attraction, or that I played a part in the creation of my life's circumstances, I listened to everyone when they said, "What's wrong with you? You should be happy. You're pretty. You have a wonderful little boy and a good job." That never helped me feel better; I still stayed depressed and empty.

The turning point came when I visited Los Angeles eight years ago. I met Fabio (the former model) while walking down the street one day. That week he took me under his wing, offering advice and words of spiritual wisdom. He could see how empty, unfulfilled, and unhappy I was. He tried to convince me that I was *supposed* to be happy and that I didn't have to settle for an empty life with a "good job" that I didn't like.

He took me to meet with modeling agents and even booked me a job. That week, I was the happiest I had ever been. I felt like L.A. was where I belonged. I felt so at home and at peace. I had always told myself that one day I would live in L.A., but didn't know how to make it happen since I was a single parent with a lot of limiting beliefs.

After returning home to Ohio, I thought about what Fabio had said. I started reading books by authors I had never heard of or even knew existed (Deepak Chopra, Gary Zukav, Wayne Dyer, Tony Robbins, etc.). I didn't want to quit my nine-to-five job for fear of what everyone would think of me. Within weeks of my L.A. trip, the company I worked for was bought out by another and was moved to another city. This was the perfect time to make a move. I couldn't believe it was happening!

To make a long story short, my son and I moved to L.A. I got tons of acting and modeling jobs right away. Then I met a man and immediately moved in with him out of fear of being alone. His insecurity led to mental and emotional abuse. I was filled with worry and anxiety every day. My acting and modeling jobs immediately started to fade away. I stopped evolving and reading the inspirational books. I hadn't saved a dime from all the work I had done, not realizing at the time he had wanted it that way. I lived in fear every day and didn't know how to get out of the relationship. If I tried to make a plan to get on my feet, he would threaten to throw all of our things out in the street. My good friend, Fabio, tried to help, but I never responded.

One night, while the man I lived with was away on business, I awoke with a thought: "If you love yourself and your son, you will not stay here one day longer." I got out of bed and immediately packed everything we owned into my car. We were now homeless and penniless! We got emergency help and stayed at a motel where the residents were homeless people, crack addicts … you name it! I was frightened but didn't want my son to know, so I tried to be happy for him.

My son was the happiest I had seen him in a while. The fact that we didn't have a home wasn't as important as the peace of mind I had and that my son felt loved. On our fourteenth and last day that we were allowed to stay at the motel, I dropped my son off at school. I went back to the motel and packed everything we owned into my car and prepared to drive back to Ohio after school.

While trying to stay sane and prepare myself to break the news to my son that we were leaving L.A., I drove around for a little while. I prayed that something would happen in the next few hours. I stopped at a Starbucks and sat down. A man approached and asked if he could sit down with me. I recognized him from TV, so I figured it was safe. We had a talk that lasted about thirty minutes. It was about spirituality and having faith. He told me to do what my heart tells me—not my mind, which decides out of fear.

I realized that God brought this person to me at the moment I needed him most. I felt like a weight had been lifted from my shoulders. I left and went back to the motel inspired and excited. I knew that my heart wanted me to stay in L.A.

I just couldn't leave! Within an hour, I got a phone call about a cocktail waitressing job and was asked to start immediately.

To sum it all up, I saved enough money to get our own place. I earned my real estate license and sold my first million dollar property in the first month. I soon realized that everything that was happening and had happened to me was a result of the Law of Attraction. After studying more, and evolving further, I saw so many things come into my life that I had always wanted.

I am now married to a wonderful man with whom I travel quite frequently. I live in my dream home. I have a wonderful lifestyle that allows me to follow my passions without fear. I am now a life coach, helping others overcome their limiting beliefs and achieve their dreams. I have even written and published my first book, *The Life of Your Dreams in 30 Days or Less!*

Although I practice and teach it on a regular basis, I am still amazed by the Law of Attraction!

Message: No matter what you've experienced in the past, it is important to remember that the past does not have the power to determine your future. Your present thoughts and emotions create your future.

Cindy Day is a writer, life and dream coach, and entrepreneur. She wrote her first book, *The Life of Your Dreams in 30 Days or Less!: The Ordinary Person's Guide to Extraordinary Abundance,* to teach others to apply the Law of Attraction in a simple, quick way to live the life they dream of. To find out more about Cindy, visit her Web site at *www.CindyDay.net.*

LIFE IS WHAT YOU MAKE IT

By Melissa Owens

Hope is always available to us. When we feel defeated, we need only take a deep breath and say, "Yes," and hope will reappear.
—Monroe Forester

Here's a tiny bit of background about my life. For reasons that have never been entirely clear to me, although I do have a pretty good idea, I was adopted by my grandparents at the age of four. I spent my childhood living back and forth between my grandparents' house and my parents' house. The majority of the time, I lived with my retired military grandfather and frequently ill grandmother.

I was brought up in a middle-class neighborhood in a medium-sized city in North Texas. My parents were alcoholics and were constantly in violent arguments, which I was regularly subjected to. My mother had spent a lot of time in and out of a psychiatric hospital due to suicidal threats. Not only did she have issues with alcohol, but prescription drug abuse as well. My parents loved me very much; I do know this. But I believe they chose to turn to alcohol and drugs in order to mask the pain they had caused each other rather than making raising their only child their number one priority.

My father was murdered in 1987, when I was twelve years old. I'll never forget that day when, after school, my aunt (my father's sister) broke the horrific news to me. That was definitely the worst, most painful day of my life. In that single moment, my whole life came crumbling down. Every hope and dream that I had with my beloved father was shattered. At the time I felt there was no reason to live. My mother made the decision to abandon me very shortly after.

Thank God I had my loving grandparents to raise me. My grandfather was such a brave man and did so much for my grandmother and me. My grandmother suffered from diabetes as well as several other serious health issues. After my father's death, my grandmother's health became even worse than before. My grandfather had to spend most of his time caring for my grandmother. This, of course, took a lot of time away from me.

I had no choice but to grow up quickly. I began to do my own laundry and even cook my own dinners. It was definitely a rough time for me! There were times when I felt so alone, so empty. I felt like no one really cared. Eventually, by the age of thirteen, I began to spend a lot of time going to church with my friends. I got involved in youth groups, etc. This was a point in my life when I knew I needed to be positive and to believe that life does go on.

Fast forward twenty years. My grandparents had since passed away, and I had pretty much been on my own ever since. I moved to California in 1995, when I was twenty-one. I met a wonderful man and shortly afterwards was blessed with two beautiful children. Their birth dates just happen to surround the death dates of my beloved father and grandmother. Their father and I were very young and pretty much grew apart. We split up in 2002.

I allowed myself to focus on my failed relationship and felt like a complete failure at the time. I then focused on, and allowed, my current and past circumstances to create my reality. I allowed myself to be involved in abusive and neglectful relationships. I allowed myself to settle for just barely scraping by financially. I figured that coming from the background I came from, every thing, every person, and every situation in my life was the best that I could get. Come on, look where I came from! Well, thanks to *The Secret* and learning how to apply the Law of Attraction, today, as quoted in *The Secret,* I call that "So what!"

I was introduced to *The Secret* DVD by one of my very best friends in November of 2006. I was at one of the lowest and darkest points of my life. I went from being homeless, living out of my car, and staying on friends' sofas, to finally moving into my own tiny one-bedroom apartment. I was laid off from my job as a corporate recruiter soon after I had moved into my apartment. In a hopeless panic, I took whatever I could get. It was a commission-only position in the field of job recruitment, which, by the way, is very slow during the holiday season. I did have a $1,500 per month draw to live on. However, my rent was $1,300 per month. Not to mention, I had a car payment and other bills. My life was going down the tubes rapidly, or so it seemed. I became extremely behind on all of my bills. I was scared and felt very alone, and of course, had no family to turn to.

My friend invited me to her home one night to watch *The Secret*. She told me that it was life-altering. Thank God for my open mind—I watched it with no hesitation. I was enamored by it! My way of thinking quickly shifted, and from that moment, my life began to quickly move in a completely different and positive direction. In exactly one month, I actually started to attract unexpected checks in the mail exactly when I needed the extra money. In two months, I landed another corporate position, and my income quadrupled. I quickly got caught up on all of my bills and even began the process of cleaning up my credit.

Fast forward another ten months. I have since attracted an even better-paying career in executive recruiting. I am moving out of my tiny one-bedroom apartment into a bigger and nicer place with an ocean view once my lease is up. I have a new car (the one I had visualized in my head by the way). I've since attracted an amazing and respectful man who fits all of the qualities on my list that I wrote and read daily. All of my close friends live by the Law of Attraction. I continuously attract positive, like-minded individuals into my life!

Since February 2007, I have been miraculously cured of hypoglycemia, which I have struggled with on a daily basis since I was in elementary school. Seriously, one day I woke up and "poof," it was gone! I am so excited about the Law of Attraction that I am now even looking into starting a non-profit organization (which I have always wanted to do) in order to help spread the word to the world.

I could go on and on about how dramatically my life has improved. I wake up every morning filled with gratitude. It has only been ten months since I was first introduced to the Law of Attraction. I am extremely excited to see what tomorrow holds for me. My life just gets better and better every single day! I am so very grateful for my life and the abundance that I have and will continue to attract.

Please, if your life is tough at this moment, read, watch, learn, understand, and apply the Law of Attraction. I am living proof that miracles do happen! I truly hope that my story, as well as the others, will inspire you to alter your way of thinking.

Message: You deserve everything that is amazing and beautiful. Don't ever lose hope.

Melissa Owens was born in Los Angeles, California. Shortly thereafter, she and her parents moved to a small military city in North Texas where Melissa was raised mainly by her grandparents. Since 1996, she has been living in Southern California where she has learned to apply the Law of Attraction to her everyday life and has created miracles she thought could never happen. Melissa can be contacted through MySpace at *www.myspace.com/melissalanetheactress* or by e-mail at *actressmelissalane@gmail.com.*

THE LITTLE VOICE THAT COULD

By Lessia Bonn

Every blade of grass has its angel that bends over it and whispers, "Grow, grow."
—from The Talmud

I spent my childhood chained to a very large musical instrument. I sat at that stupid piano for hours and hours while my friends were outside having fun. Jeez, it just wasn't fair. I didn't even like classical music. Well, Beethoven was okay, maybe. At least he was dramatic.

But I wanted to sing, not play. I had a ton of songs in my head. I was never inspired by the piano; it just felt like typing to me when I played. But to everybody else it seemed I was an endearing little keyboard prodigy. They all had so much fun watching me, they assumed I was having fun too. But I wasn't having fun. I hated my fast fingers! Big deal—fast fingers. Everyone was impressed, but I was totally depressed. I wanted to sing.

When I think back, I can still feel the ouch—I still feel sorry for the little kid who was too scared to use her voice, or at least the part of her voice that really mattered. I just wish I could have said, "I want to do something else. Can't I please learn something I really like?" I wish I could have said, "Can't you see I'm just doing this for you? Can't you see who I really am?"

Truth is, I had a little voice that sounded very ordinary. My family assumed—like most people assume—that if a person has a so-called "singing" voice, everyone can tell right away. Bet even you believe that—but you're wrong. Seriously.

Here's the real truth. Everybody has that kind of "singing" voice. It just hasn't been discovered yet. People sing "Happy Birthday" badly and then give up saying, "Ugh! I can't sing. Forget it." And their friends usually agree. "Yeah, take up cello."

But hey, "Happy Birthday" is actually hard to sing because it's full of funky consonants. Somebody should really explain *that* before a person gives up on singing. It's helpful information. But there isn't ever any real explaining going on now, is there?

Only Simon Cowell seems to get listened to. Whenever he harshly proclaims one person can sing while another shouldn't even try, it just makes me crazy. I always feel like hitting him. A lot of people don't know how to find a pretty vowel, a lot of people don't breathe, especially when they're nervous, and those are the things that can make a voice sound yucky. A lot of people just don't know the tricks.

Our culture also dictates that people, especially kids, should stifle their voices and emotions. If a person's voice carries across the room, hey, that's just embarrassing. Ugh. Find yourself some manners. Put a lid on it. Yet we're supposed to be able to sing. Just how exactly?

Sure, sometimes there are people who are great copycats. They listen to the radio, then mimic the singers they like and end up sounding great themselves. Most people are not great copycats though. Most people end up sounding like squeaky little church mice when they try to sing, but it's not their fault. Truly it's not.

I was one of those church mice. When I blurted out, "I want to sing" to my piano-oriented family, they answered back, "But you don't have a voice." End of discussion. That really hurt my soul. And in just one instant, those six little words shut me down. At that age a kid soaks in her parents' truths and really wants to please them. Because I was little and impressionable, I believed what was handed to me. My voice stayed small, in every sense of the word, for a very long time. I didn't ever feel brave with it. I kept apologizing right and left for just being me.

This is why I'm telling you my story. Maybe you don't want to sing. Maybe you want to write a big fat novel, sell floating beds, or open yourself a dude ranch. Maybe your biggest dream is to live in Paris, but everyone keeps telling you you're crazy—you don't even speak French!

So tell them you'll learn French. *Ooh lah lah.* There are three words already. Couldn't be that hard. Tell them, "I can learn French," and pack your bags for Paris.

"You're crazy, you can't do that! That's not the way it's done!" Don't you just hate it when people say that kind of stuff? All those geniuses out there on the subject of *you!*

Well hey, I'm here to urge you to aim for whatever the hell you please. Don't you dare go dumping all your dreams just because a few people around you have no vision, no insight, or are simply ignorant of one basic fundamental fact of life: There are tricks to most everything. Learning those tricks will let you rock at whatever it is you want to do. So educate yourself!

Take it from me—I was a little voice who couldn't until I figured out that I surely could. I just kept on believing. And here was my chant: "I know I can, I know I can ..." and then ... yay! I found the voice I always knew I had.

Now I not only sing, record, and give concerts, I coach others. I'm the expert. I'm the highly-paid consultant. What a hoot! I take other singers into the recording studio and make them sound awesome because I'm a whiz at singing tricks, and also I'm pretty darn cool at producing tricks. And I've always been able to write a song, so hey, throw that in too. And seriously, I don't think Beethoven misses me much.

And do you know what I've discovered along my path? I've discovered that the tricks to singing are actually a whole lot like the tricks to life. In order to sing, a person has to cut out the worrying, collect helpful data, relax, and then simply fall into her own voice. Trusting one's deeper self is important because there's a sweet spot inside us that already knows how to sing. When we find it—oh, wow—we're there. Singing's easy! Sure, it takes faith and practice, but so what? Challenges keep life entertaining. Don't tell me you'd rather be bored.

My stepfather announced to me once, "There's nothing special about your voice." He was really certain. Years later, he showed up at one of my sold-out concerts. His updated review: "Oh my God, you're great! I'm so embarrassed I ever said you couldn't sing! Your voice is awesome! I was so wrong!"

No more Beethoven for me. Now I sing. But the funny thing is, deep down inside, I always knew I was a singer.

She knew she was a singer.... She knew she was a singer.... She knew she was a singer.... And then—*voila!*—(another French word). Laugh out loud. Hooray for every little voice that can!

And take it from an expert: Every little voice really can.

And *kudos* for the Law of Attraction:

I *knew* I was a singer. I *knew* I was a better singer than piano player. I *knew* deep down—all those things—so I believed and believed *and imagined* placing my faith in what I knew until ...

My voice came out in spades one day. It said, "Hello. How you doin'?" And it was a cool voice. Laugh out loud. So yay for me! Because I knew I could.... I knew I could.... And now I can!

It just took a bit of uncovering.

Message: Know you can.

Lessia Bonn is a prize-winning singer-songwriter-producer-arranger-recording artist and author. She's the driving force behind Vocals by Locals, a very colorful group of gifted Santa Barbarian teenage songbirds. A movie is now being scripted around VBL's lively adventures. She has recently penned, with the help of many fun friends, a wonderful new book called *The Little Voice That Could.* For music, book, and CD information, please visit *www.thelittlevoicethatcould.com* or *www.myspace.com/vocalsbylocals99.*

MANIFESTING AN IMMIGRATION

By Wayne Botha

The most beautiful thing we can experience is the mysterious. It is the source of all true art and science. He to whom this emotion is a stranger, who can no longer pause to wonder and stand rapt in awe, is as good as dead; his eyes are closed.
—Albert Einstein

On January 19, 2001, a snowstorm hit the Northeast United States. At the same time, on the other side of the planet, a plane was boarded on a hot summer evening in Johannesburg, South Africa. On January 20, 2001, amidst piles of snow and bitterly cold winds, two tired parents and an exhausted four-year-old landed at JFK airport after a seventeen-hour flight. The exuberance replaced all anxiousness and fatigue. We are in America because of the eternal Law of Attraction.

Let's first go back a few years. In early 1999 my wife and I were living in South Africa and were dissatisfied with the future prospects there. We were looking for a new country to call home and decided that the "Land of Opportunity" was where we wanted to settle. I traveled to Dallas, Texas, to survey the United States and meet with prospective employers. In May 1999 I reached an agreement with a contracting house and began the process to file for an immigrant visa. Over the next year, we handed over our entire life savings for the various filing costs and attorney's fees, only to cancel the process when the contracting house demanded a large amount of cash to continue the process. We suspected illegal immigration activity and were devastated. Our life savings were gone, and our dream of living in the United States seemed unreachable.

At this low point in my life, I stumbled upon segments of the Law of Attraction in books by authors such as Napoleon Hill. Although *The Secret* articulates the Law of Attraction very clearly, *The Secret* was not available in 1999. I later realized that I had used the Law of Attraction to manifest my desires. Although

The Secret had not yet been written, portions of the Law of Attraction found me through various books I had read over the years. I realized after watching *The Secret,* that I had been guided over the years to study books proposing autosuggestion, affirmations, and the power of programming your subconscious mind. Many biographies of successful people hint at the Law of Attraction. You find phrases from people such as Henry Ford and Albert Einstein in their writings that hint at their awareness of the Law of Attraction.

When we thought our desires were destined to never be fulfilled, and we believed we would never live in the USA, I implemented the Law of Attraction. We had nothing to lose at this point and everything to gain. At this time, I worked for a banking institution in South Africa and dreamed of living in the United States.

Below is a list of actions that I took to manifest our desire:

- Every morning, when I got to the office, I watched a Web-cam of Verrazano-Narrows Bridge in New York City. I visualized us traveling over that same bridge in New York City. I looked at the Web-cam and closed my eyes, took deep breaths to be still and imagined that I would drive over that bridge. I imagined us touching down at an airport, and felt the joy and pride as we touched down, realizing that our dreams had come true.

- I created a vision board with photos of cars and houses in America and imagined, twice a day, what our lives would be like in America. I imagined our four-year-old son going on a yellow school bus to school every day. There are no school buses in South Africa, and a yellow school bus signifies America.

- I went further and created a mock household budget, estimating our monthly income and expenses when we lived in America. I researched the price of cars, houses, and groceries.

- I spoke to everyone I could about what it was like to live in America, including family and friends and acquaintances who I met over the Internet. I spoke to ex-South Africans who had moved to America and people who had lived in America and were now living in South Africa.

- I put a map of the United States on my wall, next to my computer. I saw the map every time I glanced up from the screen. I created a special binder with a list of affirmations to repeat to myself during the day, stated in the present tense, which reminded me to keep believing we would one day live in the United States.

- We also took physical steps when necessary to play our part in the master plan from the Universe as opportunities came before us. We received an offer on our house and sold it. We sold all of our household goods and belongings that we could not transport to the United States. I applied for positions with employers who offered postings in the United States and assistance with immigration procedures. I accepted an offer from an employer who scheduled our flights and informed us that we would be leaving South Africa on January 19, 2001, and reporting to their New Jersey office on Monday, January 22, 2001.

On January 20, 2001, our desires were manifested in reality. We landed at JFK Airport and were in the United States of America. My family and I are now established and live successful lives.

After we settled in the USA, I realized that continually sending out our desires to the Universe, charged with emotion and visualizations of what we desired, resulted in the Universe responding with opportunities to manifest those desires. I was overjoyed when I watched *The Secret* on DVD, because it helped me to explain to my family how the Law of Attraction had brought us to the United States.

Lessons I learned from this manifestation:

- The Law of Attraction works. You need to do your part and put your request out to the Universe. Put images of your desire on your vision board and visualize receiving the object of your desire with strong positive emotions.

- After selecting your desires, don't give up. Manifestations sometimes take years. Keep on believing and continually increase the energy that you send to the Universe by imagining what your life will be like after your desire is manifested in your life. If you want to attract money, visualize the checks coming to your mailbox. Visualize giving money to charity. Mock up budgets that reflect your desired income. Research and find out how people with the income you want spend their leisure time. What golf clubs will you belong to with that money? Where will you dine? Where will you vacation? Put out increasing amounts of energy to the Universe until your desire is manifested.

- Use all avenues available to implement the Law of Attraction. Use your vision board. Speak about your desires. Enlist the help of professional financial planners if you want to manifest more money. Do everything you can to engage the Universe and make your desire known. Study *The Secret* and learn everything you can about implementing the Law of Attraction.

- You can't see the entire path ahead of you, but you can influence your life through the Law of Attraction. We faced challenges and obstacles during the two years we implemented the Law of Attraction in our lives for this manifestation. Although we could not see the entire path, the Universe manifested our ultimate desire. When implementing the Law of Attraction in your life, expect the manifestation of your desire, but also be open to short diversions along the way when things don't go exactly as you planned.

- Continually put whole-hearted positive images and emotions of your desires out to the Universe. If you don't put positive desires out to the Universe, your mind will allow negative energy to infiltrate your desires. Prohibit negative energy by keeping your desires fully positive all the time. Don't leave any room for negative energy or desires to creep in. Any gap in the positive energy you send to the Universe will be filled with negative energy.

- Visualize your desires in colorful images. Use your vision board to help you see your desires in full color, with the textures and sights that you want to bring into your life. Imagine all the details including the sounds, smell, and taste of your desires. Don't describe your desires in limiting verbal description only. Feel, smell, and taste your desired manifestation.

To put the magnitude of this manifestation into perspective, the chances are infinitesimally small that our move from South Africa to the United States could have manifested without the Law of Attraction. Only a small number of people are able to emigrate from South Africa to the United States each year. In order to immigrate successfully, we needed to accept an uncertain future in a foreign country while maintaining financial liquidity. In addition, I am an information technology professional, and we arrived in the United States shortly after the Wall Street crash caused by the "tech bubble" burst. I firmly believe that my family and I owe our futures in the United States of America to the Law of Attraction.

I have since used the Law of Attraction many times to manifest permanent employment, an MBA degree, and a position as project manager. The more I implement the steps to manifest desires in my life, the easier it becomes and the more faith I have in the Law of Attraction.

I sincerely hope that by sharing this manifestation with you, you gain fresh appreciation for the Law of Attraction. I hope that our experience gives you renewed enthusiasm to implement the Law of Attraction in many areas of your own life.

Message: The Law of Attraction has always existed and will continue to exist for-ever—especially for those who choose to use it.

Wayne Botha is a speaker and author. He holds an MBA in e-business and now lives in the United States. Wayne continues to attract wealth and people into his life since learning how to apply the Law of Attraction. He can be contacted through his Web site at *www.waynebotha.com* or by e-mail at *Wayne@waynebotha.com*.

THE SKY'S THE LIMIT

By Cindy Ulmer

Optimism is the faith that leads to achievement.
Nothing can be done without hope and confidence.
—Helen Keller

Fasten your seatbelts and grab an oxygen mask. If you think you can't have everything you want in life, or that it will take too long, you need to hear me out. My story will make you believe.

It began with a simple declaration stated with much feeling and emotion: "I have beautiful teeth." You would not have agreed. If you'd seen what I saw in the mirror every morning, you'd have called me crazy—crooked teeth, chipped and yellow, and a face aged prematurely by fatigue and stress. My skin was drawn and pale as a storm cloud, my brow etched with pale threads. I was a woman who looked far older than her years. To say the least, my looks needed a serious overhaul. But beauty has a price—a high price. I had done research on cosmetic dentistry and was shocked to learn that $1,000 per tooth was the norm. I have thirty-six teeth. You do the math.

Instead of throwing up my hands in defeat, as many people do when faced with a seemingly insurmountable challenge, I used the Law of Attraction. Instead of looking to a financial advisor, I looked to the Universe.

Every day, I made the same affirmation over and over again—"I have beautiful teeth." And I truly believed it. I felt it. Within three weeks, my faith was rewarded. Things began to happen. I was approached, out of the blue, by a national TV makeover show. Their proposal: I'd get a head-to-toe makeover, including cosmetic dental work. The value of the package was over $100,000. My dream had come true—or so I thought.

There was one small glitch in the plan. I live in Vancouver, and the show was produced in Toronto. At the time, I simply couldn't afford the travel expenses associated with the numerous trips back and forth. So I began my belief affirmations (said with feeling and emotion) once again. I simply said and felt, "I am on

150

that show." I knew the money would come from somewhere, that the Universe would work its magic. And it did. After numerous failed attempts at selling our home, we finally sealed the deal—at a profit no less—providing me the extra money I'd need.

After several weeks of plastic surgery, cosmetic reconstruction, and esthetic refinement, I looked fifteen years younger. Now, when I look into the mirror, smile, and say "I have beautiful teeth," it is absolutely true.

But my story doesn't end there. The Law of Attraction provided me with more riches than I could have ever imagined or achieved with a plan of my own, no matter how carefully laid out. For years and years, I had hoped to meet world-renowned philosopher Bob Proctor (from *The Secret*). During my makeover, I was given that opportunity. You can imagine my elation when, during a day of television shooting, in walks Bob Proctor. I must tell you, while I was excited, I wasn't the least bit surprised. The Law of Attraction was at work, the way it always is. The first thing Bob Proctor said to me was, "You must be really good at this (Law of Attraction) because you brought me here to you." In fact, I had been saying for the past several months, "I know Bob Proctor." Yet another declaration that became a self-fulfilling prophecy.

Let's recap: In less than a year, over a $100,000 literally fell into my lap. I knew for certain that you don't set the route, you set the destination. The Universe will look after the rest. Some people would call what I experienced a miracle. But I know better. It was the Law of Attraction.

Message: It is not your business to know "how" or "when." It is your business to make a decision. The how and when will reveal themselves to you in the perfect time and in the perfect way.

Cindy Ulmer is a visionary, power speaker, and coach/trainer. She is a certified *LifeSuccess* consultant based in Vancouver, British Columbia. She helps people world-wide achieve the life they want. She is a sought-after public speaker and a past recipient of the Coach of the Year award from SuccessTracs. Cindy can be contacted through her Web site at *www.cindyulmer.com*.

EMBRACING THE JOURNEY

By Sandy Lee Jones

Whatever you can do, or dream you can do, begin it. Boldness has genius, power and magic in it. Begin it now!
—Goethe

The birth of my son was the most amazing experience of my life. It was also the most heart-wrenching because I knew I was entering into single motherhood. It would mean that along with the overwhelming joy and love I felt as a new parent, I would have to face the overwhelming challenge of going it alone. It was something I never could have imagined would happen to me. But I was determined to make it a positive experience for both of us.

Bringing my son home was a very special moment. For the first three weeks we bonded very well. It was an absolute pleasure to have this little man in my world and to embark on our new adventure as mother and son.

And then, one day it hit me. I was sitting down, holding my son in my arms. He was sleeping peacefully. I could not move. I had a pain on the left side of my chest and I couldn't breathe properly. It was a blessing that I was close to the phone so I could make the call to my family. I needed to go to the doctor because something was very wrong.

I was taken to the doctor, and they immediately sent me to the hospital. They were not sure but suggested that I could have a blood clot. In the emergency ward I was asked many questions. I found it very difficult to describe what was going on inside me, just that I was in extreme pain, could not breathe properly, and was very concerned I was "checking out."

With my son only three weeks old, and just before Christmas 2003, there was no way I would be leaving this earth anytime soon! Thankfully, the doctor was very intuitive and treated me immediately for both a blood clot and pneumonia.

Later, the results did indeed show that I had both. I was truly grateful that they did not wait to find out—and that the blood clot did not travel anywhere else.

Being very aware of the Law of Attraction, I knew that there was a definite reason why I created this. On the surface, events like this always seem very bad and depressing. Many people feel that they did something wrong to cause this. I do not subscribe to this belief. What is necessary to see in life is that experiences are created to support us to achieve what our biggest dreams are—not to hinder us from living a great life! What is on the surface is only a portion of the bigger, beautiful picture of our lives.

I spent a week in the hospital, and my mother took full-time care of my son, bringing him into the hospital to see me every day. I was concerned about losing the bond with him and missing out on moments as he was growing. And I felt bad that I couldn't breast-feed him. But in those moments, I needed to take care of me. I was thankfully given the okay to go home, to enjoy Christmas, and have nurses come to my home regularly to check on my progress.

It took many months of healing, but I progressed through my illness. It was emotionally challenging as I was raising my son and healing at the same time. Then I was admitted to the hospital a second time with chest pains. I declared to the Universe again that I was here to stay and that I would create the best life for my son and myself.

My life changed in a very big way after those experiences. I vowed that I would not put my son in childcare nor return to full-time work in an office. I wanted to experience all the wonderful moments of his growth. I wanted to create a strong bond with him. And I wanted to support him and love him through all these moments. I believed that I would find a way to work from home, doing what I loved, and being with my son every day. I would find a place for us to live to start our new adventure together.

Up until that point, I was sharing an apartment with family. We were surrounded by a lot of love and support. But we needed our own space. It was time to move forward and trust in the vision that I could create a beautiful life for us.

So I looked for areas where I wanted to live. I looked at sharing accommodations and met up with people to share with. But I truly did not want to share and trusted there would be a way I could avoid this at all costs. It was actually on a day trip with my grandmother that I knew I had found my new location. I felt at peace, like being on holiday.

I had many fears at the time of what people thought of my being a single mum on welfare. I traveled to the location, had many knock backs, and was told that I could not get a two-bedroom house. I was losing hope in my vision. But I decided to shift my focus and think loving thoughts about the real estate agents. Instead of seeing them as knocking me back, I imagined them supporting me and assisting me to find the perfect place for me and my son. I let go of seeing any perceived competition, knowing there was a home that was our home!

I moved out and briefly shared a house in the city with a friend. It was a joy to have our own space, and this was just what I needed to refocus my energy and decide on my next course of action. It was then that I got a job offer. It was full-time work, and I was seriously considering it. I went for the interview and I filled out the paperwork. I called the child care places and found there were limited spaces and the costs were very high for a child the age of my son. I felt very uncomfortable about going against my vision and my intention to raise my son and work from home. Although I had no idea how to achieve this!

I woke up one morning and had made a decision in my mind. I would achieve my dream, and inside me, I already knew the way. I had all the resources available to me. Then came the inspired thoughts. I was guided to start my own business. I had trained as an energy healer and an Angel Intuitive™. I had been assisting people for years online through message boards, Web sites, e-mail, and in person. I realised that I had never valued my work or understood that I was already working at my job. I realised it had meaning to people and how much inspiration came from my unique way of thinking and intuition. I had received countless messages from people around the world thanking me; yet somehow, because it wasn't a mainstream job, I never registered its impact.

Immediately, when I signed up under my name, registering as a sole trader, I received further guidance. I knew that by the end of the week I needed to go and stay in the location in which I wanted to live. It didn't matter where we lived, even if it was a hotel, but I had to take my son and go that weekend.

That day, I spoke to my mother about my plans. She mentioned that my grandmother had a friend living up there. She had a cabin in the backyard of her home, and she agreed that we could stay there for one week. Being an Angel Intuitive™ I said to the Angels, "Well, you better give me a lot of help, because I've only got one week!"

That Sunday, my best friend and her mum drove us to the cabin. Not long after I arrived, I reminded the Angels that I only had one week. I pulled a card from the Mermaids and Dolphins Oracle cards which stated, "You're being helped—heaven is working behind the scenes to help you, even if you don't see results yet."

So I trusted and let go of the concern about time. That afternoon, after I unpacked and settled in, I went to the first available real estate agent. I saw three advertisements of places to view. I asked about them, and it just so happened that the first one I asked about was available to be looked at the next day. They told me I could pick up the keys in the morning and go look at the house.

I was intrigued as I was not aware that they did that with houses—just gave you the keys! We traveled to see the home and were greeted by our next-door neighbour. The house was just what we needed, and I imagined the two of us living there. That day, we applied for the place, and by Wednesday we were approved. On Friday we signed the documents. And on Saturday we moved in. Exactly a week and no more! Michael was gifted with his own room by his second birthday, which I had declared to the Universe was absolutely essential.

Since we moved in, I have worked with many people from around the world. I inspire people to create a life that they truly love living and to feel good about who they are in all ways.

I have attracted many opportunities, such as writing regularly for a magazine about the adventures with my son and how we both learn from one another. I've also been interviewed for a mainstream magazine about my work. I now do sessions from a shop where I live. I'm also starting my own publishing company to publish my own books and an inspirational magazine. It is an absolute joy to meet people in my local community. I'm constantly receiving inspired ideas and trying out new things.

Every day my vision unfolds perfectly. Things are continuously working out behind the scenes as I intend our lives to be filled with lots of joy and love. I hold much gratitude every day for the strong bond I have with my son, for the opportunity to be healthy, to work at a job that I love doing every day, and to enjoy a beautiful life with my son.

I believe that life became beautiful the moment I saw everything as an opportunity. The contrast only aided me to clarify and to realise just how blessed I am.

Message: I trust in my vision and am creating a life I love!

Sandy Lee Jones lives with her son just north of Sydney, Australia. She works as an intuitive/energy healer, conducting sessions in person and online with people all around the world. She has started a "Circle of Love and Light" online inspiration group to provide constant support for all who are consciously journeying. She is currently writing her first book. You can contact her through her Web site at *www.lovecreateinspire.com* or by e-mail at *sandyleejones@gmail.com*.

TUNED TO THE KEY OF LIFE

By Dana Agnellini

Show a little faith, there's magic in the night.
—from "Thunder Road" by Bruce Springsteen

I have been a guitarist for many years, since I was a teenager. I enjoy singing and accompanying myself, as well as songwriting. It is an enjoyable release for me, and I always get great feedback.

Well, within the past ten years or so, my music has shifted as I have grown spiritually. I began writing songs with spiritual content, not religious, just songs that affirm our oneness and reach to the heart of who we are as spiritual beings.

I began performing live at events that support this kind of music, and I noticed that my music was having some significant impact on people. Many have shared with me the healing quality of my music. I was often asked to record them professionally. Then, one day, a woman in the audience actually handed me a check for $500 with tears in her eyes and asked me to accept it as seed money for my first CD. I accepted that money and professionally recorded my first CD, *One Light at a Time*, in Nashville. It has received critical acclaim and sold quite well for an independent release.

About a year or so later, my life really began falling apart. My high paying corporate job and my marriage were moving toward ending at a slow, grueling, and very painful pace. Day by day, piece by piece, my life was coming apart at the seams. Yet, through it all, the music kept flowing.

I was sitting at the piano one day, plunking out notes for a new song. I had always wanted to play the piano, but every time I tried, I sounded like a two-year-old playing chopsticks. I was emotionally at rock bottom ... just weeks from leaving my home, seventeen years of marriage, and three children. I was also just weeks away from being laid off from my job, and I had no other job confirmed. I was a mess.

Then I heard this voice inside of me saying that I am meant to heal lives with my music. And I sarcastically responded, "If you show me a sign, I will. I want to play the piano right now!"

What followed can only be called a miracle. I placed my fingers on the keyboard and began playing Bruce Springsteen's "Thunder Road," my favorite song. Actually, it would be more accurate to say I was being played like an instrument. I sang and played the song with tears streaming down my face. One by one, my family showed up and looked at me wondering what on earth was going on ... Daddy doesn't play piano. He does now!

Since that day, I have been accompanying myself at live engagements on the piano at the same quality as my guitar playing, which I have been doing for thirty years. No lessons, no books, no time invested, just instantaneous piano skills that haven't gone away.

I have since released my second CD, *For the Light,* and my music ministry is really picking up steam.

Is this the Law of Attraction at work or is this a bona fide miracle? I will tell you, for me, they are one in the same. The way the Law of Attraction works is a miracle.

I have always held the deep belief that I am a gifted singer-songwriter and that my music will someday touch lives deeply. Funny enough, these feelings began taking root in me as a teenager listening to the songwriting of Bruce Springsteen, particularly "Thunder Road." So it is no surprise to me that "Thunder Road" would be my sign of confirmation.

Message: The Law of Attraction is a miracle ... we have the power of the Universe at our command. All things are possible when we are aligned with the divine presence within us. Life is a constant flow of miracles.

Dana Agnellini is a singer/songwriter/speaker committed to a world of peace through personal transformation. His songs are guaranteed to open the heart to the divine presence within each of us. Sometimes contemplative and sometimes just plain fun, his songs cut through resistance and denial and take you through a range of emotions. His empowering messages are driven home with a musical style all his own, influenced by classic rock, country, folk, and blues. Dana has two CD's which were produced with top industry talent in Nashville, Tennessee. He is available for concerts, lectures with music, charitable events, church services, etc. You can contact Dana through his Web site at *www.DanaAgnellini.com* or by e-mail at *dagnellini@yahoo.com.*

MY SECRET

By Samara Toro

Only when we are no longer afraid do we begin to live.
—Dorothy Thompson

I have a secret. This is the first time I am telling my story....

For ten years I was a prisoner, held captive by an invisible force known as fear. I thought this was the way it was supposed to be. I thought I did not have a choice, and I would never live the life I desired. I was in an abusive relationship and thought I could never escape. So I surrendered to my thoughts and allowed him to control me, my life, and my dreams. Every time he destroyed my body, he destroyed my soul. I lost my self, my vision, my self-worth, my laughter, and most importantly, my dignity. I was numb and had lost my ability to love.

My mission each day was to survive, to live just one more day for the sake of my children. Until the day I watched *The Secret*. I'll never forget that day, because it changed my life forever. I first heard about *The Secret* through a beloved friend. She sent me an e-mail sharing the power of the Law of Attraction, and she suggested I watch *The Secret*. I was interested, but I thought my life was never going to change. I was dealt these cards ... this is my fate ... so what is the point of watching this movie?

It wasn't until about twelve months later when my twin sister gave me *The Secret* DVD as a birthday gift that I finally watched it. I cannot explain in words the way I felt as I was watching the movie. I was intrigued. I was hypnotized. I was in love. I fell in love with the great power of the Law of Attraction. I was on a mission, and this time it was not just to survive; this time it was to *live*. To live my life exactly how I desired it.

I began researching, reading, and devouring this great power. I finally understood that I must love myself in order to attract love and the wonderful goodies I desire. I finally understood that it was all about the *feeling*—that if I felt wonderful, I would attract the same vibration. I understood the power of gratitude. I understood the Law of Attraction.

I decided. I made the choice to release this invisible force, this fear, this negative energy that was controlling my life. I knew it was going to be hard. I did not know *what* it was going to look like, or *how* it was going to happen; I just knew I had to let it go. So I let him go. The man who abused me, the man who controlled my life, the man I created, the man I *attracted*.

I forgave myself. I fell in love with myself and began listening to my heart. I am finally ready—ready to share my story, ready to empower others, ready to inspire every person who thinks they don't have a choice, especially women who are, or have been in abusive relationships. Now I have a new secret—the powerful Law of Attraction! Now I know that I am powerful; I have a choice; I have a voice; I am love, and everything I ask for I will receive!

Message: Believe! I had to let go, trust, and believe. I fell in love with myself and believed in the power within. Once I surrendered and allowed the Universe to do its work, the blessings started pouring in.

Samara Toro is a native of Puerto Rico. She celebrates her life experience by sharing her inspiring story to motivate women who have been, or are currently in, abusive relationships. Samara is the proud mother of two boys. She currently lives in Rockville, Maryland, and can be contacted by e-mail at *smt_n@yahoo.com*.

WHO ARE YOU?

By Eric Martin

Hope is a good thing, maybe the best of things, and no good thing ever dies.
—from *The Shawshank Redemption*

My name is Eric, and I am so happy and grateful to be sharing this space and time with you in order to help both of us experience the greatest gifts the human experience has to offer.

My journey on terra firma started almost thirty-eight years ago, but the last four have been the most astounding. Four years ago, I was living in a trailer in my backyard with no running water. I had rented my house to summer tourists to pay off an $80,000 debt I had accumulated while running blindly through my life. I had lost my job, my driver's license, every one of my friends and family, all self-dignity, self-esteem, and any ability to function in reality. To this day, it was the darkest, loneliest, and most confusing place I have ever been. To be in a state where I wanted so desperately to kill myself each and every day for years, but not having the courage to do so, is quite a painful place of existence.

I was in this position from a drinking and drugging career of almost thirteen years. Beyond my comprehension, I had become totally unable to deal with life on life's terms; a major part of me was controlled by constant fear. Alcohol and drugs were the only answer to me, and I used them until the "wheels on the bus fell off."

Over time, I have come to realize that those years were everything I needed to get to the place I am today. I also came to realize that I was in this dark hole because I lacked the knowledge and understanding of myself as a spiritual being living a human experience. The "gift of desperation" that I received in those challenging times had actually given me the key to unlock the door to the infinite potential that I truly have.

The first day I walked into a room of recovery was the first day in thirty-four years that I had ever been aware of the feeling of hope. I did not know that at the time, but others were able to sit calmly with me and gently love me until I could begin to love myself. Every meeting I went to, I heard something I had never heard before, but somehow I felt as if I had known it forever. Little did I know that this new knowledge was allowing me to discover working with the laws of the Universe.

The folks in the rooms of recovery "suggested" that I give their program a try for ninety meetings in ninety days, read daily from an inspirational book, and share my thoughts and experiences with others. What I experienced is that by participating and taking action with those suggestions, I began to understand I could participate in my life rather than just exist. For so many years, I had given up the ability to learn and grow. This program and the gift of desperation that it took to get here was as it was meant to be.

On my second anniversary into this new lifestyle of clean and sober living, I was sharing my experience, strength, and hope at a meeting in a neighboring sea village. After that meeting, a fellow traveler came up to me and handed me a DVD that had "Bleep" hand-written on it and said, "I think you should watch this." This is when the laws of the Universe started working their magic ... and most importantly, when I was *ready* to receive the abundance of the Universe that had always been there.

I could not believe my eyes and ears. How could this be? Where was this information coming from? It was just like those first months in sobriety. I was hearing things I had never heard before, but they were resonating with me as if I had known them forever.

Six months later I was on a plane to Ecuador by myself heading to an eight-day retreat with Ramtha's School of Enlightenment. As the plane was taxiing down the runway in Miami, my old paradigm jumped in and yelled, "What the hell are you doing?" And instantaneously, for the first time, I was aware of a new paradigm that said, "Go, you are doing everything you have always wanted to do. Be free my friend." What a moment; it still brings tears to my eyes today.

Another six months went by and my perception of life continued changing in ways beyond anything I could imagine. A friend from the retreat sent me an e-mail telling me that I had to watch the movie, *The Secret*. Here, another group of folks shared their experience freely with me and simply tried to help me find the freedom and joy within. Not too long after, I was blessed to watch the movie, *ONE*.

Learning about the laws of the Universe through all of these mentors has given me the ability to work on the powers within. I am actively involved with many of them and discovering on a daily basis that I am co-creating this journey of mine. I have been practicing daily, and start my desire and wishes off with, "I am so happy and grateful now that I have continuous sobriety and carry the message to others on a daily basis like it was always meant to be."

Several months ago a thought came into my head. The idea for a 365 daily inspirational book that includes all the teachers and mentors from *What the Bleep Do We Know!?, The Secret, ONE,* and many other influential people, felt as if it had been in existence forever. As a self-employed contractor, I had no idea how to go about publishing a book, but this idea was so organic and uncomplicated in my mind. My greatest desire for so long has been to carry the message to many more, and here it was coming from my thoughts to my reality. What a feeling to realize your thoughts have become your reality!

The book is titled *Who Are You? One Quantum Leap at a Time,* and will be on shelves this year worldwide. I share with you this story as others have done with me, to allow someone else to find their truth in the way I did, naturally and organically, just as it was meant to be. If only one person discovers the vast and beautiful powers of the Universe, it will add to my infinite happiness and freedom.

I ask you to step out of your self-inflicted box, get off the couch, shut off the TV, and give yourself a gift of a lifetime. Get these movies and watch and listen with your friends and family. When someone resonates with you, go online and see what they have to offer. And of course, get a copy of *Who Are You?* New knowledge daily is the key to your freedom. To have doors open in a room in which you thought had none is one of the greatest experiences available.

Message: Accept all obstacles with a positive attitude and perseverance, and live in fear and doubt no more!

Eric Martin has come to realize that his journey is the exact path he had to travel in order to learn and receive the gifts he has today. The gift of knowledge and repetition makes all things possible. If you are filled with a great sense of curiosity, determination, and adventure, go to *www.onequantumleapatatime.com* and enjoy the freedom! Eric can be contacted by e-mail at *Erictruro@comcast.net.*

TO HAVE THE MIND OF A CHILD

By Gudmundur Sigurdarson

In this life we cannot do great things. We can only do small things with great love.
—Mother Teresa

It is funny how some things just seem to hit you like lightning out of a clear sky. How one story, one thought process, or one conversation can start changing the way everything works in your mind. Today I recall one of those moments, simply because it put things in perspective, which in turn made me seek out more of those conversations. It wasn't a conversation about me, which is often the way we make discoveries about ourselves. Rather, it was while I was talking with a few friends about the great people of our time and times past and what makes us any different from those people.

The conversation that night started with a simple question, "What makes those people different from us, and why are they attracting more positive things into their lives than we are? Why does it seem that they are getting more of what they want?" The first question was easy to answer. They aren't any different from any of us; they are just utilizing what they have in a different way. They play on the same playing field as we do, they abide by the same laws that we do, and they have to deal with the same general things in life that we do. Then why do they seem to be getting more of what they want in life than we are? This was the question that really set off the conversation. The first person up for discussion was Mother Teresa. Did she really lead a great life? Did she get the things she wanted in life?

The first comments were quite interesting. When you set a goal to heal a world that has plenty of misery, it's easy to always feel accomplished. Then again, it could also be very easy to feel bad because there is always plenty of misery to feel bad about. But what really drove her; what gave her pleasure in life; and, what did she need to believe in order to keep going and never stop pursuing her passion of making a better world? Those were the questions that really got the discussion going. In fact, those were the questions that would be the key questions about everyone we discussed that night, including ourselves.

When looking at someone like Mother Teresa, working in that kind of environment, it would probably be easy to fall back and get upset, get angry at what goes on in the world, and want to give up. But why did she keep going? The answer was the same for her as for everyone else—have a vision big enough that you can get up every morning and work toward it. Then set a rule that says: "Every day when I get up and do something about making my vision a reality, I feel a little more fulfilled than I did before." Now, that doesn't really seem like a hard thing to do. Most of the group agreed with that.

But what was our vision? What did we have that was so big that every morning we could get up and work toward it, feeling better about ourselves every day, knowing that we had moved closer to accomplishing our grand vision? What were the things we wanted to accomplish, and what were we doing to take action toward those things? A long silence hit the room. It seemed to last for several minutes while we looked around the room at each other, until finally the silence was broken by a little boy that none of us had noticed. "I want a blue bike for my birthday, and I am going to let all the kids who don't have a bike try mine, and let them use it when they want to because that would make them happy."

There we sat in a room, a few adults and this child. The child was the first one to express a vision. Was it a vision the size of world peace or ending world hunger? It may not have been. But at that age, he might as well have been stating that he wanted world peace. What made this child any different from Mother Teresa? Was the child doing the same that Mother Teresa had been doing? Did he have a vision of making others happy using what he could and what he had, helping one person smile at a time, in the hope that it would improve the quality of their life?

It is amazing how little it takes sometimes to make you realize we really do know more than we thought; we just tend to forget things over time. After all, how many of us still remember the table of elements unless we still work with it? Didn't we use the power of a vision as kids? Didn't we let our imagination run wild and do what we desired to do? Do kids utilize things like the Law of Attraction to the fullest extent with no boundaries and no thought of it? Did we really know the big secret to life and getting the things we wanted as kids, and for some reason, forget it as we grew up?

What made us limit ourselves instead of setting bigger visions like Mother Teresa, like Donald Trump, Robert Kiyosaki, Henry Ford, Emerson, and other great people of our time? Maybe they didn't discover the secret to getting what they wanted; maybe they just never forgot how to fully utilize it. What has happened in our lives that we gave up on dreaming big and creating visions for ourselves? What happened when we grew up and started learning about the way things "really" are?

What is the Law of Attraction? Why do we attract things into our lives? Why did the adults sitting at the table attract certain things, all of us different things, but yet none of the great things like what we had wanted when we were younger? As we sat there and talked, we could all recall the things we wanted as kids, and how many of those things we actually got! As the conversation continued, we realized that one of the main differences is that we have gotten afraid to ask for big things. We stopped voicing what we want—that new bike, the pony, the new action figure. What is the point of telling others what we want as adults? It worked brilliantly when we were kids. Why stop doing something that is working? Why stop telling the Universe what it is that you truly want? What is holding us back, and why do we limit our imaginations? As we sat there and discussed these questions, we found that many of us were driven by our fears, that they controlled more of what we did and how we decided to approach life.

What happened after that night was amazing; having had this realization with other people was probably one of the greatest gifts I had ever gotten. I had for a long time wanted to improve the quality of my own life, get a better job, and have an opportunity to travel and to have more time to spend with those I love. I had been afraid to dream like a child again. I had been afraid to fail, and therefore, I couldn't completely let go and fully envision a future filled with all the things I wanted in life. Just like children come up with all the things they want before their birthdays, I now started talking about the things I wanted in life, not only to others, but more importantly, to myself.

I started looking online for a few books that could possibly help me in the process of changing my thinking. I figured in order to change things around me, I would have to change what was inside of me. I started talking to a few people about my revelation, started asking who they would recommend to read, who had done this journey that I was about to embark on. I knew deep inside that the answer was in my mind, that I would simply have to change the way my mind worked. As I started asking, my boss at the time got wind of what I was doing. He called me to let me know that I would be attending a seminar that following week, since I was now seeking out this kind of information. What happened during that seminar completely changed my life and has been doing so ever since.

I learned about how my subconscious mind works, how my fear works, what limiting beliefs I had, and how to identify them. All this information and explanation made me think about what my mind was really capable of and what I had really been focused on. It was during that time I realized that what I attracted in life had little to do with what I focused on consciously, but rather the things I focused on subconsciously. I had to get rid of my fears, limiting beliefs, and doubts. Sound easy? Well, I was surprised how easy it was when I started learning how to do it.

To give you a little more insight on what was going on in my life at the time, I had recently gotten out of a relationship where I left with close to nothing. My financial situation was bad. I had more debt than I thought I would ever get out of, and my extended family was falling apart. Immediately after the seminar, I started focusing on what I wanted. The first thing was to go see one of the great motivational speakers of our time.

I didn't have a ticket, didn't have money, and didn't have a way to get to England where he was speaking. So I figured this would be a good time to try a new approach. I started saying to myself and others that I wanted to go see him, I just hadn't figured out quite yet how I was going to do it. A couple days later I got a phone call. A friend of mine had four tickets that he would not be able to use. He made me an offer that if I could sell three of them, he would give me the last one for free. Needless to say, I sold them the same day. Now I had my ticket, but still needed the flight and accommodations while in England.

A few days later, as I was now telling people I had tickets but had not found a way to get there yet, a potential client called and wanted one of our team members to meet with him—in England! My boss came over to me and told me the news, adding that if I wanted to extend my stay there, he would give me the money the hotel would have otherwise cost, and I could use it for an alternate hotel if I wanted to. How did I really make this into reality? Because I know that not long before, I probably never would have gotten this. I never would have started telling people what I wanted until it was almost set in stone.

That was such an amazing experience that I now wanted to learn how to help others in the way I had just been helped. I decided to set out to follow my passion in life with no boundaries, to live with no or limited fears, and just go for it. So I started doing what I had done before and forgotten along the way: I started dreaming like a child again. Using my experience as a sales trainer, I started preparing to become a speaker and a life coach. I attended seminars, read books, and listened to audio programs. To my own amazement, in this process, my life kept getting better. I understood myself better and learned how to control not only my conscious thoughts but also my subconscious mind. I started setting goals about moving to the United States, setting up my own businesses, and finding the person I would want to spend the rest of my life with. Within a few months of setting these goals, I had achieved more than I thought possible in such a short amount of time. Once I started asking big and without any hesitation, it seemed as if the Universe lined everything up for me to grab and take advantage of.

Within four months of setting the goal to move to the United States and set up a business, I was there. Within eight months of being in the United States, I had two businesses up and running. Within a year I had found the woman of my dreams, or should I say we attracted each other at a time in our lives when we were both ready to receive and knew exactly what we wanted. We are now planning our wedding, and both of us are extremely excited about spending the rest of our lives together. I can truly say that dreaming like a child, taking every chance, using every opportunity, and being willing to take massive action has attracted more things into my life than I ever thought possible.

I live my life to teach others how to be fearless, how to dream big, how to think like a child without limitations, and to challenge what they believe to be true today. Maybe the most important thing I teach people is how to ask for what they want and truly believe that asking for something will eventually bring it around. I am truly living my passion, all because of a willingness to improve how I think in order to attract all the things I want into my life. I made a decision to stop being a "victim" of my circumstances, and to start creating my own circumstances and life by simply using the infinite power that lies within all of us.

Message: Never give up on your dream. If you want it and if you are willing to work for it, things always show up. Sometimes these things show up in a different way than you expected, so think about what you did to attract what you have.

Gudmundur Sigurdarson is the founder of Mindformula and Redknight Marketing. Born in Iceland, Mr. Sigurdarson has relocated between Denmark, Iceland, and the United States since the early 1980s. He made a final move to the United States in early 2006. He has successfully established two businesses, spoken in front of thousands of people, and helped thousands of people reach their personal and professional goals. He can be contacted through his Web site at *www.mindformula.com* or by e-mail at *info@mindformula.com*.

THE WONDERFUL SPIRIT IN THAT GUY GIVING YOU THE FINGER

By Larry Hochman

Look beyond people's appearances. Look beyond the roles one plays and the mask they wear. Look deep into their eyes and peer into their soul. There you will find their true essence. There you will find your true essence. And that essence is love.
—Rich German

I found a wonderful little trick to change the way I see other people. Along the way, I found the person it had changed the most was me.

Here's how it started. My wife and I were talking about how everyone has a spark of the divine in them, no matter what path they may have chosen in life. Each of us has done something, at some point, we can be proud of. It may not have been something momentous or long-lasting. But all of us can look back at our lives and say, "Yeah, I did a good thing that day." Each of us can also look back on a point in our lives where we were profoundly distressed and vulnerable. We lost a lover, a parent died, or something so bad happened it shook us to our spiritual core. Everyone has had such an experience, even people who don't cultivate their spiritual nature to any extent.

We all know this, yet it seems that very often we don't honor these traits in the people we meet in our daily lives. What would happen if you perceived in everyone you met their ability to do something wonderful or to experience real vulnerability? Most likely, you would look at them with a new respect and see their potential for greatness.

It was a great conversation that we had, and I put it to the test the next day. As I was driving, I came to an intersection with a four-way stop sign. Another car and I came to the intersection at about the same time, although I was there a second or two earlier, and I was the driver on the right. By all accounts, I was the car who was supposed to go first.

The young man in the other car didn't see it that way. He rolled past the stop sign and flipped his middle digit out the window of his pick-up truck. It was quite a sight. The sleeveless t-shirt, tattoo on the biceps, cigarette dangling from the mouth, and the rap music on full blast made for an interesting combination.

I was all set to offer my conditioned response to the gentleman, which would have been a similar greeting. But the conversation from the night before stood out in my mind. At that moment, I actually got a mental picture of him crying because something bad had happened. It changed my perspective immediately and entirely.

A moment later, I got a vision of him laughing with joy over something fantastic that had happened in his personal life. Shortly after, I envisioned him helping someone small move a heavy piece of furniture. Did these things really happen in this man's life? Probably, at some point, or at least something very similar had happened.

They may not have been his defining traits, but the fact that he has access to these emotions told me that there's something lovable and valuable in all of us. Under the right circumstances, these qualities come out.

In my perfect world, this man feels the love and acceptance radiating from my spirit. He continues on to his destination, stopping to buy flowers for his significant other. He drops the change from his purchase (plus a ten dollar bill) into the charity cup on the florist's desk. He makes complete stops at all intersections with a smile and a wave to every driver he encounters. He presents the flowers to his sweetheart and then does all the household chores. Finally, he calls his parents and three of his closest childhood friends to express his love.

Of course, these things won't all happen. But perhaps interrupting the usual pattern of stimulus-response may get him thinking. "Am I happy with how I'm living right now? Is there a better way to conduct my life on a daily basis? Can I make different choices?"

And the process begins. A new and better energy is stirred up. This energy seeks out similar energy in others. He approaches a driver whose wonderful spirit is hidden behind the conditioned response of middle finger flipping. And he breathes new life into that individual. And so on and so on.

Message: See the good in everyone. See it even when they're not showing it. At the very least, it will reduce your own tension and frustration with the silly behavior you encounter. You'll be able to detach from your own patterns of hostility. At best, *you* will become the kind of person who brings out those qualities in others on a regular basis. And in the process, you'll attract more good things into your own experience.

Larry Hochman helps people break out of self-imposed limitations and move toward their individual, business, and group goals. He is a long-time educator, counselor, author, and entertainer. He has been a guidance counselor at a nationally-recognized high school in Connecticut since 1992 and has trained graduate students in counseling since 1996. Get Larry's Free 30-Day Joy and Happiness course at *www.NoMoreHoldingBack.com*.

THE POWER OF THOUGHT

By Jerry Mooney

Jump and the net will appear.
—Robin Crow

A couple years ago, I hit a low point. I hated my job. I suffered through its daily grind for six years. Although it was a high paying job, I was bouncing checks and strapped for money. I was out of shape. I was stressed-out and depressed. I made excuses to not do things I enjoyed, like skiing and kayaking. I was stuck in a boring, unsatisfying rut. My logical side continued to justify my misery. I told myself, "Jobs like this are hard to find." I felt obligated to stick with it for my family, for my future, and to prove I wasn't a quitter. The entire time, my heart, my intuition, my body, my friends, and my family were telling me, "You have to quit that job. Who cares about the payday if you're miserable?"

Eventually the message soaked in. After a dramatic conflict with my supervisors over an unconscionable way of treating customers, I couldn't take it any more. The corporate bottom line had pushed me too far from my personal values, and I couldn't stomach it any longer. I took a leave of absence. In the three months that followed, I received psychological counseling. I became introspective and analytical about the status of my life. I decided I didn't know everything about what I wanted to do, but I was sure what I was doing was not it. I labored over the idea of leaving the company; it seemed like there were so many practical reasons to stay. It felt like I was contemplating jumping off a cliff with the hope I might be able to fly (or at least land without too much damage). The logical part of my brain vigorously rejected the idea of leaving such a "good job." My logic had me in a stranglehold. I came from a background of poverty and irresponsibility, and I was unwilling to continue the chain. Working at a respectable job, regardless of its emotional toll, was easy for me to justify.

The counseling allowed me to reexamine my values and my relationship with my job. Finally, I summoned the courage to quit. I not only quit, but my exit was so colorful, I wouldn't be concerned with returning. I burned the bridge down and did so intentionally. I did not want to look back, and leaving the door open to a return might be too tempting in the face of adversity. Instead, I jumped. I quit. I left without knowing what was next. I didn't have a new job lined up. I didn't have a lead on any possibilities. I took a leap of faith. I did a summersault into the abyss.

I felt really good and decided to focus on that. I admonished myself to look forward and become excited about the possibilities ahead of me. Moments of doubt and pangs of anxiety crept into my mind. I quelled them and directed my thoughts to possibilities.

Shortly after my exit from the workforce, my mother and I went to my aunt's for dinner. She was thrilled about a book she recently stumbled upon, *Ask and It Is Given: Learning to Manifest Your Desires*, by Esther and Jerry Hicks. My mother, my cousin, and I politely acknowledged that it sounded like a fine book and continued to direct the conversation toward our regular topics of discussion. My aunt was unrelenting, however. She didn't want us to simply agree the book sounded good. She wanted us to read it right then and there. I was more interested in discussing the fact that I left my job and really needed some projects to work out. I promised to read the book, hoping to return the conversation to my dire situation.

My aunt wasn't satisfied. She wanted us to read it immediately—at the dinner table. She decided our consent was no longer necessary, and without regard to our resistance, she fetched the book and began to read. We listened as she read aloud. The first chapter didn't take long to read. Once I got over my incredulousness and listened, I realized she was right; this was important. She then passed it to me, and I read the second chapter. We did this for a few hours. The book outlined how we are vibrational creatures living in a vibrational world. Our thoughts are more powerful than we realize, and our attention to this would change our lives for the better. The dynamic of the table grew energetic. We discussed this new way of thinking after each chapter or when moved by an idea. It became clear I must get my own copy. Although the material was completely foreign to me and contrary to the way I thought up until then, it was also intuitive. It was the opposite of everything I was taught and everything I heard on TV, the radio, or read in the papers. It made too much sense to ignore. It rang true inside of me, and this was a voice I was learning to listen to.

I took the book home and tried to read it all at once. I found each chapter made me very tired. The chapters were not long or exhaustive, but I couldn't read more than one at a time. After each chapter, I had to set the book down and allow it to sink in. These ideas were paving new roads in my brain, and that was exciting, but exhausting. There were no complicated words or exasperating sentences, yet I could have read Kafka at a faster clip.

Since I wasn't working, I dedicated my days to reading and absorbing this new material and insight. Once I finished, I immediately started rereading. Each time, I was able to take on larger chunks. I began doing the exercises in the book. I really trusted that this stuff worked, but I had no history with this insight. I must confess, my habits and old thought patterns persistently crept into my mind. I would derail, but I used this new insight to help me get back on track. I had plenty of bad mental habits, and these habits were hard to recognize, let alone put down. I still had habits of worry, habits of concern, habits of anger, and habits of fear. These habits kept demanding my attention, but I was committed to my new path. My conscious self wanted these ideas to work. I needed it to work. I dedicated myself to making a mental shift. I immersed myself in the subject. I knew I had a lot of work to do.

Just before I left my job, I had bought a very nice, but modest home. The house was surrounded by beautiful landscaping. The layout was friendly and sound. Behind the main bedroom, a beautiful pond and waterfall provided a place for koi to swim, squirrels to drink, and birds to land. It was a serene sanctuary for my thoughts and me. The yard was bordered by enchanting trees and plants that overwhelmed the senses with aesthetic beauty and fragrant aromas. This house had a healing effect on me. Because of this, I placed tremendous value in it. One of my most persistent fears was that I might lose this beloved house. I knew whatever I did, I had to hold on to it. I had about $9,000 to work with. I figured that would buy me a few months while I plotted my next step. I didn't want to exhaust my modest savings and be confronted with the fact that I was broke and out of time.

At this point, the people who told me to quit my job were clamoring that I had to make money. Some were pressuring me to get a new job. Others wondered, "Where are you going to get money?" A cacophony of doubts surrounded me, pushing me deeper into my determination to make this work, my way. I had embarked upon a new path, and those questions and concerns were married to my old way of thinking. I did my best to keep them at bay.

I knew I had to envision my life the way I wanted it in order to get it. That meant no dumb job. No more doing it the way others expected. I had to be as committed to my transformation as I was to my old story. I continued to reread *Ask and It Is Given* and do the exercises. After reading it a few times, I wanted more on the subject but had no idea if there even was more. I had never heard of these concepts to this point. As I contemplated the idea of getting more perspectives, I noticed the foreword was written by Dr. Wayne Dyer. I figured I ought to get some of his stuff. The same day, I was cleaning my living room and found a box containing four cassette tapes I had never listened to. It was the *Power of Intention* program ... by Dr. Wayne Dyer. What a miraculous coincidence! I immediately ceased cleaning and listened to the tapes. I kept them on auto-play for days. I began feeling very good!

As good as I felt, my little bank account was dwindling. I continued to worry about money. Instead of letting this worry infest my thoughts though, I began consciously dismissing my fear. This was new. I was beginning to assimilate this information. Wayne spoke to me every day (although, he kept repeating himself), and I was reading inspirational material. I knew something would work out.

One "ace up my sleeve" was a speculation home I had started months earlier. Once finished, I would have some financial breathing room. However, as if to test my faith, my builder called to inform me of a glitch. Poor structural planning required us to scrap the original blueprints. My house was another five months out. I immediately found myself back into old thought patterns. I began to fret. I began to freak out. I began to panic. But I caught myself. I became calm. I decided I wanted to dismiss my doubts. Then, something miraculous happened, and it cemented my newfound faith.

I lay on my bed focusing on possibilities. I tried to quiet my mind. I felt myself becoming lighter. In my mind, I saw myself floating away. I floated into the sky past the Earth's atmosphere into space, transcending the solar system. I crossed into pulses of light speeding through grid-networks. As I observed, I heard a voice ask, "What would you like?" I said, "I would like my project to finish so I'll have enough money to get by until I figure out what I'm doing." The voice replied, "You've come to the ocean with a thimble."

No joke—immediately after I heard the voice, the phone rang. It was my builder. Since I had referred so much business to him, and they botched the plans for the house, they were going to give me a house that was already done. That house had $50,000 in equity and provided exactly what I asked: it bought me time.

It has been less than two years since my aunt introduced me to *Ask and It Is Given*. In this brief period, I have experienced many more of these miracles. I now own millions of dollars in real estate, I have a big, fat bank account, and I live in a million-dollar mansion. (I still have the original house.) I feel like I'm just getting started. These events are so dramatic in contrast to where I came from and what I've known that I feel an obligation to share my insight and make the method of this transformation more understandable and practical for everyone.

Message: We squander our thoughts. If we use their power, we can create more amazing lives.

Jerry Mooney was born in Idaho to an illiterate father and teenage mother. Little was expected of him. But he didn't share their limited vision. As a young man, he felt the need to escape his surroundings, so he traveled extensively. This included studying three semesters at the University of Munich and doing a research grant in the former East Germany for UNESCO. He graduated from Lewis and Clark College in Portland with a degree in international affairs. He is fluent in German. He is also an advanced kayaker and skier, and a meditation and yoga devotee. For more information, please visit *www.jerrymooney.com*.

IT'S A WONDERFUL LIFE!

By Lori Bowers

These are the days of miracle and wonder.
—Paul Simon

I have always lived my life with a positive outlook and attitude. I grew up in Iowa with a good family. My dad was a barber, and my mom took very good care of our family. After college, I married an alcoholic and had twenty years of drama. While I experienced a lot of ups and many downs, I lived a good life.

Then in December 2004, while at a real estate seminar, I was introduced to the Law of Attraction, and my life changed forever. Amazing things started to happen and are still happening today!

I began meditating and visualizing how I wanted my life to be. Each morning I write down ten things I am grateful for and ten things I want to attract. Then through inspired action, I manifest wonderful things and wonderful people come my way.

I had always wanted to build a beautiful new home. I could see what it looked like—five bedrooms, five and one-half baths with a casita, early California-style, overlooking a lake and mountains in a quiet, peaceful location. I could see the colors, size of the rooms, and even the furniture. I could hear the birds and other sounds. I could see the flowers and palm trees.

In December 2004 the manifestation started. I began the journey to build my dream home. I had no clue how it would happen or where the money and energy would come from. I located a lot and then discovered it had sold a few days before I found it. So I bought the lot next door. This lot ended up being the perfect lot! My second husband, Ted, and I spent two years building the house. We found a talented architect, the best contractor in our area, went through three designers, found a great landscaper, and more.

During this time, our daily life continued on. Ted played golf. We went to dinner with our friends. We traveled. I am one of the top Realtors in our area, so I kept selling houses. I survived malignant melanoma cancer, and my husband contracted a rare nerve disease. We kept going. Many of my employees left. I hired more and kept going. I kept attracting more and more good in all areas of my life.

We owned fourteen rental properties that I planned to sell to pay for the house. The real estate market took a turn, so it was not a good decision to sell the rentals. We kept going. The house was completed in December 2006. We love it! It is in a prime area overlooking a lake and mountains—incredible views! It is 4,760 square feet—five bedrooms, five and one-half baths, three-car garage plus a golf cart garage, a pool and spa, fountain, casita, and more and more. It looks just like I envisioned it in my dreams!

The week we moved in, I noticed a large cyst on my arm. I went to the oncologist for tests, consultation, and ultimately removal. I continued to focus on perfect health and safety and kept working on the house. Over a period of a few weeks, all tests came back negative, and I was fine.

Before we ever moved in, the house appraised for much more than we ever thought possible. We kept the rentals, and due to some special financing, our total monthly payments after we moved into the new house had gone down over $10,000 per month! I let it all work out the way it was supposed to work out. I went with easy flow, joy, bliss, love, and peace. The process of building was fun. Our home has wonderful energy. We are grateful every day for the fabulous life we enjoy filled with wealth, success, and love—abundance on every level.

I live my life by the Law of Attraction. I believe there are no accidents in life. We attract what we put out there. Like attracts like. I am so grateful for the people in my life, especially my wonderful husband, my health, my career as a Realtor, and all of the material blessings I enjoy. I know that all things work out as they are supposed to work out. Abundance fills my life daily. I live with gratitude, peace, joy, calm, bliss, feeling good, and happiness.

Message: Life is wonderful. You can accomplish whatever you really desire with positive energy and inspired action.

Lori Bowers grew up in Burlington, Iowa, and moved to the Silicon Valley area of California in 1989. She was in the lighting business for twenty years before becoming a real estate agent. In 2001, she moved to Palm Springs where she became a top-producing real estate agent with a team of eight agents. Her husband is a retired chiropractor. Her son is a Realtor on her team, and her daughter lives in Iowa with her husband and two young sons. For more information, please visit her Web site at *www.loribowers.com* or contact her by e-mail at *lori@loribowers.com.*

THE BIG PICTURE

By Steven S. Sadleir

Since you alone are responsible for your thoughts, only you can change them. You will want to change them when you realize that each thought creates according to its own nature. Remember that the law works at all times and that you are always demonstrating according to the kind of thoughts you habitually entertain. Therefore, start now to think only those thoughts that will bring you health and happiness.
—Paramahansa Yogananda

Early in my life, I was attracted to the spiritual. I spent many years first studying, and then teaching world religions, yoga, and meditation. This is my passion. But for many years my mind did not see how I could make a good living teaching yoga or meditation. So I pursued a career in investment banking and resigned to teach "on the side."

The origins of the Law of Attraction date back thousands of years to the ancient path of the Siddhas, yogis in India, who could manifest in miraculous ways. Over the years, while doing research on my book on world religions, *Looking for God*, I had the occasion to meet and study with dozens of enlightened masters and witnessed, first hand, the power we have to manifest. I have seen spiritual masters produce ash out of thin air. I have seen such uncanny timing of events and synchronicities occur that you know there must have been some invisible force or power at play. And I now experience the miraculous application of the Law of Attraction on a daily basis.

Back in the late 1990s, I applied this law to my business and saw it go from zero to millions overnight. I would hold the intention to serve others, to bring about the highest good, and deals would just fall into my lap. It was as if at some unconscious level these people were being drawn to me and my internal antenna was picking up signals and guiding me to the people, places, and situations where my intention became realized. The funny thing was, the more business that was generated, the more money that was made, and the busier I got, the less time I had to teach. As I moved away from my true passion of teaching, a feeling of lack

179

of meaning and purpose crept into my life. But my mind rationalized that I could not leave a good thing. It made no rational sense to leave a business that was doing so well. I argued with myself that, after I made a certain amount of money, I could retire early and teach full time.

At the dawn of the new millennium, I got the sign I needed—the stock market crashed. It got pummeled, and almost all the money I made that was invested in technology companies disappeared forever. In my forties, with no other career to fall back on (or so I thought), my life had completely collapsed. Within months, I had spent most of my savings trying to keep my business afloat and was looking down a career path with no light in sight.

Finally, the day came when I did not have the funds to pay all my bills, and I had absolutely no idea where the money would come from. I took a walk on the bluffs along Newport Coast in Southern California; I got down on my knees and prayed. In this moment of complete surrender, I asked God how I might serve. I let go of the "me" that wanted, and I dedicated myself to serving others and then asked for a sign. In that moment, an osprey flew by, and immediate peace enveloped me along with an inspiration to teach. So I asked God for another sign.

As soon as I got home, the phone rang. The man on the phone, Matthew, called me out of the blue and asked if I would be his "spiritual coach." I had no idea what a spiritual coach was or how I would make any money coaching one man, so my mind resisted the idea at first. Then he offered to pay me $500 per month for a one-hour phone session each week. Even then, it didn't seem like a real job. But I promised God I would serve, and I took it as a sign that I was being guided. Soon, Matthew brought other people onto the calls. Within the first month of "spiritual coaching," I was not only cash flow positive again but filled with passion and absolutely loving the opportunity to serve.

The first class did so well I started a second class, created a course curriculum, and put up a Web site. In the first year, we reached thousands and made a handsome profit. Within three years, we had grown the Self Awareness Institute to tens of thousands of students in over 120 countries. As I fed this passion, opportunities began to manifest in miraculous ways. Students talked about putting together a trip to Machu Picchu, Peru, and the next day, a spiritual tour agency, Power Places, called and asked me to lead a tour to Peru. Whether it was book publishing, radio interviews, or speaking engagements, opportunities would, and still do, just fall into my lap. So much so that our Institute teaches classes in the Science of Manifesting.

Now we witness thousands of people manifesting for themselves. The more connected you are with your Self and your purpose, the more powerfully you manifest. So for me, meditation was the key to learning how to manifest power-fully. The Shakti (spirit) amplifies your attractor field and draws all the people, information, opportunities, and resources needed like a powerful magnet.

One of the best examples occurred recently at a seminar I attended, both as a speaker and participant. It was one of Matthew Ferry's *"Mental Journey to Millions"* seminars where he, too, teaches others how to manifest. At his seminar, I was inspired to use the media to reach more people and entertained the notion of creating, or participating in, a movie that would awaken consciousness. I had never wanted to be a movie star or sought to be in a film but offered to serve in that capacity if the Divine willed it. Within a week, I was asked to be in a film. Within just a few months, I was filmed for two spiritual documentaries, have been invited to be in a third, and was approached by a production company to take my *Looking for God* book and make it into a movie. Each of these movies is currently in different stages of production, and one's "in the can."

During Matthew's last seminar, he mentioned television, and this gave me an inspiration. So in my seminar workbook, I wrote out my idea for a television program. I never really thought of being on television before, either, but was inspired to get the message out. That day, I gave a talk and led a meditation to a thousand people in Seattle. In the audience were several television producers. The very next day, two different production companies came to me and suggested that I think about being on television. When I told them about my television idea, they both went nuts, and within weeks, one group had flown out to California and started shooting.

Message: What you think, you create, and you create what you think. The limitations are only in your mind. The more self-realized you are, the more powerful you are. The world is your canvas. What do you want to paint in your world?

Steven S. Sadleir is a Shaktipat Master, best-selling author, and director of the Self Awareness Institute. For more information, please go to *www.SelfAwareness.com*.

STORIES OF LOVE
AND
RELATIONSHIPS

A SINGLE DAD'S LESSON

By DP Gates

Nothing can withstand the power of the human will if it is willing to stake its very existence to the extent of its purpose.
—Benjamin Disraeli

We all have defining moments which forever alter our lives by shifting our thoughts, feelings, and actions in a new direction. Sometimes those moments look like natural disasters! And then, eventually, we see that everything took place in perfect harmony with the Law of Attraction.

I'd have to admit that my life was on a pretty comfortable track about three years ago. I was cruising along in that in-between world of no longer being the high school jock or college kid, but not yet ready to be a full-fledged grown-up, either. I always had the heart of an entrepreneur and had tried a few things and experienced some success mixed with equal parts of failure with the attempts I had made at building a home-based business. But that was okay, because I knew that I'd do something extraordinary someday. That's not to say I didn't have an idea of what I wanted. I had a nice, neat little plan to first earn a sizable amount of money with a business from home, then get married, then have kids. More than anything, I always wanted to be a stay-at-home, entrepreneurial dad so I could be an active part of the lives of my children ... but I was in no hurry. I mean—after all—why rush?

And then ... Ka-pow! I got a wake-up call. The company I worked with went bankrupt after I had invested more than a year into it. And in January 2005 I got the news that my girlfriend was pregnant. We had taken precautions and talked about the "what ifs"—so I couldn't believe it was happening. I was stunned and reacted accordingly—*badly*—as I resisted the reality of the situation. This was not the plan I had laid out for my life and certainly not the way I wanted to bring a child into the world. I wasn't ready, and there was nothing I could do about it. I was angry, hurt and—most of all—felt totally powerless.

On August 22, 2005, I was in the delivery room to watch my son, Dylan, enter the world. I kept thinking, *"Wow—I'm a dad!"* It was sobering and deeply moving … yet I was still scared and worried. I needed more time to prepare for this, I thought, to find my way in life, establish a home, and a home-based business. It wasn't going according to plan. Or was it?

During the first year of being a father, I went through a serious adjustment period. I think most fathers do. I continued to build a very special bond with my son, but the relationship with his mother ended.

The ending of the relationship with my girlfriend in the first year of my son's life was a major blow. She wasn't just someone I had dated for awhile. She was my best friend and the mother of my son. We had a serious connection that had lasted for quite some time, on and off, since college. So I was in a daze, shell-shocked, wondering what had happened and why. All the while, I was also wondering what I was going to do about my son so I could be fully involved in his life. We seemed to be working it out though, sharing the caregiver roles between us on a pretty friendly basis.

And then … another Ka-pow! In June 2006 I received court papers from an attorney representing my son's mother. The papers asked for sole custody for the mother with very limited and restricted time for me with my son. Suddenly, I realized it was a whole new ball game. I went into resistance again, after the first shockwave … and then I began to see the bigger picture. It was a gradual awakening as I was being drawn into a legal system that dictates whether a dad can or cannot spend time with his own child. I began to recognize this drama as an opportunity to affect change, from within a system that is in dire need of change, with respect to the rights of single fathers. I'm not any kind of activist, but I went to Web sites for information and advice from other fathers, and discovered a very angry and resentful group of men who had suffered the loss of their children and other rights as a result of a very slanted court system.

My own parents were also surprised at how slanted the courts are with respect to single dads. Sure, there are some "deadbeat dads" out there … just as there are some unfit mothers. Sadly, though, it is automatically assumed by our current court system that a mother should be the primary caregiver while fathers are often relegated to the role of a "babysitter"—lumped in with day care workers and pre-schools. In a case like mine, in which the mother and I were never married, there were huge hurdles to jump over in order to establish my rights as a dad.

So I quietly refused to accept any assumptions or labels that suggested I was any less capable, responsible, or loving than my son's mother. It was never my desire to restrict her time with him or to suggest in any way that she was anything less than a great mom. I followed the example of Mother Teresa who, when asked if she would march against the war, replied that no, she would not—but she would march in favor of peace. I decided to be *for* something … in this case, peace and equal parenting rights.

I discovered how perfectly—and quickly—the Law of Attraction responds to what we put out. Whenever I found myself focusing on the negative aspects of the situation, I would attract more of it. When I focused on the good, I attracted more of it. So I made a concerted effort to give my whole and entire attention to one thing and one thing only … gaining the maximum time possible with my son without violating or limiting his mother's rights in the process.

It wasn't easy, but I can tell you that I grew in the process. I had to remind myself time and time again to take the high road despite letters full of untruths and personal insults from the opposing attorney in her attempts to discredit me and limit my parental rights. Rather than engage in the legal rhetoric and offense/defense games, I quietly affirmed over and over again gratitude that my son has a good mother—a woman who loves him and provides good, dependable care. Being grateful was the key.

During some of the most challenging times, I had the benefit of coaching from a man I am fortunate to have as a personal friend and mentor, Bob Proctor. He coined a perfectly appropriate phrase that I repeated many times each day: *"The main thing is to keep the main thing the main thing."* My son, Dylan, was—and is—the main thing. So I applied the principles from the now-famous DVD, *The Secret*, and followed the advice of Bob Proctor. Despite the circumstances around me, I continually visualized my desired outcome—a peaceful co-existence with my ex-girlfriend, with the security and happiness of our son as the first priority.

A hugely defining moment occurred one day in February 2007 when Bob Proctor asked me to drive him to the airport for a return flight to Toronto. He invited me to join him for lunch, and we talked for about an hour. It was a very long hour and the best hour I have ever spent with anyone. He challenged me from every angle … he questioned my goals and aspirations and what I said I wanted. Most of all, he challenged me to be honest with myself about what I'm willing to do in order to have the life I want … including that of being an entrepreneurial, stay-at-home dad fully engaged in the day-to-day raising of my son.

I got very clear about what I wanted and began holding that image as I petitioned the court for joint custody. A fragile peace is now growing between us all.

It's still a work in process, but the lights of awareness are on full beam, and the "main thing" has grown to include helping single dads in similar situations. My message to single dads *who sincerely want to be part of their children's lives* was best stated by Winston Churchill when he said: *"Never, never, never give up!"* Be persistent in your efforts—and back your words with your actions. Come from a place of love and commitment to your child … and keep the main thing the main thing.

Today I enjoy 50/50 custody and an unprecedented amount of parenting time—quite unusual for a dad with a child under the age of two years old! What's more, I can feel great knowing that my time with him doesn't limit or violate the rights of his mother—because most of the time I spend with him is during the weekdays when she is working, so she wouldn't be with him at those times anyway. It really is a win-win scenario for both of us—and especially for our son.

I've been blessed to enjoy the stay-at-home dad arrangement I so desired, and visualized, as a result of the flexibility of my work with LifeSuccess Productions.

The Law of Attraction brought all this about with one stroke—with the "untimely" conception of a beautiful boy between two young people who each had much to learn and much to gain from an experience that might otherwise appear on the surface to be a disaster. By embracing it as a gift of love and learning, we are all growing and enjoying life with this beautiful little boy we call The Love Man—Dylan Paul Gates.

Message: Hold your vision and think the truth regardless of the circumstances around you. It works for everyone, every time … keep the faith!

DP Gates works directly with Bob Proctor as the director of the SGR Club city leader training worldwide. He recently married the girl of his dreams and moved into his dream home where he continues to raise his son. For DP, life is good and getting better all the time. For more information on the SGR Club, please visit *www.thesgrclub.com.* You can contact DP by e-mail at *dp@bobproctor.com.*

MOTHER'S DAY

We have not come into the world to be numbered; we have been created for a purpose;
for great things: to love and be loved.
—Mother Teresa

Growing up, I always knew the most important thing that would ever happen in my life would be to become a mother. This didn't happen. All of a sudden, I went from being in my twenties to a woman over fifty, and felt I had this terrible void in my life. Each and every day of my life, I thought of how my dream hadn't been realized and always the "Why me?" came up. Had I failed?

My mother was truly a gift to the world. She always smiled and was happy whether we had money or not. Somehow, she always pulled things together for our family. She taught us that our thoughts were as important as our actions. Being a young child, I don't think that I quite understood what she meant. I wanted to be just like her—always loving, giving, contributing, and helpful.

Mom was from an immigrant family from Russia that had many hardships during their life, and yet she never looked at it that way. She always spoke of the experiences they had and consistently found goodness in everything. The Depression came along when she was a young child, then World War II. She met my father in Hollywood during the war, and they married after twelve dates and remained married until her death fifty-plus years later.

The void wouldn't go away as many of my friends started having children. As I watched them grow, it hurt so much inside. My friends and family have been wonderful and shared many of their children's special times with my husband and me. Over the years we have been blessed with many fantastic godchildren, nieces, and nephews. Neighbors have always included us in their children's lives and experiences.

What was wrong with me that so many people had my dream and not me? I was able to excel in business, and I had a wonderful family and friends. I fought my feelings and had a daily mental game going with myself. I just wasn't able to find the missing piece in my life.

Then, in December of 2005, at a business seminar, I was exposed to the Law of Attraction and learned to focus on what to be grateful for. It became easy to realize that my dream had come true and was always there. By going with the flow and not fighting with myself anymore, my thoughts changed. We have beautiful godchildren, many of our friends' children share their lives with us, and we have fantastic neighborhood children as well. My volunteer projects are all done with the goal to improve the life of a child each and every day.

The following May, on Mother's Day, I received seven Mother's Day cards from the beautiful children in my life! What happened? My thoughts changed and the pity party stopped. No longer do I think, "It's not fair." Instead, I recognize all that is there for me. We all have the power to affect our lives. Mom, I have found my dream! Thank you for all you gave me.

Message: It is all there for you once you allow and are open to receiving.

SPIRITUAL AWAKENING

By Janelle Sagen

You could say I'd never had a true religious moment, the kind where you know your-self spoken to by a voice that seems other than yourself, spoken to so genuinely you see the words shining on trees and clouds. But I had such a moment right then, standing in my own ordinary room. I heard a voice say, "Lily Melissa Owens, your jar is open."
—from *The Secret Life of Bees* by Sue Monk Kidd

My journey to gain knowledge about the Law of Attraction led me to a seminar given by Matthew Ferry and Thach Nguyen in March of 2007. I also met Rich German at this event. It was an amazing weekend-long experience. I sat with bated breath every day of that seminar, lucky to witness the countless miracles that were happening all around me as people from all over the country shared their stories.

Day two came and went, and I left that day feeling especially elated with what I'd learned. I didn't realize that day's session had gone an hour over, and I had a husband and two kids at home waiting for me. It all came to a head when I glanced down at my cell phone that had been set to vibrate and saw seven missed calls from home. At that very moment, my phone began to vibrate—another call from home. I picked up, still not aware of the time, and said hello to my husband.

He immediately fired back at me, "Where the hell are you?" I was so taken back; I had such an amazing day, and to get this kind of treatment from my husband was absolutely unimaginable. In an equally annoyed tone, I asked him, "What do you mean, 'where am I?' I'm on my way home from the seminar." He asked me to look at the time and went on to really let me have it for not calling to let him know I was going to be late.

I immediately fired back at him, blaming him for ruining what was the best mood I'd been in since I could remember. I swiftly hung up on him, feeling ever so righteous for doing so. Then it dawned on me, what had I been learning for the past two days?

I immediately gave the hurt, resentment, anger, confusion, and hostility to the Universe; in my case that is God. I asked God to take away all the negative emotions that were blocking my feeling good at that moment. I began to breathe and feel the power of the Law of Attraction begin to work in my life. I declared to God that by the time I returned home, I would be back in complete alignment with my husband. Of course, I saw this alignment as my walking in the door, and my husband running over to me to greet me with a warm embrace and a soft kiss, and most importantly, an apology.

When I walked in the door, I walked up to him before realizing what I was doing, and I began to speak to him in a way that wasn't the norm for me; I am rarely the "apologizer." I went on to tell him how very sorry I was that I didn't call him to tell him I'd be late. I apologized for his having to sit around and worry about my safety. I put myself in his shoes and really thought about what would serve him, not me. He had a look of confusion on his face that told me this was the Law of Attraction working here. But just to make sure I really saw it, God inspired my husband to ask about the seminar and what was taught that day, something that isn't the norm for him.

I had shared my vision with fifty strangers that day but never my own husband. I went on to tell him my vision of being an author who writes inspirational books on self-healing that will one day save the lives of millions throughout the world. Even though a fight had been avoided, for some reason I still didn't feel completely and utterly aligned with him. However, I went to bed having taken back that feeling of overwhelming peace I'd left the seminar with earlier.

The next morning was the last day of my seminar. I hurried out of the house as to not be late. I told my husband I would pay attention to the time and let him know if I was going to be late that day. He looked at me with a look I'd never seen him give me and said, "I guess I'm going to have to get used to your being gone." I answered, "Why is that?" He responded, "Aren't you going to be on a book tour soon?" It was at that moment I realized I'd achieved perfect alignment. What a magical moment of the Law of Attraction working in my life!

Message: Look within at what you are bringing to every situation. Let go of the fear of examining yourself and how people view you. Be willing to say "I'm sorry," and smile as you reap every benefit.

Janelle Sagen's journey to spiritual awakening began about three years ago and has led her on a wonderful path of self-discovery. She knows her true purpose on this earth is to inspire and deliver this message to as many people as possible through her poetry and coaching. Her vision is to reach out and teach people their true potential in life, to raise their consciousness, and create a more peaceful world. Janelle can be contacted by e-mail at *Janelle@Buzzen.us.*

PAST LOVES

By Christine Taylor

The vision that you glorify in your mind, the ideal that you enthrone in your heart—this you will build your life by, this you will become.
—James Allen

In August 2004 I was forty-seven and questioning my lack of companionship. Finding my life partner was still eluding me, as it had my whole life. I kept asking myself why. The desire was so strong, yet I was clearly unable to actualize this deep longing. Something must be blocking the manifestation, I thought. But what could it be? After much consideration, I realized I was still holding a tremendous amount of energy in my heart for two former lovers. I felt this was the main obstacle standing in the way of my attracting my life partner.

Each relationship had lasted three and a half years, and each had played a significant role in my emotional and personal development. I had dated one man in my early twenties and the other in my mid-thirties. Both men had asked me to marry them, but in the end, I never went through with either marriage, and pieces of my heart had never been the same.

As I looked back on my life, I found myself questioning my decisions regarding these two marriage proposals. Had I made a mistake? Maybe I should have said yes. Maybe I should have gotten married. What was I thinking? Why did I keep comparing every man I dated to these two men? Was it arrogance that drove me to believe that there was someone more well-suited for me and that I should wait? Or, maybe I had been right. Maybe I knew something about myself then that I was conveniently questioning now. It had been eight to twelve years since I had seen or spoken to either one of them.

What would it be like to talk to them again? Would I still feel the same? My head was spinning. I didn't know where either of them was or how to get in touch with them. I had a few pieces of information to go on, but I was ambivalent about actively searching. Maybe they were married or living with someone.

Maybe they wouldn't want to hear from me. I just wanted to move forward, to move past all these barriers to my future and questions about my past.

So I decided to put the Law of Attraction into practice. At the end of my daily meditation, I began asking for a resolution to these doubts. I wasn't specific about the resolution, just that it be for my highest good. A part of me expected that the most that would happen was my angst would disappear and the questions would fade away. But the Universe had other plans.

A couple months later, an amazing thing happened. I called home to retrieve my voice mail. To my surprise, there was a message from the secretary of the art department at Orange Coast College. Although I had been an adjunct instructor for almost fifteen years, I hadn't taught there for a couple years. I couldn't believe she still had my number. The message continued, "A gentleman has contacted our office trying to reach you. We didn't want to give him your phone number directly but told him that we would contact you. Here is his contact information...."

Time stood still for a moment as I caught my breath and came back into my body. It was the man I had loved in my twenties. Without thinking, I picked up the phone and dialed the number. My heart was racing. The phone was ringing. He answered. Suddenly, so many feelings came rushing back as I heard his voice say hello. It was as if I had been transported back in time.

He had just been in a car accident and had almost died. His brush with death had brought about an intense desire to reconnect with me. His wife was aware that he had called me. We talked at length about our lives and sorted out the confusion surrounding our difficult breakup. I answered a lot of questions about why I had decided to end our relationship. There were tentative moments, tender moments. I came to realize by the end of the phone call that I had made the right decision and that he was meant to be with his wife. My heart was finally at peace after almost twenty-five years. My gratitude was immense.

However, I was only halfway toward manifesting the resolution to my blockage. At the end of my meditations, I kept on with my intention. Little did I know that an even more astounding rendezvous was in the making.

About four months later, I was on my way to lunch—about an hour later than usual. I had been detained by my boss. I couldn't decide where to eat. I kept changing my mind and was driving without much of a plan. Finally, I was near a favorite restaurant I hadn't gone to for quite some time. I thought, "Why not? They have a nice outdoor seating area, and it's a beautiful spring day." As I was walking up to the restaurant, I was intent on putting my keys into my purse. When I looked up, I was only a couple hundred feet from the door. And there he was—right in front of me, the man I had loved in my thirties! What should I do ... keep walking? Run the other way? He was staring at me, smiling, walking toward me. There was no turning back. In a few seconds, he was holding me in a very long embrace that I thought would never end. Then he kissed either side of my face just like he had always done ... his ethnic background melting my heart. And once again, the buried feelings came rushing back.

This experience was a little more delicate to navigate. I didn't have the phone to hide behind, and several of his friends that had shared lunch with him were teasing us. It was clear they knew who I was and that they had heard stories of our past that foretold of an unrequited love that still yearned for me. He was still unmarried and unattached. I was swooning inside.

He wooed me for a couple weeks. As our lives began to entwine once again, we went crashing from romantic fantasy back into reality. Little things that I had forgotten suddenly resurfaced. And just like with Laird, I realized that I had made the right decision the first time around; this relationship was not for me, and the deep wound in my heart healed completely.

The best part of this story is that I am very dear friends with both men (and the wife), and I feel so blessed to have them in my life. I have been reunited with the two most incredible people from my past. Our relationships are stronger and richer than they've ever been. Our love has stood the test of time. We talk often, and we are committed to remaining friends for the rest of our lives. With a connection as strong as ours, who would want to squander that again?

Message: When you believe in the Law of Attraction, it is easy to trust yourself and your intuition. Your intention is an incredibly powerful force that allows you to manifest things beyond what your mind can even imagine.

Christine Taylor has been a marketing and creative consultant for the last fifteen years. In her free time, she enjoys teaching yoga and meditation in the Southern California area. You can contact her by e-mail at *ctaylormail@cox.net.*

EVERYDAY
MIRACLES

MANIFESTING THE THINGS YOU DESIRE

"THE GENIE" GRANTS BOTH LARGE AND SMALL WISHES

By Mary "Ashley" Mann

Whatever you vividly imagine, ardently desire, sincerely believe, and enthusiastically act upon, must inevitably come to pass.
—Paul J. Meyer

Last fall, after watching *The Secret*, I realized I had been living the Law of Attraction my entire life with really great results; I simply hadn't put a name to it! But having watched this wonderful DVD, I decided to make more conscious choices about what I *really* want in my life. Like Aladdin, referred to in *The Secret*, I decided to "ask the genie" for not only three wishes, but for as many as I wanted, knowing the Universe will give me exactly what I am feeling, exactly what I am focused on.

So I started out slowly with some little goals. The first week after watching this incredible video, I decided to ask the genie for some flowers. With gratitude in my heart for receiving the flowers, I spent time the first day feeling how great it would feel to receive flowers from someone that week. I visualized receiving them, but I didn't know from whom I would receive them. I wanted the Universe to surprise me! I didn't share this goal with anyone, but instead kept it between me and the genie.

The next day, I did the same exercise of feeling and visualizing receiving flowers with gratitude, feeling as if I'd already received them. That same day, at the clinic where I work, I was talking to a colleague who suggested I step into her office to talk with her office partner, another hypnotherapist (like myself) who also specializes in preparing Bach Flower Essences. I told her what was going on in my life (without talking about my wish for flowers), and she proceeded to concoct a bottle of specific flowers just for me. I asked her what I owed her, and she told me it was her gift to me. For those of you who aren't familiar with flower essences, they are just that, the essence of flowers that work on deep and profound levels of healing when mixed with water and taken orally.

I thanked Helen for her gift, smiling both inside and out that my request was granted within twenty-four hours of first thinking about it. This was great as it reaffirmed what I already knew, had practiced, and had been exposed to by watching *The Secret*. I stopped envisioning flowers, but the next day, much to my surprise, when I returned home from work, my husband had a gift of beautiful spring flowers waiting for me. Hmmm ... my wish came true a second time even though I wasn't still focusing on this small goal. Amazing, I thought. The next real surprise came about a week later. No longer focused on flowers, and still not having shared my goal with anyone, my husband gifted me a dozen red roses. This, too, was amazing because after seven years together, though he's given me beautiful flowers often, he'd never given me two sets of flowers within a week's time.

I was exploding with excitement and decided to share my "small" goal with him, not only for a great laugh between us, but also because we had watched *The Secret* together and had both decided to put the principles into action in every area of our lives.

The second week, I decided to once again practice the principles of feeling happy and grateful while visualizing and affirming, "This week I will win something." I recall just feeling happy, allowing the Universe to surprise me with whatever it thought would be fun for me to receive. I affirmed this for a few days then just "let it go." That Saturday, I visited an open house for a new skin care spa where they were having special discounted treatments and a few raffle tickets for expensive treatments.

Only ten minutes or so after receiving my ticket, my number was called out as the winner of a $1,000 laser treatment for my face, something I would not have paid for at the time. Wow ... I was the only one to win anything of such high value that day. Then I remembered the "wish" I had given the genie for the week, just for fun, to remind me that following the principles of the Law of Attraction really does work. I scheduled my treatment date and felt very grateful for receiving such a wonderful, unexpected gift.

The third week, my wish was that "someone will treat me to lunch this week," and two different friends did treat me to lunch at different restaurants. I was having a lot of fun these first three weeks! Remembering the genie will grant many more wishes, I decided to put the principles into action for something much bigger and more important to me.

The fourth week, I decided to focus on living near my son, Scott. He had been out of high school for several years but never attended college. Since he lives in St. Louis, Missouri, and I live in Tucson, Arizona, I thought about it with deep longing but at the same time knew there was no way I would move back to St. Louis where I grew up. He and I spoke years ago about how much he loves Arizona, but he was married and his wife didn't want to live here. So I just let go of the idea thinking maybe someday in the future we'll live somewhere close, or at least closer, to each other.

I had forgotten about this goal when he called the day after my birthday to say "Happy Birthday" and that he had a gift to tell me about. He had applied to several universities around the country and had just that day received his acceptance letter from the University of Arizona with a $2,000 grant. He hadn't wanted to share his application process with me because he said he didn't want to disappoint me if he wasn't accepted at the University of Arizona!

I proceeded to tell him about *The Secret* and the Law of Attraction, and he laughingly said, "You didn't have anything to do with this, did you?" Then we continued our conversation focusing on how he would come up with the rest of the $16,000 out-of-state tuition. I told him to focus and visualize receiving it, and I would do the same for him. By the end of the week (three days later), he had been told the university wanted him so badly, they gave him the additional $14,000 in scholarships and grants. We were both excited and amazed that the answer came so swiftly. But then again, he had graduated near the top of his high school class and placed in the 99th percentile on the SAT, and we were both practicing using the Law of Attraction.

Now, I am happily looking for the perfect place for him to live as he winds down his life in St. Louis to head to the Southwest to begin his education here. He is happy about beginning his new life here, and I am delighted to have him live in the same city where I live after so many years apart. As mother and son, we have many things in common including our love of nature and hiking.

This is one of the most important and personally satisfying stories of my using the Law of Attraction to create more joy and happiness in my life. I will forever be grateful for knowing how to use it before, and for being reminded how to use it after viewing *The Secret*. thank you to the Universe for showing me that "you get exactly what you are *feeling*," and just for fun … Thank you to "the genie" too!

Message: Always be focused on your big goals with gratitude and patience, and practice using the Law of Attraction on smaller goals while waiting for the bigger ones to manifest! This reminds you that the Law of Attraction is always working on your behalf.

Ashley Mann resides in Tucson, Arizona, and is one of the founding members of The Center for the Healing Arts where she specializes in life coaching and hypnotherapy. Having known how to use the Law of Attraction all her life, she now teaches her clients how to use it. She is also available as a motivational speaker and can be contacted by e-mail at *ashleymann@yahoo.com* or on MySpace at *www.myspace.com/ashleys_secret10*.

THE HOUSE
ATTRACTION BUILT

By Betty Bogart

I have just three things to teach: simplicity, patience, and compassion.
—Lao Tzu, founder of Taoism

The pictures in my head were crystal clear. Our dream house would have a sunken living area with plenty of room for plants by the windows. The room's double-paned sliding doors would open to a bricked grill just beyond the covered patio. As I drifted off to sleep, I could almost smell the steaks cooking outside on that grill as I mentally built our new home.

The reality was that since the birth of our second child in 1978, we were cramped in a house the size of a cracker box. My husband's job required a home office for which he had framed in the garage's workbench space. But this provided him with barely enough room for his desk, computer, and file cabinet. Electric fans and a floor heater provided the only relief from the West Texas weather extremes.

We periodically looked at new houses in a nearby neighborhood, and my husband and I both liked a Spanish-style model that "Dub" Turner, a local Lubbock builder, constructed. With my being a stay-at-home mom, we felt that our single income conflicted with the idea of obtaining a larger, newer house. At the same time, the thought of staying where we were depressed me.

For almost a year after our daughter's birth, I fell asleep while mentally designing the four-bedroom house we wanted and needed. I pictured the wall separating the dining and living areas and envisioned a shoulder-high, arch-shaped opening with a finished wooden ledge as an attractive accent. My green thumb could produce a large hanging plant that would beautifully adorn the arched opening.

The kitchen's dark-finished custom wood cabinets provided abundant storage space—more than I could fill from our current kitchen's inventory. The model home's large kitchen opened to a casual breakfast nook that I saw separated by a raised, stool-height countertop surrounded by bar-level chairs.

The model's master dressing area was wide and held three double-door, under-sink cabinets. But I pictured a practical modification that changed the middle cabinet to three stacked drawers.

Another aspect of the builder's model particularly concerned me. The two front bedrooms that could house our son and daughter were across a hallway behind the living area. I wondered if late-night television viewing in the living room would disturb our children's sleep. A good solution was to include sound-proofing insulation in that wall during construction. After all, the mind developing all of these fantasy images was mine, and I could paint the canvas any way I chose.

Our imagined home existed only in my mind's bedtime envisioning process, but our family was increasingly cramped in the current residence. While out driving through the newer neighborhood one Saturday, we noticed for the first time that our favorite builder's sign included the message, "Will take trades," which sparked our curiosity. Could my dream become a reality?

My husband's work took him out of town on Monday, and I stopped by a vacant lot where Mr. Turner's crew was framing a house. I no longer believe that much in life happens by coincidence, and Mr. Turner greeted me in the yard. We briefly discussed my family's needs and decided it would be worthwhile for him to visit with us the following weekend.

To my surprise, Mr. Turner pointed to the vacant corner lot across the street where construction would begin in two weeks on a four-bedroom house with our preferred floor plan. I could barely wait until my husband called that afternoon, and he was as excited as I was about the news. He really liked the idea of having an extra room inside the house for his office. My husband didn't know anything about the thoughts I peacefully dwelled on each night just before falling asleep. The details of the house were my dreams, and he was a black-and-white kind of guy who wasn't curious about my hopes, dreams, and wishes for our life.

Our meeting with Mr. Turner resulted in a signed contract in which he agreed to take our house as a trade-in if he could not sell it. In the meantime, he liked the aesthetic changes I proposed—all of which matched the pictures held in my mind those many months. He had not planned to add the model's sunken living room to the soon-to-be-built house, but I had acted on my instincts and caught him just in time to modify the blueprints.

We were able to visit our in-progress home as often as we pleased over the next six months, and one such inspection proved to be another well-timed occurrence.

In his revised blueprints, Mr. Turner included the arched opening I wanted cut between the dining and living areas. The worker was about to carve the opening in the sheetrock when we arrived, but he was considering cutting a circular hole in lieu of an arched one. Naturally, we quickly quashed that idea!

Otherwise, the construction unfolded as planned, and I was able to select the decorative accents as well (e.g., ceiling fans, light and plumbing fixtures, carpet, flooring, and wallpaper). In each case, I easily found materials that matched those included in my bedtime imagery.

As the date to close on our home approached, our current house was still on the market. Without its sale, we would have to come up with several thousand extra dollars—a prospect that could kill the deal. With only four weeks to spare, Mr. Turner brought by a young couple who needed a starter home. They were the perfect buyers at the perfect time.

My Christian background never prepared me to recognize or even know about the creative visualization that made our dream house a reality. But ten years later, when I read Shakti Gawain's book, *Creative Visualization*, I recalled all the hours I spent mentally designing the home we needed and wanted. I then realized the spiritual power of the consistent imagery I had used back in Lubbock. Since the early 1990s, I've been a member of the Unity Church where I learned more about the Law of Attraction before *The Secret* was even written.

Every few years, I put together a visualization board comprised of pictures and words describing where I want life to lead me, and I've found two other homes based on this process. I've included other elements of life in my mental envisioning practices: creativity, happy relationships, and career choices. I keep my dreams pictured before me, and even if the path to them is sometimes surprising, the destination is what I've had in mind.

Message: Focus daily on images (mentally or on a vision board) of what you want in life, whether it's a larger home, financial security, or positive relationships. Respond when your intuition delivers signs and messages intended to lead you to your desired destination. Wait and be careful not to get in the way. Time and patience are your friends.

Betty Bogart has a strong background in grammar and composition. She fine-tuned her writing skills while ghostwriting for Herb Kelleher, Colleen Barrett, and other Southwest Airlines officers. Additionally, she's been a guest column contributor to the *Palm Beach Post,* and other personal pieces have received awards from The Greater Dallas Writers Association and the Florida Writers

Association. Although she's a Texan at heart, she currently resides in Florida with her husband. You can contact Betty through e-mail at *texasgirlb@gmail.com.*

MANIFESTING A
COMPUTER

By Korbe

*The purpose of life is to live it, to taste experience to the utmost, to reach out eagerly
and without fear for newer and richer experiences.*
—Eleanor Roosevelt

I am fourteen years old, and this is the story of my first big manifestation. Now,
my whole family is really spiritual, and my mother had been telling me that I was
creating my own reality since the age of four, but it had never really meant anything until I saw the movie, *The Secret*. Even then, I had to see it several times
before taking real action toward changing my current state of reality. So I decided
to make a vision board, and I started to write out all the things I really wanted
and set to work.

The first material thing on my list was an iMac computer. I had wanted one
for months because my dad had continually tried (and failed, I might add) to
build my PC computers for years, and I was sick and tired of it! So I went to the
Mac site and did a price check on my perfectly customized computer. It was
going to come to around $1,500, which is no small chunk of change, especially to
a fourteen-year-old without a job. So I made out a check to myself for $1,500
from the bank of the Universe and got a picture of my computer to put on my
board. I also put up a dollar bill and the phrases "money comes to me easily and
frequently" and "I am a money magnet."

About two weeks after I put up my board, my mom came home from work to
tell me that her client had offered me a job at a fast food restaurant of his. I was
very, very excited, to say the least, because this was the first job opportunity I had
ever had! I gladly accepted and scheduled an interview right away. This was proof
that the Law of Attraction worked, and I couldn't have been more excited to start
my new job.

I went into the interview and did great. They told me I had the job and started to schedule me for training. The only problem was that the wages and shifts I could get at my age meant it would take me all summer to get my computer. I planned on working there but decided to continue to manifest the computer and really try to focus on it more.

The next day, my mom and I went out for coffee at the bakery two blocks from our house. We were friends with the baker and the owners because we had been going there for months. I was telling the baker how I was going to be working at a fast food place all summer to buy a computer. I will never forget his response! He just sort of looked at me with this incredulous expression on his face and said, "Why on earth aren't you working here?" I honestly hadn't thought about it much, but it seemed like a much better job than the one I had already lined up.

Within the week, I was working at the bakery, having a blast, and getting paid better than I ever would have been at the other place. Not to mention, it was two blocks from my house so the fact that I couldn't drive didn't really affect me at all. I calculated how long it would take me to get my computer with my wages at the bakery, and it was only going to take me a month and a half! That was half as much time as the last job!

Now, that in itself would have been a decent story about how the Law of Attraction worked for me. I got a good job that I enjoyed, and I would have my computer in a relatively short amount of time. I would have been happy with that! But it didn't end there.

After I got my first paycheck from the bakery, my mother came home from work. She is a massage therapist and a healer, so she meets interesting people each day and gets to know them well. She came home to tell me she had a new client. He was really spiritual, nice, and he just happened to be a multi-millionaire. Just so you know, this isn't really that odd of an occurrence because where I live, we happen to have one of the highest concentrations of multi-millionaires in the country. But the fact that he was really spiritual was kind of odd. And even odder was the fact that my mother came home and immediately decided to tell me this story.

I probably should have guessed that my mother had been telling stories about me at this point—she is sort of notorious for that. She had been telling this client of hers about how I was working to manifest a computer, how I had attracted a great job, and how I was saving up for it. His response was that he had a gift to give my mother and her family so that we could enjoy the weekend. He would bring it in for her the next day. And with that, he left.

Needless to say, both my mother and I were surprised and excited. We couldn't wait to see what was going to happen. I didn't have any expectations about the gift. At that point, I would have been extremely grateful for a free dinner at a local restaurant. (That was actually something my mom and I had thought it might be. A night out to dinner would help us enjoy the weekend, wouldn't it?) So imagine my surprise when my mom came home the next day with a small box.

Inside the box were a few books and a few cards. She handed me a card and two books. The books were entitled *The Dummy's Guide to Macintosh Computers* and *The Dummy's Guide to the Internet.* This was incredible because I didn't know too much about computers, and these books would be great once I had raised enough funds for my Mac!

I opened my card and it started singing "Dancing in the Street," which is one of my favorite songs, and I started to laugh. I almost didn't notice what else was in the card because I was laughing so hard. There was a stack of bills. Upon counting, I found that there was $1,500 in total enclosed within the card.

I began to cry. I was so incredibly happy, I could not contain myself, and I broke down. A man I had never met had given me the exact amount that I had needed for my computer without asking for anything in return—it truly was beautiful. The Law of Attraction worked in so many ways to make this happen. Many different opportunities were presented to me so that my desire would manifest. Each time, the opportunities were better, until someone gave me exactly what I had asked for. I even got to upgrade my computer to the next size up because I already had some cash saved up. My next goal is to manifest $30,000 so that I can buy myself a hybrid car for my sixteenth birthday!

Message: Anything is possible.

Korbe is a fifteen-year-old high school student who uses the Law of Attraction every day to not only improve herself, but also to help her in pursuing a career in acting and singing.

MY DIVINE DESK

By Julia Rogers Hamrick

Life has its own hidden forces which you can only discover by living.
—Soren Kierkegaard

In the mid-1980s, I was at the right place at the right time to contribute my writing talents to help a graphic-designer friend who needed some advertising copy for a newspaper ad he was creating. What I wrote was a hit with the client. They asked me to do all their advertising and PR writing, and a copywriter was born! I decided to hang out my shingle as a freelancer, and the Universe let me know I was on the right track by delivering me quite a few writing jobs in very short order.

The problem was I didn't have a desk! I lived in a tiny 550-square-foot apartment and had to put my word processor on my coffee table and sit on the floor to work. This was okay for awhile, but soon I grew frustrated with not having a specific work space and not being better organized. I had the sense that if I *felt* more professional and had my act together, I would be able to attract more clients, more work, and of course, more money.

There were piles of papers and office supplies wherever I could find to stack them, and the Lilliputian apartment, which seemed to be shrinking by the day, was a disorganized mess. Though I was pretty busy with my new business, I had not yet made enough money to do much more than pay my rent and other bills. So buying a desk, however much I needed one, seemed like an impossibility. I was getting extremely frustrated and annoyed not to have what I so badly needed.

One evening, I went to a meeting of a bi-monthly support group for those, like me, who had taken a particular course in personal empowerment—a regular opportunity to follow up and refocus. As a part of the session, we did an exercise in which we expressed a challenge we were facing and let the others brainstorm ideas for us. The rule was that when it was your turn, you had to be completely quiet while the other people suggested solutions. Naturally, the challenge I put out to the group was that I had started a business but was totally unorganized and had no desk. What to do?

As the dozen or so other attendees discussed it, I was not allowed to interject any of the "yes, but" comments I felt bubbling up. I just had to listen. There were some helpful ideas tossed out about organizing. And, while I left committed and motivated to at least begin sorting through and filing my papers, no one had come up with a clear plan for me to get a desk. They had, however, concurred that one way or another, I needed to make procuring a desk my top priority. Of course, I agreed but still had no idea how I was going to do it.

On the way home, feeling both frustrated and energized, I said, "Okay, Universe, I really, *really* need a desk, and I need it *yesterday*. I don't have a clue how you're going to deliver one, but please hop to it!"

When I tried to figure out how the Universe would possibly bring me a desk, I was totally stumped. So I just gave up trying to figure it out and said to myself, "I've had enough of thinking and worrying about this for now. I'll focus on it again tomorrow. Maybe tonight I can at least sort through a few things and throw away stuff that is unnecessary." Yes, even though I had been resisting it and procrastinating over organizing things for quite some time, it suddenly seemed like it would feel good—it would be an easy, concrete step in the right direction. I relaxed as I drove, looking forward to taking that inspired action.

When I got to my apartment, I surveyed the living room to see where to begin. There was a pile of mail from a few days before that had come at a very busy time, and I had put it aside unopened. That seemed like a good place to start. As I sorted through it, I found among the bills and advertisements an envelope from the Scandinavian furniture company where a friend of a friend worked. A few weeks before, I had gone there with my friend to give the other friend a ride to pick up her car from the repair shop.

"Why are they sending me this?" I pondered as I opened it. It clearly wasn't an ad as my address had been typed, and it had a first-class stamp on it. The day we'd been there, we'd had to wait a few minutes while the one needing the ride finished up with a customer. As I had wandered the store admiring the handsome furniture, I spotted a box and some forms with the invitation to enter to win a gift certificate to the store in celebration of their anniversary. I had completely forgotten that I had filled out one of the entry slips. I didn't even remember it as I opened the envelope.

That letter that had been sitting there unopened for days was announcing that I had won second prize in their drawing—a $150 merchandise credit from the store! "Cool!" I thought. And then it hit me—*they have desks!* They *absolutely* have desks! In fact, I had been coveting a great little teak desk that day when we had been waiting around. Its price? $149! So I got my desk. Like magic. Now, years after having retired from a sixteen-year career as a freelance copywriter, and after authoring my book and a collection of spiritual articles too numerous to count atop it, I still use it. In fact, I am sitting at that very desk as I type this.

And a funny little twist and evidence of the Universe's timelessness, precision, and sense of humor: If you recall, I had said to the Universe that I need a desk *yesterday*. If I had opened my mail when it came, I absolutely could have had it *yesterday!*

Message: The Universe always supplies what you need—sometimes even before you know you need it!

Julia Rogers Hamrick, author of *Recreating Eden*, has been a spiritual-growth facilitator since the early 1980s when she experienced a radical spiritual awakening upon turning her life over to Spirit in response to a crisis. Julia now shares her insights with an international audience via teleconference and in-person appearances, as well as through articles, her blog, and other resources on her Web sites at *www.JuliaRogersHamrick.com* and *www.ILiveInEasyWorld.com*.

GO WITH THE FLOW

By Pete Hawk

*The greatest gift that you could ever give to another is your own happiness, for when
you are in a state of joy, happiness, or appreciation, you are fully connected to the
Stream of pure, positive Source Energy that is truly who you are.*
—Esther Hicks

For many years I had been searching for that one thing that would resonate
within me to "get me on track" with what I really wanted out of life. Then, in the
summer of 2006 I discovered the movie, *The Secret*. It was the first version with
Esther Hicks in it, and it was the first time I'd heard of Abraham. She just struck
such a chord within me that I was soon researching her on their Web site,
www.abraham-hicks.com. And now, months later, I guess you could call me an
"Aber."

Abraham is a collective consciousness of five beings that Esther has been chan-
neling since 1989 or so, along with the help of her husband, Jerry. Through their
book, *Ask and It Is Given,* I have found I've become quite good at creating and
attracting my desires. Small things are pretty easy for me, like getting ideal parking spaces when out shopping at the mall. And I can also help others attract what
they want by their simply telling me—what a hoot! For example, "I have such
and such a problem and don't know what to do about it." I simply and immediately jump to the end result. The problem is taken care of, and they are happily
telling me that it's done. It is really fun and incredibly rewarding for me. Money,
however, due to the power and stigma that it tends to have over most people, was
a bit harder to master. But with time and practice, I have overcome all disbelief in
practicing the Law of Attraction.

After following many of the processes in Jerry and Esther's wonderful afore-
mentioned book, and bringing myself into alignment with God/Source Energy, I
began to see more and more things come to pass that I had desired. I made a list
of ten things that I wanted to attract within a two-week time period. Several of
my top items revolved around money and having my bills paid. I was watching a

show with Bill Gates and Warren Buffet that I'd recorded on TV. They were talking to a college audience about what it was like to be a billionaire. During this show, I imagined myself sitting there on stage with them and was getting a wonderful feeling that I, too, was a billionaire. I was in the right frame of mind—doing this with a strong feeling of fun and ease. I actually felt as though I *was* one of the "super" rich.

About three-quarters of the way into the show, my phone rang. It was a call from someone telling me that, through certain circumstances, I would be receiving almost $50,000 in the next few weeks. The Universe heard my call, and because I'd spent a few minutes three times a day focused on the list I'd made and seeing all of those items as "done," it brought it to me (it's a law—it had to without fail). Instead of taking two weeks though, this happened on the fourth day. So not only did the money come to me quickly, I got more than ten times what I'd asked for! I can't imagine living any other way now.

I would like to give you another example of the Law of Attraction in my life. In early 2007 I decided to bless my mom. I asked God to bless her in a very big way. And so in my mind, I pictured her calling me with some wonderful news. Not your everyday news but some *big* news that really excited her. Well, because I was still learning all of this, I didn't put a time frame on when I wanted it to happen. A few months went by, and then she called. She said, "You'll never guess what happened today. A person we both know called and told me to go pick out a brand-new car for myself." Immediately I thought, "*Wow!*" She chose a beautiful car that was much better for her than the one she had been driving, and it was 100 percent paid for. That was my first really big "wow" moment with the Law of Attraction. Just based on the results I've seen in my life and those around me, I know without a shadow of a doubt that the Law of Attraction is real, and it does work.

So in case you are wondering how I really do all of this in detail … here's how. The first thing I learned is that you must *know* what it is that you want. Most people don't really know what they want. Take the time to ask yourself, and put some thought into it. I sat down for a few minutes and wrote out a list of things I'd really wanted. I made two lists, a short-term one (within the month) and a long-term one (over the next year). Once you know what it is you want and it's written down, don't hesitate to make changes. It's not set in stone, and it's actually good to make changes. You are sorting and sifting through things in your life and putting them in order. God/Source Energy will reward you for taking the time to do this.

So you're thinking, "I have my list, now what?" In the morning, when you first wake up, around lunch time, and before going to bed, take out your list and look at it. I'll give you an example of a couple things that I had written down. "All of my bills are paid for this month. I have an extra $2,000 in the bank." By doing this you are saying to the Universe, "The thing that I want is …" By looking at it and thinking about it several times a day as though it already *is*, you are sending out positive vibrations that will attract the end result to you. It is very important to be thinking from that new perspective. Don't think about what you see around you now. See yourself living in the end result of what you want with the expectation and thrill that what you have written down has already happened. It's important that you are excited, happy, and grateful that it has happened (even though it hasn't yet). Do your best to think from this new perspective as much as you can. *The important thing is to always feel good!*

According to Abraham, Esther, and Jerry, it's best to make your life's goal nothing more than to feel good. That's right—do the things that bring you joy, make you laugh, and cause you to always feel good about your life. A very easy thing to do is to go on a "rampage of appreciation." Just look around you for things you are grateful for, appreciate them, and give thanks to the Universe for bringing them into your life. What this actually does is turn you "downstream" in the flow of Source Energy.

Most people in the world are living "by default," meaning they are thinking, "Whatever happens will happen, it's my destiny, etc. If I work extra hard, all the things I want will come into my life." What this is actually doing is causing most people to be pointed "upstream" in the flow of well-being. But according to Abraham, everything we humans want is *downstream*. So what's the best way to flow downstream? Stop "trying" so hard and go with the flow. Drop your oars, and let the stream carry you.

You do this by reaching for things that make you feel good. Follow your emotions, or as Abraham calls it, "your emotional guidance system." If you aren't feeling good then you are pointing "upstream," and you aren't going toward the things you really want. As soon as you come into alignment with your Source Energy, you go with the flow, and the things you've wanted all your life will quickly and easily start to manifest for you.

The Law of Attraction has now brought me the love of my life, I'm pursuing my dream of flying, I'm recording my own music, and I really couldn't be any happier. This has completely changed everything for me and the future looks very bright! So now it's your turn. Go create your dream life!

Message: Stop trying so hard! Let go of the oars, and let the current of the stream carry you toward your desires.

Pete Hawk lives in Las Vegas and is in his seventeenth year with the U.S. Air Force. He is the father of two wonderful children and is dating the love of his life. Pete wants to thank all of his family and friends for the wonderful support he's received over the years. He can be contacted through his Web site at *www.pete-hawk.com*.

PICTURE IT

By Wendi Nguyen

If you can dream it, you can do it.
—Walt Disney

The first time I really experienced the Law of Attraction was back in 2002. This was before I knew what the Law of Attraction really was. As a matter of fact, I had never even heard of the Law of Attraction. I wasn't aware of its power at all. I also wasn't aware that I could create my own life. I just didn't know that what I'm about to share with you would have such an impact on my life.

I was dating a guy who had a series of cassette tapes (remember those?) from Carlton Sheets. At that time, he suggested I listen to one of the cassette tapes because I was starting to become interested in how to purchase real estate. I didn't want to buy a bunch of real estate, just my first home. And, since Carlton is known to be an expert in the field of real estate, I figured I'd give it a shot and listen to the cassette. I had nothing to lose.

I remember putting the tape in the cassette player and taking notes like crazy. I must have taken notes for about twenty to thirty minutes straight. I was like a sponge. Then I remember Carlton saying something that stuck in my head. He said that if I want to achieve any goal, what I needed to do was write that goal down on a piece of paper and look at it every day. When he said that, I just knew that's what I had to do.

I grabbed a piece of paper and wrote down four goals. Those four goals were: within a year, buy my first home, leave my job for a better job, get my dog into commercials, and save $5,000. Then, after I wrote down those four goals, I found some magazines lying around the house. I thought to myself, "Why don't I take some pictures from these magazines (pictures that resemble the goals I want to achieve), cut them out, and paste them to my paper?"

So that's exactly what I did. But I took it a step further and wrote down one goal per piece of paper. For my goal to buy a house, I cut out pictures of homes and pasted them onto the page that was titled "Buy a House." I especially remember a picture of a pale yellow house.

For my goal to have my dog in commercials, I cut out pictures of dogs that looked like they were modeling and pasted them onto the page that was titled "Train Harley to Be in Commercials."

For my goal of leaving my job for a better one, I cut out pictures of people in business suits, people who looked professional, and pasted those pictures onto the page titled "Leave My Job for a Better Job." For my goal of saving $5,000, I cut out inspirational sayings and taped them to the page titled "Save $5,000."

I looked at my goals faithfully every day for about a week or two straight. I loved what I had done. I was proud that I actually got creative and went beyond writing my goals on a piece of paper. I just enjoyed looking at those pictures so much that I would always say, "It sure will be great when these goals I want to achieve come true."

I wanted all four of my goals to come true so badly. These were what my heart truly desired. I wanted these things so much. I felt these desires with every fiber of my being. The more I would think about them and feel the feelings of what it would be like to have those goals achieved (the heart and soul of the Law of Attraction), the more I just desired them. Mind you, though, I had no clue about the Law of Attraction at this time.

Well, I'll bet you're wondering if any of my goals came true. Actually, three out of four goals came true, and not within one year like I had originally allotted for myself. I achieved all three within only six months.

The first goal I achieved was getting my own home. I was so excited when I got my first home that I really felt like I had accomplished something. I was so proud of myself!

The second goal that came true was my dog getting into commercials. He wasn't actually in a commercial, though. We went a step above that and he was on an episode of *America's Funniest Home Videos*. And up to two years after that episode aired, people were still telling me that they saw my dog on the show. *Wow!* I just couldn't believe that. Harley has since passed away and will always be loved and missed.

The third goal that came true was leaving my job for a better job. I went from a job where the schedule was erratic to one that was set, with weekends off. I received better benefits with better pay, as well. The place where I got my new job was actually a place I had desired to work for three years. I believe that putting those pictures on paper actually fueled my desire that much more and got me the job in the company in which I really, really wanted to work.

As the Law of Attraction states, you must ask, believe, and receive. And that's just what I had done for those three goals that I wanted more than anything. But it's funny that after I achieved those goals, I had forgotten that I wrote them all down on paper. I forgot that I even still had those same pieces of paper. I forgot all about them for over four years until one day I was looking through my junk drawer and found those papers. I showed them to my husband (believe it or not, a few weeks after I first saw *The Secret*). His very first reaction was, "Do you realize that you attracted all of that into your life?" When he told me that, I got goose bumps and immediately went to work on the vision board that I currently have on my desk and look at every day.

And do you remember my saying that I had a picture of a pale yellow house on my "Buy a House" paper? Well, guess what! I actually bought a pale yellow house. Not the same exact house as the one on the paper, but it's still a pale yellow house. Isn't that amazing?

The Law of Attraction truly works, especially when you attach pictures to what you want. It will help to fuel your desires.

Oh, and the $5,000 that I had originally planned on saving? Well, I'm still working on that. With the help of my husband and the Law of Attraction, I am well on my way!

Message: If you write down what you desire, and have strong, positive feelings behind it, you can have anything you want. It's up to you. Now, go live your life!

Wendi Nguyen and her husband, Tom, live in Grantville, Georgia. Together they run a Web site development business called Mr. Technique, Inc., *www.mrtechnique.com*. Wendi is an author in the *Thank God I ...* book series, due out in 2008, and has another book due to be released in 2008 as well. She loves to sing, shop, cook, and spend time with her family. Wendi can be contacted by e-mail at *Wendi@mrtechnique.com*.

HOW WE MANIFESTED
A FREE MOBILE HOME

By Taylore Vance

If you are clear about what you want, the world responds with clarity.
—Loretta Staples

In manifesting, it helps to be familiar with the object of your desire. We had rebuilt mobile homes for five years and were comfortable with fixing them up. There were very few unknowns in this manifestation.

If you want to bring your dream into reality … get familiar with it. We manifested the double-wide mobile home for only $1. It was valued at the tax office for $24,000. Here's how we did it. We ran a small classified ad in the *Nickel* paper. It stated: *Retired couple wants a mobile home to fix-up. Must be reasonable. Have some cash. Write to POB ____, Lacey 98503.* We were living in the woods with no phone and our mailbox was thirty-five miles away. Someone wanting to sell or give away a mobile home had to actually write a letter to us telling us what they had and how to get in touch with them. That's asking a lot of people these days. We received many replies. After several phone calls, we contacted the owner of the double-wide. He had already offered it to a handyman who was moving it to Idaho. We were second in line. I decided that I would not worry about *not receiving it*. I told myself, "If it is meant to be, it will be ours. Otherwise, a much better one will show up!"

Many people read our classified ad. We were offered several single-wide trailers and the one double-wide. After one long week, we received word: The double-wide was ours, free and clear! *Hooray!*

We had never actually worked on a double-wide before. We had to figure out how it came apart and how to put its axles on. We arranged an appointment with a hauler. He offered valuable information on the teardown and setup and on the paperwork and permits, etc., that were required to move it.

We went to the Snohomish County seat to secure a release and found that the owner owed $324 in back taxes. We had to pay that before we were given the permit to move it. When we showed the owner what we paid, he quickly reimbursed us for the taxes. We celebrated this victory, too!

He had lived in this mobile home while he built his new home. He really wanted it to be moved off his property as soon as possible. We had a few problems (learning experiences) in preparing it for transport and getting it out of the tight place where it was parked. Trees and bushes had grown, water pipes had broken under the ground sinking the mobile axle deep in mud, etc. The owner was actually afraid we'd give up. As the obstacles came up, we overcame them one by one. We were not giving up on our prize! We were winners!

So you can get a sense of what it takes to manifest objects, here are some important steps we took. Try it yourself:

1. Decide what you want.

2. Write what you want on a pad or piece of paper. You could make it like a letter with a list of things you choose.

3. Write out why you want this object.

Dear Life Manager,
I desire a better place to live because I have too much stuff—I'm tired of living in a '73 Dodge van. I think a mobile home would be good because we could park it on the rented land where we are now located. We know how to do this.
I am open to receive God's abundance. I am worthy of a better life. You are bringing us all this stuff. (I'm very grateful for the many things you've brought, but I have no place to keep them, yet.)
Thanking you in advance, I am your faithful co-worker.
(signed)
Taylore Vance

4. Find a place to put your object.

5. Visualize what it might look like, always leaving room for Spirit to make it even better or bigger.

6. Make it real to your mind. Become familiar with your goal.

7. Know that your goal is possible.

8. List action steps for getting the process moving. Start immediately, acting on your first action step. (We wrote a small three-line classified ad to announce what we were looking for. We placed the ad in papers, on bulletin boards, etc.)

9. Don't worry about the details. Let the Universe fill them in, allowing your dream to be even better.

10. *Start celebrating* the accomplishment of your manifestation as if it were already finished. Tell yourself, "It's a done deal!"

11. Thank the "higher powers" for helping align you with your desired goal.

12. And finally, celebrate and express gratitude again, both when it is completed and on a continuous basis.

We manifested our mobile home with ease *because we were familiar with them.* The manifestation skids were greased. If we had asked for a million dollars, it probably wouldn't have been so easy. Why not? At that time, my energy field was not a vibrational match for a million dollars. My energy field would contain lots of unknowns and maybe some fear about having a million dollars.

Your manifestation is easiest when you *know* your subject well. We knew about mobile homes. We had worked on them for five years.

If you don't know your subject well, you have some studying to do and/or you need to find a mentor who has walked the path before you—someone who can show you how it's done. If you are blazing a new trail for yourself, all kinds of internal fears may pop up (e.g., fear of success, fear of failure, and fear of moving forward into the unknown).

I'm not saying that being able to manifest a million dollars is difficult. It is no harder than getting the Universe to align you with a parking space when you go into town. The difference is that you *know* you *deserve* a parking space. When the stakes get higher, all kinds of old fears come up and interfere with your abundance. I was a novice at manifestation when I manifested the mobile home. I figured that since Spirit wanted us to go west with no money, it had to support us by helping us get settled. I thought that I *deserved* a place to live.

Message: It is important to release the root cause of your fears and other obstacles on your path to success.

Taylore Vance is a Reiki Master and energy healer. She has been teaching Reiki for Abundance at the Reiki Ranch in Chehalis, Washington, since 1994. She has figured out how to help a person to be able to receive all of God's abundance—it is free for the taking. Taylore is the author of *How to Attract Wealth*, published in paperback, and *How to Triple Your Home Business Income*, an online eBook. Her Web site is *prosperity-coach.blogspot.com*.

THE 52-HOUR DASH TO THE MILLENNIUM

By Namaste Faustino

Dreams are illustrations ... from the book your soul is writing about you.
—Marsha Norman

In 1997, I was nineteen years old and living in South Pasadena, California. I had quit college my freshman year in order to start a business. I was running a cellular phone store during the day and working on my business at night.

One day, I was reading a book in which the author explained the concept of dream boards. A dream board is a big, poster-size board with pictures of your goals on it. You buy a bunch of magazines, cut out all the pictures of your dreams (e.g., house, car, girl or guy, etc.), and you put them on the dream board. The idea is that by having the pictures of your goals in a place where you will see them every day, they are more likely to come true.

As soon as I was done reading, I ran out and spent $50 on magazines, a poster board, some glue, and a pair of scissors. I cut out all my dreams, put them on the board, and hung it on my wall. I was so excited to start getting the things on my dream board! One month passed and no results. Then another month passed and still no results. A few months turned into six months, and soon a year had passed without results. At that point, I took my dream board down and trashed it. I figured it was a nice idea, but the results spoke for themselves.

It was November 23, 1999. Josh Hillis and I had quit our jobs in late 1998 to start a new business on a shoestring. One thing led to another, and soon we were doing really well. We started making more money than we ever had before. I'll never forget what it felt like the first time we made more money in three hours than I used to make in two weeks. We were out of our minds with excitement. Unfortunately for us, we made a classic mistake. We landed one really good account, and that was where we made all of our money. We treated the client like gold, which was great for the client, but bad for us. One day, we woke up and got a call that the client had gone out of business. We were stunned. All of a sudden we had no money coming in, and we hadn't saved anything.

Like they say, "When it rains, it pours!" Josh totaled his car and didn't have the insurance coverage necessary for the insurance company to replace the car. I was driving down the street one day in my truck, and when I shifted, it stuck. The transmission was toast. At this same time, a lot of our friends were graduating college and getting jobs with large starting salaries. It sucked.

Shortly after, we were hanging out, and the question of what we planned to do for New Year's came up. The more we talked about it, the more we realized that there was only one place we could be on New Year's Eve 1999; we had to be partying in Times Square. The only problem was that we were broke. Neither of us had been able to bring ourselves to get a job, and what little we had left to sell was just enough to cover our basic expenses.

Now, here comes the interesting part. The next day, I woke up and couldn't get the idea out of my mind—I *had* to be in New York for New Year's Eve. I had this picture in my mind of the New York City skyline at night all lit up, and I wanted it so badly I could taste it. It's all I thought about. I had that picture of the New York skyline with fireworks going off in my mind constantly. One week turned into two, which turned into four, and then Christmas came and went. You would have thought that I'd given up hope at that point, but I hadn't—I wanted it that badly. I just kept thinking of that picture of the skyline in my mind. The twenty-sixth passed, and then I woke up on the morning of December 27, 1999.

I walked into the living room and saw my mom and sister arguing (my family had come to visit for Christmas). I asked them what was going on. After a good fifteen minutes of waiting, I finally got it out of my sister what had happened. A few days ago, in the middle of the night, a big butcher knife had been thrown through the window of her room that she shared with her college roommate. She and her roommate had called the police and filed a report. I was shocked. I asked her if she knew why it had happened. She said she didn't, but I could tell she wasn't telling the whole truth. Then I asked the question that changed my life for the next five days and her life for the next six months.

I asked her, "When are you moving out?" She said, "I'm not." I said, "Are you nuts?" She said, "I'm not moving out!" I turned to my mom and said, "If a big butcher knife was thrown through my window, I would be out of there that day. There is no way she is staying!" My mom got the point. My sister hadn't told the whole truth, as I had suspected. I found out what had really happened years later. Her college roommate was dating a complete loser with a criminal record. He was the one who had thrown it because he was mad at her roommate. Her roommate didn't want anyone to know, so she made my sister promise not to tell anyone.

It went from bad to worse for her. I went and woke up my dad. I asked him if he knew what had happened. He said, "No." I told him to get dressed and come out into the living room. When my dad found out, it was over for my sister. He called my aunt who lived right outside Philadelphia, and they agreed that my sister should move back east and go to college there immediately. My sister was understandably upset, but my dad wouldn't budge. He called the airline and got her a one-way ticket. Next, he began calling car transportation places to find out how much it would cost to transport her car back. The best quote he got was $900. When he told me that, I saw the opportunity and I took it. I said, "Josh and I would be happy to drive the car back there for $600." He agreed. I called Josh and said, "Get packed. We're leaving for New York in three hours, and the trip is paid for."

Josh and I drove fifty-two hours straight through from Santa Monica, California, to Springfield, Pennsylvania. We got there, slept at my aunt's for a few hours, and took off the next day for New York. We got to Times Square at 11:00 AM, and the crowd was already beginning to form. We were totally unprepared for being there. One hour turned into five which turned into ten. I was exhausted and hungry. I couldn't leave or I would lose my spot. My back was absolutely killing me. I wanted to sit down, but people had been urinating in the street for hours. It was a mess. Finally, I couldn't take it anymore so I left. I took the ferry back across to where I had parked. I sat in the car, turned it on, and flipped on the heater. Next, I reclined the seat and dozed for a little while. I woke up about ten minutes before midnight, put the seat in the upright position, and looked out the window. Then it hit me.

Do you know what I was looking at? The *exact* picture of the New York City skyline all lit up that I'd had in my mind for the last six weeks!

A few minutes later, the fireworks went off, and I spent the Millennium alone in the car. I couldn't believe it. It was so absurd that I had to laugh or I would have cried. When Josh got there at 1:00 AM, January 1, 2000, I told him what had happened. We talked about it on the long drive back. While it had sucked for me, we now knew why our dream boards hadn't worked in the past.

The reason our dream boards hadn't worked in the past actually came down to two reasons:

1. We weren't specific enough. Sure we cut out pictures of cars, houses, women, etc., but we weren't specific enough. Did we want the blonde or the brunette? Did we want the house to be located on the beach or in the mountains? We'd just cut out random pictures, slapped them on a board, and expected results.

2. We weren't emotional enough about our first dream boards. White hot emotion, burning desire, that feeling that you absolutely have to have it is the key. With it, you don't even need a dream board to get what you really, really, really want. White hot desire is the key!

Message: Be specific about what you want and have a strong desire to attract it.

Namaste Faustino is a thirty-year-old entrepreneur living in Las Vegas, Nevada. His father raised him as a Rosicrucian, so he began manifesting at the ripe old age of eight. His first success was manifesting a little red radio. As the years passed, he successfully manifested money, trips, and relationships into his life using the techniques he'd learned. Namaste can be contacted through his Web site at *www.privateernation.com.*

THE SWEEPSTAKES

By Cindy Coury-Broadhurst

Ordinary people believe only in the possible. Extraordinary people visualize not what is possible or probable, but rather what is impossible. And by visualizing the impossible, they begin to see it as possible.
—Cherie Carter-Scott

I discovered *The Secret* in February 2007. I was immediately filled with a sense of excitement and delight. It all made perfect sense! Scrapbooking is my passion, so I sat down and created a little book in which I placed pictures of things I would like to have. I included all of my blessings and added positive reaffirming statements to the pictures. I also created a vision board that I placed on the wall in my bathroom, the only place that I know I will get a few minutes to myself several times a day. I write down five things every day that I am grateful for.

I tried sharing my excitement with family and friends but did not receive a very warm reception, except from my sister and my ten-year-old son. I tried to share with my husband, but he didn't quite grasp what I was so excited about. I did not share my scrapbook or gratitude journal with him. But, nevertheless, he was affected by the Law of Attraction.

Entering sweepstakes is another one of my hobbies. Back in November, I had asked him if he did not use his laptop much at work, perhaps I could use it at night to enter contests. He said he needed it enough that he had to leave it there. I forgot all about it. One day late in February, he said to me, "Let's go down to Best Buy and get you a laptop." It was completely out of the blue and out of character for him. He and I looked through the ads and drove to the store. We found the laptop that was in the ad. But as he was chatting with the salesman, he saw another laptop and asked the man to compare the two. Even though the second one was $100 more, he decided in the long run it would be a better deal, so we got that one.

Later that night, I was looking through my *Secret* scrapbook and realized I had created a page that said something like, "Entering sweepstakes is easier with my laptop." I had printed off the Internet a picture of a laptop—no rhyme or reason to it—just a picture to go with the statement. The laptop we purchased was the *exact same* one as in the picture! At the time, my husband did not know about my scrapbook and almost fell out of his chair when I showed him the picture!

Around this time, I purchased the book, *The Secret,* and watched the DVD again. There is a point where Dr. Joe Vitale states, "Your job is to declare what you would like to have from the catalog of the Universe." His example is "$25,000 within thirty days." So I said out loud, "I would like to have $25,000 by April first." I believed it would happen. Several times over the next few weeks I would say, "$25,000 by April first" to myself. On *March 29,* I received a letter via Federal Express informing me that I had been chosen as the Grand Prize winner of a 2007 Toyota Prius hybrid car. The value of the prize? *$25,627!* I believe I was more shocked by the fact that the prize was valued at $25,627, than I was that I had won a car!

Recently, my mother-in-law came to visit. The next morning, she called and told me that she had gotten her late husband's affairs settled and would like to purchase us a few things so she could see us enjoy them instead of just leaving us money when she was gone. She decided to buy us a new refrigerator, two sets of "movie" couches for our living room that we are going to transform into a home theater, plantation shutters for all of our windows, a new grill to replace the one that was destroyed in a monsoon storm last summer, and a few other items. She knew nothing of my scrapbook or vision board. The refrigerator, movie room couches, and shutters were *all* on my vision board! We had spoken of these things in the past, but she picked them out herself. I didn't give her a shopping list … she just *knew!*

Trust me when I say that people around us are now very interested in *The Secret* and the Law of Attraction! We are living proof that the Law of Attraction works, and with all that has happened to us in just a couple of months, how much more proof do you need? However, we will be happy to continue manifesting and give you more!

Message: Start each day in gratitude and visualize the things you desire.

Cindy Coury-Broadhurst is married to a police detective. She is the mother of four children, two girls and two boys.

BLESSINGS IN SURPRISE

By Georgia Williams

Sometimes things happen to you that may seem horrible, painful, and unfair at first, but in reflection you find that without overcoming those obstacles you would have never realized your potential, strength, willpower, or heart.
—unknown

Every morning in February, after my neighbor told me his car (the same make and model as mine) was stolen, I jumped out of bed and ran to the window to see if my car was still in my driveway. About two weeks after his car was taken, my purse was stolen. After this happened, all I had the energy to do was go home, cancel my credit cards and checks, get into my bed, and cover my head. Everything was in my purse! On that day, I had gotten my tax return portfolio and my daughter's portfolio from my accountant. Both of them were in my purse.

The next day, I went to the bank to get a replacement debit card, made a police report at the local station, and then went out into the world and replaced everything I could replace with money—makeup, a makeup bag, my iPod, wallet, purse, and checkbook holder. The only thing I didn't replace was my digital camera. I couldn't find what I wanted, and I honestly didn't know enough about them to buy one just based on the recommendation of a salesperson.

I am quite a talker, but I only told my mother, my cousin, my daughter, and one of my friends about what happened to me. Before I told each person, I prefaced the story with, "I am going to tell you about something that happened, but I don't want you to say anything to me because I refuse to worry." I didn't tell my friends, as I would have in the past when even the slightest mishap occurred, because I knew they would say things to make me worry. And I refused to be drawn into negativity. As I was replacing my things, I kept thinking how lucky I was to have the funds and time to make the purchases. I remembered there was a time when I would not have been able to do anything except borrow a purse and wait to replace my things little by little.

After work the next business day, I went to the Department of Motor Vehicles to replace my license and registration. Again, I thanked God that I had a car to drive myself to the office and that the lines weren't long and brutal. After that, I started to tell myself I was going to get my things back. Every day, when my stomach was getting tight with thoughts of identity theft, I thanked God for giving me back my things, and I forced myself to think good thoughts so I wouldn't worry. I fantasized about how incredible it would be to get back my things, daydreamed about possible scenarios, and visualized the looks on people's faces when I told them the whole story.

Three weeks later, after a long, long day, I found myself driving home at about 9:30 PM. I called my home phone to check my messages. I rarely do this because I have a cell phone. Sometimes, I don't check my home messages for days. There was a message from someone named Jennifer saying she had found some of my things. I called her and met with her immediately. She gave me a handful of personal items—insurance card, pictures, some store discount cards, roadside assistance card, half of my registration card, and a little inspirational prayer I'd kept in my wallet for years. I drove her to where she had found my things. All over the ground, I saw lipstick, mascara, gum, and other personal items. In a garbage can that had been put out for pick-up the next morning were the two sealed envelopes with the tax papers inside. I didn't even have to dig through the garbage to reach them.

Now, here's the crazy part. Jennifer had gone to the Salvation Army to drop off some clothes her son had outgrown. She could have gone on any day, at any time. She bumped into one of her friends on the way out. She took a different route home so she could walk with her friend. As they walked and talked, Jennifer saw all my things on the sidewalk and said, "Wow, someone got robbed, what a shame." She continued walking and then saw a little folded-up piece of looseleaf paper and picked it up. It was a prayer I had handwritten years ago to remind myself to pray and had kept in my wallet for nine years. She read it and said, "I have to give her back her stuff." She picked up everything that was salvageable, and though my license was not there, she found half of my registration card—the half with my name and half of my address on it. She called information and left a message for me.

Had she not called on that day, I wouldn't have gotten my things back. Had she not left the message, the garbage would have been picked up the next morning while I was at work. Had I not checked my messages, I would have missed the window of opportunity. I'm convinced it was my positive thinking, gratitude in advance, the application of the Law of Attraction, and God's supernatural mercy and grace that made a bad situation turn into many blessings.

These are the blessings I believe I received: After being robbed, I felt mad at the world and trusted no one. Jennifer restored my faith in humankind. I struggled with worrying, and as a result of forcing myself not to worry at a time when I normally would have been beside myself with grief, I received my final lesson about worrying (I've had some others). I could move on believing the Law of Attraction is real and employing it in conjunction with my faith in God and Jesus Christ. You see, it was God and the application of the Law of Attraction that brought my things back to me. It was my faith in God that moved her to pick up my things and return them to me. I had been struggling with how to combine the two in my mind—still thinking they were somewhat separate—still questioning many things. Now, I feel good within my soul with regard to my beliefs.

After this happened, I told everyone. I was testifying all around and seeing the expressions on faces, just as I had envisioned. I thought I had seen the end of the story, until one day, I was at my cousin's house telling her about all that had happened. Her husband came down the steps with a digital camera in his hand. Without knowing anything about what had happened to me, he said, "I bought a new digital camera because I'm going to sell my baseball cards on eBay. You can have this one if you want it."

I started to become very interested in this Law of Attraction, and as a result, my faith grew all around. I started to believe in the impossible. I started to expect good things. I started to pray for deeper understanding and expected to receive it.

In May, my mother told me that I had a cousin who was on a speaking tour in New York. She told me to call him so I could meet him. I teach high school English, and I am the co-advisor of the senior class, so between planning for the prom, graduation, and grading papers, I was overwhelmed. I didn't call him. Finally, she told me she had invited him for dinner, and I had to call him to give him directions. I called and ended up having to pick him up that day. As soon as he got into the car, I loved him. He brought peace, warmth, and unconditional love. He is my third cousin. I never even knew he existed, but we are both named after my grandfather, his great-uncle. He is a traveling, nondenominational doctor of theology who has spoken in over eighty countries and has written a powerful book, *Eternity Invading Time*. I showed him *The Secret*, and he thought it was great. He said, "I've been preaching this for thirty years, but I call it faith." That was enough for me. I had come full circle. It was the ultimate confirmation for me.

Since my exposure to the Law of Attraction, which ultimately strengthened my faith in God, I've changed many things in my life, and I have seen miracles. I took and passed the New York life insurance test with almost no effort. I was able to refinance—a miracle for a single woman with my income. Without the recovered tax papers, I would have missed the window of opportunity in which I had to get it done. Within about six weeks, I received over $11,000 in unexpected income. The money did not come from one place; it came from many places. For example, I used to work for the New York City Board of Education. They owed me money for nine years and finally paid. I took three classes during the summer which gave me credits above my master's so I could qualify for a salary increase. For years, I'd wanted to work on credits above my master's, but at first I could not afford it because I had to work extra to support my family. When the time came that I could take a class every now and then, I felt fear about being the oldest person in the class. Those fears have gone out the window. I even got "A's" in all three classes!

I visited my cousin and his family in Texas and now have even more people to love. I started to read the Bible—something I had tried to do many times, but always gave up after the list of who begot whom. I have been able to inspire and be inspired by two women, a good friend and a close cousin, who are both battling and winning the fight against breast cancer. I've started to write poetry again, and this time my focus is positive, not trying to save the world or highlighting its social injustice, but shining light on its beauty and showing my gratitude for all that we have. I'm happy in a way I've never been. In the past, I thought I was happy, but compared to the peace I feel now, I know I am truly happy. I feel more in control, though I've been able to let go of so many things. I feel at peace for the first time in my life. And finally, I have always daydreamed about writing and being published. It is ironic that this is the topic that has made it possible.

Who would have ever thought that being robbed could turn into such a wonderful, life-changing experience!

Message: Don't worry even when the worst seems to be occurring. Always think positive.

Georgia Williams has been a New York State high school English teacher for nineteen years. She was born in Toronto, Canada, to Jamaican parents. She enjoys writing poetry.

THE QUARTER

By Chasity Smith

If you're going to doubt something, doubt your limits.
—Don Ward

My name is Chasity Smith, and I am a thirty-one-year-old single mother of two children. I have no formal education and received my GED in 1994. I divorced my husband in 2003 and struggled to make it on my own. With no experience and no education, the going was tough. I made some very poor choices along the way and wound up in a bad financial situation. I had come to the conclusion that I would always be working two low-paying jobs just to get by. Until recently, I had been working an average of sixty to sixty-five hours a week for the past two years. What made it worse was that I was still barely able to pay my bills and there was never anything left over. The Law of Attraction is what changed all of that.

Over a year ago, I started hearing about something called *The Secret*. It was just in passing and in casual conversations, so I didn't pay much attention to it. Then it felt like everywhere I went and everyone I talked to was telling me I needed to see this DVD. From the lady at the post office to a co-worker reading the book in her car, *The Secret* was everywhere I looked. I finally gave in and ordered the audio version of the book. I didn't have much spare time so I thought it would be easier for me to listen to it than it would be to watch it. Buying the audio book was a big deal for me because, as I mentioned, there was no money left over after the bills were paid. I started listening to the book in March. I listened to it over and over, on my way to work, on my way home from work, on my way to the grocery store, and even at work on my computer.

It took a few weeks, but slowly my mindset changed. I stopped focusing on how broke I was and started being thankful that I had enough to pay my bills. I started printing out pictures of things I had asked the Universe for and taping them to my desk and the wall in my office. The first thing I asked for was very small and very specific. It was a quarter. Not just any quarter, but a 1976 quarter. I printed out a picture of a 1976 quarter and taped it to my desk. Within days, I started finding quarters everywhere. I even had one lady just hand me two quarters at the gym because she had no pockets and didn't want to carry change. For me that wasn't good enough. None of the quarters were my 1976 quarter. I knew that I had put out a request for something specific, and I knew it would be received. I did not waiver in my belief.

After about two weeks of this, I came home from work, and my roommate told me that she had figured out the reason why I had not received my quarter. "It's not just a quarter," she said, "It's a collector's piece because it's a bicentennial quarter." Then she went to a little box that her friend had sent her a couple months before and pulled out my 1976 quarter in its very own protective plastic covering. We had had it the whole time! We both just stood there in amazement. What was even more strange is that when I went back to work the following Monday and looked at the quarter I had taped to my desk, it looked like there was a perfect plastic covering around it.

After that, I was hooked! I have always wanted to be able to help people and guide them in their lives. I put out to the Universe that I wanted a job in which this is what I would be doing. Two days later, I was introduced to a man who had heard that I give great advice and I was a good listener with a bit of an intuitive ability. He is a very prominent businessman here in Birmingham. He said he wanted to interview me, and he would pay me as a consultant. I thought this was odd but went along with it. What turned out to be a chance meeting has launched me on a whole new journey. I started my own Web site, *www.Lifecoachforprosperity.com,* and through referrals and word of mouth have already obtained over twenty clients.

It's now three months later and my life has changed drastically. I write down every day what I want to accomplish. I want to be a successful life coach who helps to empower women. My success with this has grown by leaps and bounds! I now coach women all over the United States and just recently coached a woman from Japan. It has been truly amazing. The second thing I asked for was to bring home $3,000 per month. At the time I was only bringing in around $1,700 per month and things were very tight, so $3,000 per month to me was like winning the lottery.

Today, I am currently the marketing director of a large company in Birmingham, Alabama. I bring home $1,497 every two weeks. This does not include any income, which has become quite substantial, from the coaching I do. Now, I want to live abundantly, coaching for a living, and helping to guide and empower women everywhere. If I can do it, anyone can! The Law of Attraction is a powerful force, and I am definitely a walking testimony.

Message: The only limitations we have in life are those we set for ourselves. Remove those limiting beliefs, and you can achieve anything.

Chasity Smith is a single mother of two boys. The Law of Attraction has changed her thinking and her life. She now has a thriving life-coaching practice that helps men and women accomplish their goals. For more information, please visit her Web site at *www.Lifecoachforprosperity.com.*

PAYING THE BILLS

By Darrell Borza

What you have in your life must correspond exactly to who you are being.
—Darel Rutherford

It had been a slow year for work and almost a year since I had seen *The Secret,* which had begun to change my thinking on a daily basis.

On a Sunday evening, my wife and I discovered we had both paid the same bill for a threat of shut-off. This error left us strapped for money in a budget already strained. I felt myself slipping into darkness, so familiar, such murky energy. My wife went to bed, and I stayed up to wrestle with old demons trying to reclaim a hold on my mind and heart. I knew I had money coming in the next day for work I had done, but it was not enough. I was short $500.

At times the decree to think only good thoughts, to stay in happiness, and not go into despair seems almost impossible at best. It takes effort to rid the mind of desperate thinking; it is so natural to fall off the emotional deep end. I thought, "Well, the one bill is paid." A point of gratitude.

The next day, I went to the office to pick up my money at the appointed time, only to discover the man I was to meet was not there. The doors were locked, and there was no one to be seen, not even a receptionist. I felt my energy dive like a whale from a whaling ship—anger, frustration, all of it trying to entrench itself into my life again.

Just then a truck pulled in, and a man got out and tried the door as well. It seems he was there for the same reason. He vented for ten minutes about the thousands of dollars the man owed him for work. He then left, leaving gravel flying the whole way. This day just kept getting better and better.

I got out of my car and slammed the door with extreme vigor and started to walk toward the woods behind the building, another thing to be grateful for, I thought. I walked into the woods and found an old tree in the middle and sat down against it. It felt good somehow, like it was trying to tell me to breathe, relax, and calm down. I closed my eyes and let it talk.

I thought of the day as it was, not good, not what I wanted, and not what I had been practicing. Then I thought of how I wanted it to go. I began seeing it in my mind, with the old demons still trying to shred my vision.

I saw myself getting my money and leaving feeling happy and grateful. I saw it clearly and precisely. I then let my mind go to delegating the other $500 I needed. I said it to the Universe, even commanded it. Then I switched my thoughts to my kids and granddaughters I had seen the day before, remembering the laughter and the fun. I pictured each of my children happy, then myself happy.

The knot of energy in my solar plexus was disappearing, and the demons were quieting. I thanked the tree and headed back to the parking lot, with "trust" as my mantra as I walked.

I reached my car and looked back to see another car had arrived. I went and tried the door again and it was open. I walked out fifteen minutes later with my money—and $500 more than I had anticipated; the job paid a bonus I was not aware of. I was also assured of more work in the future.

I went home, paid some bills, took my wife to dinner, and told her this story. She is not a believer of life without struggle and miracles being mundane occurrences, but I felt it important to tell her anyway.

My feeling of gratitude when I left there was off the chart. I visualized my happiness going to everyone I knew and cared for and even to people I was passing on the street.

I know many success stories regarding *The Secret* are ones of millions, rags-to-riches sagas. I, too, look forward to that kind of wealth. But what I was going for was a life that was not a struggle daily, hourly, and even moment-to-moment; not having to monitor my thinking for negativity; and for the way I chose to handle that day to be the norm. And I chose the results of that day.

I discovered that I *am* a powerful creator, yet more importantly I discovered I *am* a magnificent creation, and it's okay to feel that way, regardless of life's examples to the contrary.

I learned nothing new in *The Secret* movie. I have been practicing spiritual arts all of my life. I have searched all the ancient treasures of wisdom and the newest scientific ones as well. But *The Secret* gave me permission to live it, not search for it any longer. It is where I can merge science and God in a powerful union called … me.

To tell most how I chose to handle that day's demons and needs is clinically delusional, but it was the most practical approach to the day's dilemmas, and it worked. I didn't just get the money I needed; I got real solutions for a real-time life.

My grandfather once said, "The best place to hide a secret is where everyone can see it."

Message: You cannot get there—you can only *be* there.

Darrell Borza is the father of five children and grandfather of seven. He was a pioneering stay-at-home dad and a single parent to all five of his kids. He has studied most religions, philosophies, and spiritual approaches to life. This led him to the sciences of biology, physics, and related ideas of expansion and potential of the human mind. He taught meditation and related fields for twenty years. He recently published the first in a series of books titled *Beyond the Moment*, describing the changes we are encountering in a changing world. He is a master of meditation, yoga, tai chi, and other martial arts. Darrell can be contacted by e-mail at *zensunni7@neo.rr.com*.

MY NEW CAR

By Marion Williams

Be careful what you wish for, 'cause you just might get it all.
—from "Home" by Daughtry

Not too good to be true! Have you ever heard the saying, "If it's too good to be true …"? That is simply not the case! On December 3, 2006, I watched *The Secret* from my computer. Being a visual person, I was thrilled to do an experiment where I closed my eyes and envisioned myself in my new car. I knew the year, make, model, color, and also that I would want the newest salesman at the dealership. I even imagined how thrilled he'd be to make the commission. I genuinely felt the excitement!

I couldn't wait to share "how to visualize" with my two children while eating at our favorite Mexican restaurant. My twenty-four-year-old son is quite the comedian. After I demonstrated, he replied, "I can't see it; I am still on my Chevro-legs!" I quickly answered him saying, *"No,* you will always be stuck like that if you continue to say and think those things." That was December 21, 2006.

On Christmas Eve, my daughter and I drove to my brother-in-law's house. Everyone kept calling and wanting to know when we would be there; we were holding things up!

When we arrived, my husband came out to help unload the car. He stopped me and said, "Honey, put those down. I will get them in a minute. There's something I want you to see." I was in a bit of a rush and just wanted to get the presents into the house. He took me by the hand, and we walked toward the closed garage. When we were only steps away, the door opened and everyone in our family yelled, "Merry Christmas!" What do you think was parked in there? My brand-new 2007 Lexus RX 350! It was loaded, the color I wanted, everything. It was perfect in every way. For the first time in my life, I was speechless! Not a single soul knew about my private visualization, yet there it was, right before me. Nobody had a dry eye; they all knew it was the first time I had ever owned a brand-new car.

I cried as my husband shared the details with me. He had called the dealership and asked to speak to the *newest* salesman they had. I was in the car business and had even owned my own lot. Therefore, I know what it means to have such a profitable sale and commission. What blesses one, blesses all!

And what about those checks in the mail? For me, it wasn't a check, but a car title. I had no idea until then if it was financed or even how it was paid for. We aren't supposed to concern ourselves with that. As it turns out, it was my title, and there were no lien holders.

My family now pays closer attention to what we think about, dream about, and wish for!

Message: You were given the tools to build your dream. They won't work unless you take them out of your toolbox.

Marion Williams is a wife and mother of two. She shows and breeds champion Maltese dogs. She also enjoys painting, decorating, and meeting people and hearing their stories. You can contact her through her Web site at *www.moonstruck-maltese.com.*

TRUST THE PROCESS

By Darren Jacklin

Simply open your heart to receive and miraculous gifts will descend upon you like raindrops dripping from the wings of angels.
—Rich German

Picture yourself in a room full of highly-successful entrepreneurs and business owners, collectively brainstorming to create new strategies specific to your business, special project, or your lifelong dream. This is your creativity think tank. Now picture your dreams becoming reality.

You attract into your life whatever you give your attention, energy, and focus to, whether positive or negative.

At my "Trust the Process" Idea Party Events, I ask people to tell me something that they really want in their life and I will show them how to get it. I get all kinds of responses. I can actually help most of the people in the room, and I routinely accomplish miracles with them. I have witnessed many miracles of people's lives changing. Here are a few I would like to share with you:

I had a woman say that she wanted to go on her honeymoon someday when she was out of debt and able to afford it. I asked her why she hadn't taken her honeymoon yet. She said that they spent all of their money on the wedding day.

I told her, "We don't have money problems in life; we only have thinking problems." I asked her where she would like to go on her honeymoon. She didn't really know. So I asked her some more questions. She came up with Puerto Vallarta, Mexico. I asked the room full of people who had been there, and a few hands went up high in the air. I made a request to these people, "Would anybody be able to help her out so she can go away on her honeymoon for a few weeks?" I believe that for every question that you don't ask, the answer is no. A woman raised her hand and said she was a businesswoman who had accumulated thousands of air miles and was scared to fly anywhere. She would be willing to "pay it forward" and donate enough air miles to fly this woman and her husband to Puerto Vallarta. The woman accepted.

Then, a man in the room raised his hand and said he had a two-week time-share that he wouldn't be using this year, and he would be willing to "pay it forward." Another person in the room said she had a brother who was an executive chef living and working in Puerto Vallarta, and she would contact him to see if he would prepare a beautiful, complimentary honeymoon dinner for the two of them. The recipient of all these gifts now believes that when you are open to receiving, anything is possible.

Another woman came to one of my public events, and her dream was to one day be able to afford to buy a horse. She had dreamed of owning her own horse since she was a little girl. She grew up in a single-parent home, and money was often tight. I asked her how she planned on getting this horse. She said, "Well, someday if I am lucky enough to afford one, I will get one." Then, toward the back of the seminar room a woman started laughing. At first I thought she was rude to laugh at someone else's dream. I asked the woman what was so funny. She said, "I knew there was a reason for my being here today. My husband and I have been thinking for the past few days about how to get rid of our daughter's horse. She has gone away to college and doesn't want the responsibility any more. So it is up to us to make the decision of what we are going to do with this horse. We believe in the Law of Attraction, and we have been putting out the intention that an answer would come." She said to the other woman, "We would love to give you the horse. Do you have a place to take care of it?" The woman said yes, that she lived on a small acreage just outside of town. So the woman with the horse called her husband on his cell phone, and at the end of the seminar, the horse was delivered. The woman was brought to tears. "A complete stranger helped me today to achieve my childhood dream. How can I repay you for this?" And the response, "You don't have to. Just 'pay it forward.'"

At one of my events, there was a woman who had always dreamed of riding on the back of a Harley-Davidson motorcycle. Growing up, her father always said motorcycles are for men and not for women. So she never went on one, but in the back of her mind, she always wanted to. When you put out your intention to the Universe with feeling, the Universe will bring people, events, and situations into your life. This woman was in for a thrill of a lifetime. That day, there was a gentleman who worked at a Harley-Davidson dealership. He made a telephone call to the dealership, and at the end of the seminar, she got to ride all the way home on the back of a brand-new Harley-Davidson motorcycle. The Law of Attraction works ... you just need to "trust the process."

I have seen many people come to my "Trust the Process" Idea Party Events, and their lives have changed in the span of a few hours. Opportunities will present themselves to you. You'll be in the zone—the flow of life—that magical, miraculous place where everything seems to work in your favour without any effort.

Message: Never underestimate the difference it can make in your life to meet someone with a piece to your life's puzzle.

Darren Jacklin empowers people around the world to make a difference in their lives. Tell Darren what you really want in your life, and he will show you how to manifest it. You can contact him through his Web site at *www.darrenjacklin.com*.

AFTERWORD

We hope you enjoyed this first collection of Law of Attraction stories. Just like the story contributors found their inspiration, our hope is that you find your own inspiration which leads you toward truly living the life of *your* dreams.

Our intention in creating this book was that our readers would experience life at a higher level by incorporating the principles of attraction. You are here on this planet to enjoy all the mystery and wonder that this existence has to offer. Additionally, we hope you are here to help other people experience a better life as well. The best way to improve the world is to improve *you*.

The purpose of this book is two-fold:

- To encourage you to live life at a higher level ... a life full of love, joy, fun, peace, and prosperity.

- To inspire you, through the power of stories, to listen to that voice inside of you that is silently screaming for you to declare whatever it is you desire and to have the courage to act and attract it into your life.

So now the question is ... what do you do next?

Consider the following process:

1. Each day, spend as much time as possible engaged in activities that make you feel good. Make *feeling good* your number one priority in life!

2. Create a vision for your life—decide what you *really* want.

3. Take action toward your intentions.

4. Don't be attached to *how* things will occur.

5. Be a *"yes"* to life!

6. Allow what you desire to come about.

(Please refer back to the Introduction for more details on this process.)

The truth is, as you begin to create your vision and act upon it, your mind will act up in its quest to keep you safe and secure. In order to really live your possibilities, you must be able to move beyond your mind and its self-imposed restrictions. So any time limiting beliefs begin to dominate your thoughts, or any time you simply need a boost of inspiration, come back to this book. Flip it open and read some of the stories. Reread the introduction and implement the techniques offered.

Looking ahead:

Our intention is to create a series of books similar to this one and we would love for you to be a future story contributor. So go out and practice the principles, create your own magic, and let us know about it. You can tell us your story by going to our Web site at ***www.Living-the-LOA.com***. You just might find *your* story in the next edition of ***Living the Law of Attraction!***

Thank you and happy manifesting,

Rich and Robin

ABOUT THE AUTHORS

Rich German is the Founder and Creative Director of *True Wealth Unlimited (www.richgerman.com)*. He is one of the top business and life coaches in North America. Since 1999, he has conducted over 15,000 individual coaching calls and has led numerous trainings and seminars. He helps his clients dramatically increase their creativity, greatness, happiness, and of course, their results. He is also certified as a meditation teacher through the Self Awareness Institute and leads weekly classes.

Rich has been applying and teaching the principles of the Law of Attraction in his business, life, and spiritual coaching for many years. Additionally, Rich is studying to get his PhD in preventative medicine. His passion is to help people raise their energy and expand their consciousness. In his personal time, Rich enjoys playing guitar, painting, writing, and photography. He lives in Laguna Beach, California.

Robin Hoch graduated from the University of Michigan with a BBA in marketing. She spent ten years with IBM, first as a systems engineer and later as an account executive. She left to start her own printing, publishing, and graphic design business where her clients included brokerage firms and condominium associations as well as the local performing arts center and newspaper. She has served on the boards of Kids in Crisis, NCJW, and the PTA. Robin lives in the Orlando, Florida, area with her husband and two daughters. She loves working out, traveling, skiing, scuba diving, going to the beach, watching movies, and being a soccer mom!

SHARE YOUR STORY!

If you have used the Law of Attraction to manifest something in your life ... we want to hear from you! Have you experienced a great healing miracle? Found the love of your life? Created wealth or business success? Are you living the life of your dreams? If so, tell us about it!

If selected, your story may be published in an upcoming book in the *Living the Law of Attraction* series. Your experience will help other people better understand how the Law of Attraction works. People reading your story will be inspired and realize that they, too, can achieve similar success in their lives.

If you have a story to tell, or know someone who does, we'd love to hear it. Stories should be approximately 1,000 words in length. Please e-mail them to us at *Stories@Living-the-LOA.com* or visit our Web site, *www.Living-the-LOA.com,* for more information.

978-0-595-47411-0
0-595-47411-X

Printed in the United States
208893BV00003B/28/P

9 780595 474110